TABE

Test of Adult Basic Education
The First Step to Lifelong Success

Phyllis Dutwin, M.A.

Carol Altreuter, M.Ed.

Kathy Guglielmi, Ph.D.

McGraw-Hill

New York   Chicago   San Francisco   Lisbon   London   Madrid
Mexico City   Milan   New Delhi   San Juan   Seoul   Singapore
Sydney   Toronto

CONTENTS

TO THE READER

Welcome to TABE, Test of Adult Basic Eduction: The First Step to Lifelong Success. TABE is an academic test that measures a person's ability and skill in mathematics, reading, and language. This book has been designed to help you succeed on the TABE, but as the title suggests, the authors want you to acquire even more than test-taking skills. When you finish the book, you will have identified some of your goals. You will also know more about your learning preferences and the strategies that make learning and test taking easier for you. In other words, the book will help you succeed in the challenges of work and study that follow.

HOW TO USE THIS BOOK

The TABE tests cover basic skills that you use in your everyday life. You may be surprised to find that you know more than you think you do. You may also be surprised to discover skill gaps you do not know about.

This book is all about helping you target and master the skills you need to succeed

- On the TABE
- In future situations as a lifelong learner

Before You Begin

Before you begin to use this book, take some time to explore it. The book offers much more than question and answer material. Read the Table of Contents. As you browse through the book, notice the following:

- Skills Assessments beginning each section
- Scenarios recalling students the authors have known
- Skill building in every subject
- Word study
- Study Tips and Test Tips and FYI's

All of these elements give you a process, or way of learning. In fact, because each section builds skills, you should read and do all the exercises in order.

What if you think you have great strength in one of the subjects? Take the Skills Assessment for that subject anyway. If your results are 90 to 95 percent correct, you probably don't have to study that section. However, be sure to take all the posttests when you have finished all the sections.

One section, "Spelling," needs a special comment. *You should not study this section straight through* from first page to last. Correct spelling is best learned slowly and through repetition. Take the pretest. If you find that spelling is not your strong subject, start the section. No matter what else you are working on, study a *small* part of the spelling section at the same time. If you use the tips provided and study consistently, you can improve your spelling.

FYI

Learning how to succeed in test-taking situations makes good career sense.

You will be expected to take tests throughout your adult life, both on and off the job. Standardized tests are everywhere you look: drivers' licenses, technical certification, educational placement tests, financial aid qualifying tests, job placement, and advancement exams.

Use This Book as Your Personal Trainer

You should approach this book as you would any fitness regimen you start.

Step 1: Develop a fitness plan.
       Complete Section 1: "Work Smarter, Not Harder."

Step 2: Warm up:
       Take each of the subject area Skills Assessments.
       Target skills you need to strengthen.

Step 3: Work out:
       Pace yourself through the exercises.
       Achieve optimum results.

 TEST TIP

Do not study for the Skills Assessments that begin each subject section. The results of each assessment will help you

- *Compare what you already know with what you need to know*
- *Make a learning plan for choosing and using the lessons that follow.*

Look for these tips throughout this book:

 STUDY TIP   **TEST TIP**   **FYI**

Succeed At Learning

Before reading about what *other* people have to say about learning, how would you complete this sentence?

"The best learning experience I ever had was ——————————— "

You do not have to write it—just think what you would say if someone asked

"I *see* and I forget, I *hear* and I remember, I *do* and I understand."
An Old Chinese proverb

Research into how people learn and remember has proven the truth of this ancient proverb. When we learn something new, and do something with that knowledge, understanding comes more quickly.

After two weeks, we tend to remember:

- 10% of what we read
- 20% of what we hear
- 30% of what we see
- 50% of what we hear *and* see
- 70% of what we say
- 90% of what we say *and* do
- 95% of what we help someone else learn and understand

The higher our level of involvement, the more likely we will remember.

Increase Your Percentage of Success

- **Put it to work.** *Doing* something with new knowledge means *putting it to work* and getting results.
- **Results are valuable feedback.** You may be unhappy with your first results, but making mistakes is all part of the learning process.
- **Mistakes** are *learning opportunities.* Welcome mistakes as a chance to figure out "what is not working and why." Then make it your business to try again.
- **Just do it, step by step.** The path to acquiring new knowledge or skills is a series of steps. Sometimes these steps are baby steps, especially if you have had no previous experience in this area. Other times these steps may be giant steps, as when a new bit of information connects with knowledge you already possess.
- **Use it to make it yours.** The understanding of how to do something new is first stored, *temporarily,* in your short-term memory. Perhaps it will stay there for a minute, an hour or a day. If you do not take it out of temporary storage, and *use it within that time period,* it will not be there when you need to use it again. You will have to start the process over again.
- **3 may be the magic number.** Each time you put a new bit of knowledge to work, you help guarantee that it will move from *temporary* storage to *permanent* storage in your memory. *Rule of thumb:* Use your new skill successfully 3 times, on 3 different occasions, and you'll probably find yourself saying, "I've got it."
- **Use it again, or risk losing it.** A stored skill, like a stored metal tool, may rust or become stiff with time. Then, when you need to use it, you'll find it doesn't do the job easily or well. Then again, you may forget where you left the key! Plan to open that storage door regularly, and put your skill to work.

How do you prefer to learn something new?

- See it; read about it; write it down?   (See TIPS A)
- Hear it; talk about it?   (See TIPS B)
- Watch it done, then do it yourself?   (See TIPS C)

Lead with your strength. If you have a strong preference for a certain style of learning, it makes sense to connect with new information in that way *first*.

TIPS A

1 Think in pictures, colors, and shapes. Make movies in your mind about new ideas.

2 Think on paper. Organize your thoughts by making diagrams, charts, and flash cards.

3 Watch videos, TV, or films about subjects you are learning. Search for study books that have lots of graphics and photographs.

4 Ask yourself questions in writing; reply to yourself in writing. Doodle your ideas.

5 Work in a quiet place, with a clear study space that is pleasing to your eyes.

TIPS B

1 Think out loud. Explain things out loud to yourself as you study.

2 Read out loud. Read *under your breath* - as you move your lips, you will *hear* the sound of the words in your head.

3 Make your own tapes of information you want to remember. Get the *sound* of standard English *in your ear* by taping your voice reading from a textbook or novel.

4 Study with other people. Talk things over. Hold question-and-answer sessions.

5 Listen to information about a topic on video, TV, film, or recorded books.

TIPS C

1 Connect to things you are studying with *movement* and *touch*. Act out ideas. "Talk" with your hands.

2 Watch someone *do* what you need to learn. Then, *do* it yourself.

3 Use the computer as a learning tool. Go for programs that are multimedia and interactive. Create your own study notes using a word processor.

4 Write about, draw, or build models of what you are learning.

5 Exercise before you sit down to study. Take 5-minute *movement breaks* between 30-minute study sessions. Play background music as you study.

Don't Limit Your Options

Learning different subjects may mean using different approaches. Consider all the tips above. Ask others about their tips for learning. Watch for study and learning tips in the subject lessons that follow.

On Your Own, or With Others?

If you work together with a partner, or with a small study group, you can benefit in these ways. You have the opportunity to

- Pool your experience and knowledge
- Exchange strategies and study tips
- Ask and answer questions of each other without fear of embarrassment
- Give and get suggestions when the going gets tough

Ask

Questions are like fishhooks.

Information you hook with your own questions tends to "stick around" in your memory better than information you have received without fishing for it.

Learn how to ask good questions. Keep your hook baited and in the water long enough to catch some information.

Take time to do some fishing. Chances are, you will be hooked on learning for a lifetime.

One Final Observation

The more you understand about the way you learn best, the more you will be able to get what you need to succeed.

Good luck at discovering how to unlock your potential!

Work Smarter, Not Harder

LESSON 1 Identify Your Target

Where Are You Headed?

My Goals

I am studying to upgrade my basic academic skills to: (*Check all that apply*)

Score well on the Test of Adult Basic Education, Level A

- ☐ Enroll in an associates degree program
- ☐ Enter a vocational certificate program
- ☐ Obtain admission to a job training program
- ☐ Obtain admission to a career advancement program
- ☐ Qualify for a promotion at my workplace
- ☐ Be eligible for federal financial aid under Ability to Benefit guidelines
- ☐ Qualify for certification in _____
- ☐ Complete graduation requirements for _____
- ☐ Successfully exit the Welfare to Work Program _____
- ☐ Become more independent in handling my affairs
- ☐ Attain personal satisfaction
- ☐ Help family members with their schooling
- ☐ _____
- ☐ _____
- ☐ _____

After I upgrade my skills and/or score well on the TABE, I plan to

_____

_____

A vision I have for my future is _____

_____

_____

When Do You Want to Get There?

My Timeline

Today's date: _____

I want to upgrade my skills by this date: _____ because that is when _____.

That date is _____ (months, weeks, days) from today.

If I do not improve my skills as much as I want to by that date, my options will be to _____.

Do You Need to Achieve a Certain Score?

Programs vary in their TABE score requirements.

Are you already in a program with score requirements? _____

Do you want to enroll in, or qualify for, a program that has test score requirements? _____

Do you need to take a test to qualify for scholarship aid? _____

If your answer is yes to any of these questions, make sure you know what those requirements are. Take the time to find out this information right now. It will help you focus on your goals for studying the subjects in this book. The information will help you be realistic as you plan your timeline.

Turn to Appendix A for specific information on TABE scoring.

Do Your Research

Fill out the blank that fits your situation.

1. The program *I am already working in,* requires me to _____

    _____

2. The program I want to get into requires me to _____

    _____

For my own satisfaction, I would like to _____

What Do You Already Know about Your Skills?

Take a moment to think in general about the academic subject areas covered in this book, and tested on the TABE: Reading, Math, and Language.

Would you say your level of skill is about the same in each area, or is it quite different? _____

How about your level of comfort using and learning about these subjects? Are you just as comfortable learning in one subject area as another, or is there a significant difference in the way you feel about them? _____

Rank Your Levels of Skill and Comfort

Skill Level:
Strongest subject area first

1. _____
2. _____
3. _____

Comfort Level:
Most comfortable subject area first

1. _____
2. _____
3. _____

Why do you think your skills are stronger in some of these areas than others?

_____

_____

_____

Why do you think you are more comfortable with some subjects than others?

_____

_____

_____

What Do You Need to Succeed as a Test-Taker?

Reflection: Past Experiences with Tests

The last time I took a standardized test was _____

My results were ___OK ___Good ___Excellent ___A disaster

I think my performance on that test was due to: _____

In general, I consider myself a ___Good ___Fair ___Poor test-taker.

My biggest problem with taking tests is _____

I think I need to _____

Test-Taking Strategies

I am familiar with, and am able to put into practice, the following test-taking strategies. I know how to

Visualize success for self-confidence and best results.	___Yes	___No	___Need Practice
Prepare physically for the test day.	___Yes	___No	___Need Practice
Identify key words in questions and directions.	___Yes	___No	___Need Practice
Recognize pitfalls of multiple-choice tests.	___Yes	___No	___Need Practice
Use process of elimination to check multiple-choice questions.	___Yes	___No	___Need Practice
Relax by using breathing techniques.	___Yes	___No	___Need Practice
Take 1-minute vacations to relieve stress during the test.	___Yes	___No	___Need Practice
Pace myself during the test to finish within the time limit.	___Yes	___No	___Need Practice
Know when to leave a question that is giving me trouble.	___Yes	___No	___Need Practice
Use time that is left at the end to check my work.	___Yes	___No	___Need Practice

 FYI

Don't worry yet about getting ready for any of the assessments or tests in this book, or the TABE. There are test-taking tips throughout the lessons. Turn to Appendix A for an explanation of each of the strategies mentioned in the preceding list.

Take time to complete the next unit: Analyze yourself as a learner. You will meet another student in the next few pages. Learn how she uses this analysis to help herself prepare for studying to be test-ready.

LESSON 2 Analyze Yourself as a Learner

Self-Assessment and Planning

In this section you will take steps to better understand yourself as a learner. You also need to examine and manage the time you have to prepare for the TABE. In addition, you will be able to identify, understand, and develop strategies to overcome the barriers that many adults face as learners. The result will be a plan of action that will help you target success.

To help you through this process, read Alice's story and then walk through the worksheets with her. Once you see how the process is done, complete your own.

Alice

Alice has been employed for the past 18 years in a small safety products manufacturing plant as an assembler. She recently saw a supervisor's position opening in her department posted in the lunchroom. Alice thought about applying for the job. The poster said that she should see the Human Resource's Department Manager for job specifications. She went to the department and picked up the qualifications statement.

Assembly Supervisor
Qualifications:

The qualified applicant will possess

- Excellent communication skills (oral and written)
- Leadership abilities (able to manage the different personalities in the department)
- Ability to schedule workers, understand department budgets, and operate within them
- Ability to assist with new product setup
- Ability to read, analyze, and report on computer printout data regarding scrap rates
- Ability to implement the quality control process on a daily basis
- Ability to make adjustments to work processes

The successful candidate will

- Assist department employees with information regarding the performance of their jobs
- Provide employees in his or her charge with an annual review of their performance, including goals and professional development activities
- Possess specific skills to be used in the quality control and process improvement include ability to
  - Understand algebraic equations used in the quality control process
  - Compute fractions (used in measurement of product outcomes)
  - Understand the geometry (area, perimeter, volume) needed to set up new products
  - Understand the basic statistics used in this process

Alice had been working in the assembly department for many years; however, she lacked many of the skills the supervisor's job required. She was especially worried about her lack of math skills and wasn't sure that she could do that job.

What Kind of a Learner Are You?

Because people learn in different ways, it is important for you to understand how *you* learn best. This information will help you develop a learning plan that targets success on the TABE and your other learning goals. Alice reflected on her learning experiences. The last math class she took was a disaster. She remembered having trouble, being confused, and feeling alone. The way the teacher expected her to learn did not work for her.

The following is an example of how Alice might complete this worksheet.

Learner Preference Worksheet

1. *What time(s) of day or night do you feel better able to study/work/read/write?*
   Early morning ✓ Afternoon ____ Early evening ____ Late night ____

2. *Do you prefer to study or learn by yourself or with others? (Check one)*
   I like learning about new things with a study group. ____
   I like learning about new things by myself. ____
   I like learning something new with one other person to help me. ____
   It depends on the subject matter. ✓ (I need help with Math)

3. *Do you learn best by (Check all that apply)*
   Reading about something? ____
   Seeing a picture or graph? ✓
   Hearing someone explain something? ____
   Doing what I'm learning about? ____
   Writing it down? ____
   Talking about it with or without someone else? ✓

4. *What length of time do you prefer to spend studying?*
   I prefer to work for periods of two hours or more ✓
   I prefer to work for shorter periods of time (less than an hour) ____
   I can work whenever time permits ____

5. *How's your concentration? (Check all that apply)*
   I need complete quiet when I study or read ✓
   I can study or read with some background noise ____
   I can study or read in any environment, quiet or noisy ____

Examine the items you have checked to get a picture of how you best learn. Use the information to fill in the blanks in the Learner Preference

Statement that follows.

Learner Preference Statement

I prefer to study in the _early morning_ with _the help of others_
(when I'm doing math) . I learn best when I _see something in a_
picture or graph and by _talking about it with other people_ .
I prefer to spend _at least 2 hours_ studying, and I prefer to study
in complete silence .

Now that you have seen an example of a completed worksheet, complete
this one on your own to get an idea how *you* prefer to learn.

Learner Preference Worksheet

1. *What time(s) of day or night do you feel better able to study/work/read/write?*
   Early morning ____ Afternoon ____ Early evening ____ Late night ____

2. *Do you prefer to study or learn by yourself or with others? (Check one)*
   I like learning about new things with a study group. ____
   I like learning about new things by myself. ____
   I like learning something new with one other person to help me. ____
   It depends on the subject matter. ____

3. *Do you learn best by: (Check all that apply)*
   Reading about something? ____
   Seeing a picture or graph? ____
   Hearing someone explain something? ____
   Doing what I'm learning about? ____
   Writing it down? ____
   Talking about it with or without someone else? ____

4. *What length of time do you prefer to spend studying?*
   I prefer to work for periods of 2 hours or more ____
   I prefer to work for shorter periods of time (less than an hour) ____
   I can work whenever time permits ____

5. *How's your concentration? (Check all that apply)*
   I need complete quiet when I study or read ____
   I can study or read with some background noise ____
   I can study or read in any environment, quiet or noisy ____

Examine the items you have checked above to get a picture of how you learn best. Use this information to fill in your Learner Preference Statement.

Learner Preference Statement

I prefer to study in the (1) _____ with (2) _____.
I learn best by (3) _____.
I prefer to spend (4) _____ studying.
I study best with (5) _____.

We will use this information to develop your Personal Learning Plan later in this chapter.

You have thought about how you learn and study best. Now you should be aware of, and plan for, obstacles that might get in the way of your success.

As adults, we are all faced with a variety of life issues and challenges that can, if we let them, sabotage the accomplishment of our goals. These barriers can be overcome if we are aware of the supports that we can draw upon to help us with them.

You can categorize barriers in three ways: institutional, circumstantial, and individual. Read the discussion of barriers that follows. An exercise follows the discussion to help you plan for and overcome some of these barriers to your success.

Barriers

Institutional barriers are those over which we have no control. They are put in place by a school, a program, or a class. Institutional barriers can include inconvenient class times, difficult registration procedures, financial aid deadlines, and other things that keep us from taking a class or continuing with one. These barriers may be overcome in some cases.

Circumstantial barriers are difficult but are more often within our control. These barriers may include lack of time, money, child-care, or transportation. They can make it difficult for us to reach our learning goals.

Personal barriers are mainly in our control, yet they are typically the most difficult to overcome. They include long-held beliefs about our abilities as a learner or student.

Personal barriers include the following:

- Feelings of being too old to take classes or to learn
- Feelings that we are not smart enough to do well in class, or even in one particular subject (many people have a fear of math and feel they cannot do well in that subject)
- Negative feelings about school or learning because of poor experiences with school earlier in life

These barriers may keep some people from even attempting to go back to school or to take a course. They might also be the cause of someone dropping out of a class or program. The good news is that there are ways to deal with, and overcome, many of these barriers.

Supports

Many sources of support exist for you. Identify these within your own family, within your circle of friends, and within your neighborhood and community.

Family

Try to identify people within your close or extended family whom you can ask for help if you need to. Ask yourself these questions:

1. Do I have a parent, sibling, aunt, uncle, or anyone who can provide child-care, even on a short-term basis, so I can study, go to the library, or to a class?

   I can ask _____. Telephone: _____.

   I can ask _____. Telephone: _____.

2. Is there anyone in my family that I can call on short notice to help me with a ride if I need one, last minute child-care, or financial needs?

   I can call _____. Telephone: _____.

   I can call _____. Telephone: _____.

Friends

Identify those people closest to you that you can count on to help you with child-care, studying, or a ride if you need one. Are there things you can offer to do for them in exchange? Can you offer them child-care or other support at times when they need it? Sometimes, friends set up an informal child-care exchange program where they develop a schedule of support for each other.

I will ask my friend _____ for help with _____.

In exchange, I can offer _____. Telephone: _____.

I will ask my friend _____ for help with _____.

In exchange, I can offer _____. Telephone: _____.

Neighbors

Do you have one or more neighbors that might consider helping you on short notice if you need it?

A neighbor I might call on for help is _____. Telephone: _____.

A neighbor I might call on for help is _____. Telephone: _____.

Community

Many social services are available in the community to assist you. These services include child-care, transportation, clothing, food, shelter, financial aid, and counseling. Check the community service telephone numbers at the front of your telephone directory. Many communities offer

- Health centers
- Family services
- Educational financial aid services

I will check out the following community services:

_____

_____

_____

_____

_____

Before working with your own barriers, read what Alice has identified as her barriers. See how she plans to overcome some of these barriers with supports.

Balancing Barriers and Supports Worksheet	
Barriers	Supports
Institutional	**Family, Friends, Neighbors, Community**
Some of my classes will be at work, but I've never taken classes anywhere else before. So I'm not sure where I go to register.	I will ask my friends if they can help me.
Circumstantial	
I'm not sure I can afford these classes. I'll need help with my kids while I'm in class.	I will try to get financial aid to help me. I will ask my friends if we can trade baby-sitting with each other.
Individual	
I'm really afraid that I can't do this math. I think I'm too old to learn it now.	I want to try for the supervisor job so I need to try to get over my fears. I have never been good at math. I have to start thinking more positively about the future.

As you can see, Alice has some issues that are more easily handled than others. She can try to ask her family and friends to help her with her institutional and circumstantial barriers. She is going to have to really work hard to get over her fear of not being able to succeed in math. That is something for which she must take the major responsibility. Once she gets started, an instructor can help her develop more confidence in herself. Now it is time for you to try this exercise for yourself.

1. List the institutional, circumstantial, and individual barriers you might face. Use the descriptions on page 8 to help you identify the different barriers. Write these in the spaces provided on the left side of the form that follows.

2. Match sources of support that you might use to help you overcome the barriers you have listed. Write these on the right side of the form.

Balancing Barriers and Supports Worksheet

Barriers	Supports
Institutional	Family, Friends, Neighbors, Community
_____	_____
_____	_____
_____	_____
Circumstantial	
_____	_____
_____	_____
_____	_____
Individual	
_____	_____
_____	_____
_____	_____
Notes to Myself:	
_____	_____
_____	_____
_____	_____

Make Time for Learning

A common complaint of adult learners is that they lack time for studying and other learning activities. This section will help you document and analyze how you currently spend your time. It will also help you develop a plan to include your learning activities. Notice how Alice filled out her calendar: She used an X for fixed activities—working, in her case. She used a ◇ for flexible activities that could be scheduled at another time.

Alice filled her calendar out this way:

	Mon	Tues	Wed	Thurs	Fri	Sat	Sun
6:00 AM							
7:00	XXXX XXXX	XXXX XXXX	XXXX XXXX	XXXX XXXX	XXXX XXXX		
8:00	XXXX XXXX	XXXX XXXX	XXXX XXXX	XXXX XXXX	XXXX XXXX		
9:00	XXXX XXXX	XXXX XXXX	XXXX XXXX	XXXX XXXX	XXXX XXXX	Children's Sports Events	
10:00	XXXX XXXX	XXXX XXXX	XXXX XXXX	XXXX XXXX	XXXX XXXX	XXXX XXXX	XXXX XXXX
11:00	XXXX XXXX	XXXX XXXX	XXXX XXXX	XXXX XXXX	XXXX XXXX	XXXX	XXXX
12:00 PM	XXXX XXXX	XXXX XXXX	XXXX XXXX	XXXX XXXX	XXXX XXXX		
1:00	XXXX XXXX	XXXX XXXX	XXXX XXXX	XXXX XXXX	XXXX XXXX		
2:00	XXXX XXXX	XXXX XXXX	XXXX XXXX	XXXX XXXX	XXXX XXXX		
3:00	XXXX	XXXX	XXXX	XXXX	XXXX		
4:00	Library with children						
5:00							
6:00	◇◇◇	◇◇◇	◇◇◇	◇◇◇		◇◇◇	◇◇◇
7:00	◇◇◇	Weekly Food Shopping	◇◇◇ ◇◇◇	◇◇◇ ◇◇◇	◇◇◇ ◇◇◇	◇◇◇ ◇◇◇	◇◇◇ ◇◇◇
8:00					XXXX		
9:00					XXXX XXXX		
10:00					XXXX XXXX		
11:00					XXXX		
12:00 AM							

Step One: Look at this weeklong calendar. Place an X through the times when you know you have fixed activities, such as job hours, family meal times, and other schedules that cannot be changed.

My Weekly Calendar

	Mon	Tues	Wed	Thurs	Fri	Sat	Sun
6:00 AM 7:00 8:00 9:00 10:00 11:00 12:00 PM							
1:00 2:00 3:00 4:00 5:00 6:00							
7:00 8:00 9:00 10:00 11:00 12:00 AM							

Step Two: You have identified time slots that are *not* available for learning. Now ask yourself the following critical questions to help you plan your best times for learning during the week. Use the information you recorded about yourself on the Learner Preference Worksheet, page 7, to help you.

Here are Alice's responses:

When do I learn best? _Early Morning_

How much time do I need during the day/week to study? _At least 3 hrs a week_

Are there any times available when I will be able to study without interruption? _Before 7 am or at night weekdays. Weekend mornings._

Write *your* conclusions here:

When do I learn best? _____

How much time do I need during the day or week to study? _____

Are there any times available when I will be able to study without interruption? _____

Step Three: Use the answers to the preceding questions to help identify the best times for you to study. If there is a conflict, use your Barriers and

Supports Worksheet to help you identify your supports. Make time in your schedule for studying by calling on your supports for help with tasks that must be done daily or weekly.

Write these times in on your preceding weekly schedule and on the lines that follow:

_____

_____

_____

_____

LESSON 3 Put It to Work—Here's How

Create a Personal Learning Plan

Now that you (and Alice) have reflected on your situation, put all this information to work for you. Complete this learning plan as directed. Next, photocopy it and put it in a place where you will see it every day. The refrigerator is a good location.

My Learning Plan

Goal/s: (page 1) _____

_____

Timeline: (page 2) _____

Supports I need to reach my goals: (page 9) _____

_____

_____

My Promises:

I will study at the times, and in the ways, I learn best.
Write your Learner Preference Statement here: (page 8)

I will refer often to my Barriers and Supports Worksheet (page 11).
I will continue to try to find and use the supports I need to overcome obstacles.
I will consult my Weekly Calendar (page 13) and use the study time I have scheduled.

I WILL SUCCEED

2

Reading

LESSON 1 The Challenge

In Lesson 1, you will join Mike Rinaldi on a new and challenging journey. Mike graduated from high school not knowing how he would use his considerable computer skills. After almost a year of going from one unsatisfying job to another, a friend told Mike about an ad for a job that required computer skills.

Mike was in for some surprises, as well as satisfactions, as he pursued employment at The Ace Computer Chip Company.

Words to Know

Human Resources Manager	A business title for a manager of people in the workplace
Non-exempt employees	Hourly employees
Mentor	Advisor, coach

Job Hunting

After Mike Rinaldi graduated from high school, he immediately started looking for a job. Mike wanted to do something with his computer skills. The jobs he found, including his current job, had no use for his skills. In the meantime, he had two goals. He wanted to learn much more about the computer programs used in business. Mike also wanted to make enough money to live on his own.

He had been looking for a new job for weeks, using the newspaper as well as the Internet. Then a friend told Mike about an opening he had seen posted on their state's Internet site. The Ace Computer Chip Company was advertising for entry-level employees. The employee would be trained to handle information storage tasks.

Knowing that he, undoubtedly, was equipped to handle the entry-level assignment, Mike immediately called about the job. He was invited to come in for an interview with Sue Mendez, Human Resources Manager. Mike learned that the job did require some computer skills that he had mastered and some that he had not. The new employee would be hired to enter data on new customers into the information system.

During the interview, Sue also asked Mike many questions. She included questions about his favorite subjects in high school (Mike's was math and computer science). She also wanted to know about his least favorite subjects (English, especially writing). He wondered why Ms. Mendez wanted to know so much about what he liked and didn't like. He soon found out.

Ms. Mendez asked Mike if he wanted to fill out a complete application, and Mike replied, "Yes, absolutely. When can I start working?" Sue smiled and said that he needed to take one step at a time. At Ace Computer Chip Company, all new non-exempt employees needed to take the TABE, Tests of Adult Basic Education. Sue watched as Mike grimaced. She said, "We need to know more about your reading, language, and math skills." Mike thought to himself, "I hate taking tests. I'm terrible at taking tests! I'll never get this job!" Ms. Mendez explained that Mike needed to demonstrate more about his strengths in English, math, and reading. She said, "Mike, don't worry about the test right now. We'll provide you with a mentor—we do this for all new employees. The mentor will tell you what to expect and how to prepare for the TABE. Also, you can take one test at a time, starting with the reading test." Mike sat quietly for a while, thinking about what he should do. He knew one thing: He had two important goals and he needed to do whatever he could to reach them.

Ms. Mendez followed through on her promises to Mike. The first thing she did was to introduce Mike to Alicia Buchanan. Alicia worked as an assistant to Sue in the Human Resources Department. Her job was to explain all the steps Mike would take as he walked through the pre-employment process. Alicia knew that Mike was very concerned about taking the TABE, so she immediately introduced him to his mentor, Dave Elliot. Over a cup of coffee, Dave assured Mike that he could accomplish his goals. Dave would make another appointment with Mike after he had time to consider his goals, strengths, and weaknesses. Dave took Mike back to Alicia's office, where he started the employment process.

If you think about what you read in Chapter 1, you can relate to all that Mike did to look at himself as a learner and new employee. In fact, Mike eventually took a test that looked very much like the one you, the reader, are about to take. First, think about your reading habits and skills.

Reflection: Reading in My Daily Life

I read approximately _____ hrs a day/ _____ hrs a week to keep informed of current events and other issues that concern me.

I read approximately _____ hrs a day/ _____ hrs a week for workplace tasks.

I enjoy reading _____.

I would like to improve my ability to read _____.

Comprehension

I am able to understand, analyze, and use these types of materials:

Newspapers	___Yes	___No	___Need practice	___I don't know
Instructions	___Yes	___No	___Need practice	___I don't know
Maps, charts, and graphs	___Yes	___No	___Need practice	___I don't know
Stories and novels	___Yes	___No	___Need practice	___I don't know
Business letters	___Yes	___No	___Need practice	___I don't know
Manuals, handbooks	___Yes	___No	___Need practice	___I don't know
Standardized forms	___Yes	___No	___Need practice	___I don't know
Indexes, table of contents	___Yes	___No	___Need practice	___I don't know

Vocabulary Knowledge

I know how to figure out the meaning of words from their *context* (the way they are used in a passage).

___Yes   ___No   ___Need practice   ___I don't know

I know how to identify the meaning of words by analyzing their *structure* (roots, prefixes, and suffixes).

___Yes   ___No   ___Need practice   ___I don't know

TEST TIP

Before you start this test (and any test):

- Breathe. You probably think that you do this without thinking, and most of the time you do. However, when you are in a stressful situation (as tests are for Mike), you tend to hold your breath. So, start this test-taking opportunity by taking and releasing four deep breaths. Breathe in through your nose and out slowly with a slightly open mouth.
- Read the directions, including any time limitations.
- Don't linger on any one question. You can always return to it later.
- Use a process of elimination to check multiple-choice answers.
- Use time that is left at the end to check your work.

Reading Skills Assessment

Take a look at this chart. Use it to answer Questions 1 to 5.

Calories Burned in 5 Minutes According to Body Weight

To use this chart, locate the activity in which you are interested. Then locate the number of calories burned in five minutes that corresponds to the weight that is closest to yours. If you perform the listed activity for 10 minutes, multiply the calories listed by two. If you perform the activity for 15 minutes, multiply the listed calories by three, and so on.

Activity	110 lb.	130 lb.	150 lb.	170 lb.	190 lb.	210 lb.
Badminton	25	28	33	37	41	46
Basketball	35	41	47	53	60	65
Carpentry, general	13	15	18	20	22	24
Cleaning, general	15	17	20	23	26	29
Cooking, general	12	14	17	19	21	23
Cycling, 5.5 mph	16	19	22	25	28	30
9.4 mph	25	30	34	38	43	47
Dancing, ballroom	13	15	17	19	22	24
Fishing	15	18	21	24	26	29
Food Shopping	15	17	21	24	25	28
Football	33	39	45	51	57	62
Gardening, digging	31	39	43	48	54	60
planting seeds	17	20	24	27	30	33
Golf	21	25	29	32	36	40
Horseback Riding, walking	10	12	14	16	18	20
trotting	27	32	37	42	47	52
Ironing	12	14	16	18	20	22
Judo	49	57	66	75	84	92
Jumping Rope, 70/min	40	48	55	62	69	77
125/min	44	52	60	67	76	84
Lawn Mowing	28	33	38	43	48	53
Mopping Floors	15	17	20	23	26	28
Music Playing, conducting	10	12	14	16	18	20
piano, sitting	10	12	14	16	18	20
brass, standing	8	9	10	11	12	14
string, sitting	11	13	15	17	19	21
Painting, inside	8	10	11	12	14	16
outside	19	22	26	27	34	36
Raking	13	16	18	21	23	25
Racquetball	44	52	60	68	76	84
Running, 11 min/mile	34	40	46	52	58	64
9 min/mile	48	57	65	74	83	91
Scrubbing Floors	27	32	37	42	47	52
Skiing, downhill	26	31	36	43	46	50
cross-country, moderate	36	42	48	55	61	68
cross-country, slow	30	35	40	45	50	55
Snowshoeing	41	49	56	64	71	79
Stairs (walking upstairs)	65	76	87	99	110	122
Step Aerobics Class	42	46	51	57	64	70
Swimming, back stroke	42	50	57	65	72	80
breast stroke	40	48	55	62	72	77
crawl, slow	32	38	43	49	55	61
Table Tennis (ping pong)	17	20	23	26	29	32
Tennis	27	32	37	42	47	52
Vacuuming	12	14	17	19	21	23
Walking, slow (2.0 mph)	11	13	15	17	19	21
fast (4.0 mph)	20	26	31	37	42	48
Window Cleaning	15	17	20	22	25	28
Wood Chopping, slow	21	25	29	34	36	40

1. In the directions at the top of this chart, find the word *corresponds*. In this context, corresponds means

   A Writes to

   B Is correct

   C Is closest to

   D Is less than

2. The main reason for reading this chart is to discover

   A Which exercises are best for you if you are less than 110 lb

   B How much you should weigh at any particular height

   C Your body index

   D The connection between calories, exercise, and body weight

3. According to the directions for reading this chart, the first thing you should do is

   A Locate your weight

   B Choose an activity

   C Multiply your weight by two

   D Divide your weight by two

4. You can conclude from the directions that

   A Skiing slowly or moderately uses the same number of calories.

   B Golf and judo use the same calories.

   C Painting outside is better for your health.

   D The longer you do an activity, the more calories you will use.

5. If you weigh 150 lb and you walk upstairs, you use how many more calories than your 110-lb child?

   A 22

   B 11

   C The same

   D None of the above

Here is an excerpt from a work procedure at a manufacturing firm. Read the document and then answer Questions 6 through 10.

ABC Inc.
Manufacturing Engineering Procedures

The **purpose of this procedure is to document methods ABC Inc. uses to control manufacturing processes.** The procedure applies to ABC Inc. documents used at any of ABC Inc.'s facilities.

Responsibility
The **Industrial Engineering Supervisor is responsible for the maintenance, interpretation, and implementation of this policy/procedure.** It is the **responsibility of all ABC Inc. supervisors and managers to enforce the use of this policy/procedure.**

Procedure

Location—Shop Floor

1.1 **Product drawings will be filed in a centrally located cabinet.** The machine operator will assure that the drawing number and revisions match the shop order prior to running the job. **If a new drawing is required, the operator shall notify the department supervisor.**

1.2 **Process, test, inspection and set-up instructions** will be available to production either **electronically via the ABC Inc. Intranet or through paper documents** kept in binders in the department they are used in.

1.3 **The supervisor or lead person can print out electronic documents from their local printer or paper documents may be removed from the binder they are stored in.** Under no circumstances should documentation remain at workstations after the process defined in the documents has been completed. **Paper documents must be returned to their proper location and any electronic document should be destroyed after it has been used.**

1.4 **Any drawings used on the manufacturing floor must be logged out at the central file to identify the drawing, revision, and location of the document.**

It is the **department supervisor's responsibility to assure these drawings maintain the current revision.**

---

6. The purpose of this document is to

   A Provide information about engineering

   B Explain ABC Inc.'s business

   C Outline the methods used to control manufacturing processes

   D Explain where documents are kept

7. In the purpose statement at the beginning of this document, the word *processes* means

   A Policies

   B Products

   C Operations

   D Inspections

8. Who is responsible for enforcing this policy/procedure?

- **A** The department supervisor
- **B** The industrial engineering supervisor
- **C** All ABC Inc. employees
- **D** All managers and supervisors

9. What should be done with used electronic documents?

- **A** Print them out
- **B** Remove them from the binder
- **C** Destroy them
- **D** Remain at the workstation

10. Who should make sure the drawings are kept current?

- **A** The lead person
- **B** The supervisors and managers
- **C** The department supervisor
- **D** The Industrial Engineering Supervisor

After you read this advertisement, answer Questions 11–14.

Secretary Wanted: Busy Office

Must be able to word process 80 words per minute, take dictation, know Microsoft Word and Excel, and keep files up-to-date. Important: Person must know how to greet and direct clients and handle inquiries and requests of incoming phone calls.

11. Which of the following is a correct inference based on the job advertisement?

- **A** The new employee will answer the telephone and keep files organized.
- **B** The new employee will take dictation, but not have to word process.
- **C** The new employee must be comfortable handling more than one task at a time.
- **D** The new employee can plan on a one-week vacation after the first year's employment.

12. In this advertisement, the word *inquiries* means

- **A** Incoming messages
- **B** Requests
- **C** Incoming questions
- **D** Quirks

13. One of the computer applications the new employee must know is

- **A** PowerPoint
- **B** Algebra
- **C** Freelance
- **D** Microsoft Word

14. You can tell the main idea of this advertisement by

    A   Looking at the heading

    B   Reading the first half of the first sentence

    C   Knowing who applied for the job

    D   Writing an application and cover letter

Read this letter and answer Questions 15 through 19.

Cal Meinhard, President
Insurance Services of America
10 Afton Boulevard
Hartford, CT 00000

Dear Senator Ross:

A vote is coming up on increasing the funds for Worksite Training, and I am writing to ask you to cast a positive vote. Many factors, including economic, social, and technological, argue in favor of increased worksite training. We have moved to an information age of high technology, global competition, and a multicultural workforce. All of these changes require upgraded employee skills.

Although we are still concerned with graduating students who can read, write, and use math skills, we know now that there are job/work specific skills that need to be addressed. We need to work together to define those skills and implement the training. As a start, we should concern ourselves with employees' ability to value different cultures in the workplace. Inherent here are implications for teamwork as well. In addition, because of the automation of technology, our entry-level workers have to make decisions, use critical thinking skills, and work with much less supervision. Finally, Senator, we must do a better job of bringing the workplace together with the schools—public, technical, and advanced—to ensure that our newest employees benefit from all of our experiences. Please vote for the bill.

Very truly yours,
Cal Meinhard

15. The reader can easily tell what this letter is going to be about because

   A   The letter was written by a businessperson to a senator.

   B   The letter talks about how industry wants an additional million dollars for programs.

   C   The letter works because it uses humor to make a point.

   D   The topic is introduced in the first sentence.

16. In the second paragraph of the letter, the opposite of the word *inherent* is

   A   Included

   B   Inherited

   C   Excluded

   D   Invited

17. You can infer from what you have read that Mr. Meinhard needs employees who can

   A   Devote more hours to a longer workweek

   B   Work independently

   C   Use technology in their jobs

   D   B and C above

18. According to this letter, employees need to work on

   A   Getting to work on time

   B   The Internet

   C   Valuing different cultures

   D   Thinking less, doing more

19. You could say that this letter's purpose is to

   A   Entertain

   B   Persuade

   C   Interrogate

   D   Insult

Telephone message forms seem like simple items. In fact, they can include essential ideas, details, and inferences that require reading skill.

Read the messages below and answer Questions 20 to 25.

Message 1	Message 2
To _Jason Chou_ ☐ URGENT Date _6/23/02_ Time _10:00_ A.M. P.M. **WHILE YOU WERE OUT** From _Eli Blum_ of _Accurate Prints Corp_ Phone _999_ – _111-2222_ _196_ Area Code Number Ext. Fax _Do Not Fax – Send email confirmation_ Area Code Number _Alan @ AccPrint.com_ Telephoned ✓ Please call Came to see you Wants to see you ✓ Returned your call Will call again Message _He says it is essential he show you the changes on the plan. Needs your OK on additions + documentation. He'll be in until 6 PM today. Can you meet over lunch_ Signed _April Lang_	To _Jason Chou_ ✓ URGENT Date _6/23/02_ Time _11:30_ A.M. P.M. **WHILE YOU WERE OUT** From _Eli Blum_ of _Accurate Prints_ Phone _999_ – _111-2222_ _196_ Area Code Number Ext. Fax ___ Area Code Number Telephoned ✓ Please call ✓ Came to see you Wants to see you Returned your call Will call again Message _His schedule has changed. He'll leave office at 4 PM sharp. Hopes you'll be able to see him at 1 P.M._ Signed _April Lang_

20. Look at the words "email confirmation" in Message 1. What does this mean?

A Say yes by e-mail.

B Phone me if you can come.

C Do not reply by fax.

D Phone me if you can't come.

21. Jason Chou has two messages from Eli Blum. Which one is more urgent?

A Message 1 is more urgent because it arrived first.

B Message 1 is more urgent because it requests lunch at 12 noon sharp.

C Message 2 is more urgent because the caller will be leaving the office shortly.

D Message 2 is more urgent because the caller will be leaving earlier than he first said.

22. What is the first clue to the urgency of the message?

A The caller's name

B The time of the call

C The Urgent box is checked

D The date of the call

23. You can conclude that Eli Blum's first choice is to

A Meet and work over lunch

B See Jason at 4 P.M.

C Meet Jason at 6 P.M.

D Cancel his request

24. In Message 1, the caller has asked Jason

    A   To please fax instead of calling back

    B   To fax and call him

    C   To fax, call, and e-mail

    D   Not to use the caller's fax

25. You can infer from the two messages that Eli wants to see Jason

    A   No later than a week from now. There's plenty of time.

    B   No earlier than 9:30 A.M. He's sleeping late.

    C   No later than today. He needs Jason's input in order to go forward.

    D   No earlier than 2003. He wants to delay the project for as long as possible.

To the Student: As you check your answers, record the results in this chart. Use the three columns next to the Answer Key to mark your answers as *Correct, Error,* or *Skipped.* Use the other columns to record additional information you want to remember about the individual questions. Total the number of your responses in each column at the bottom of the chart. Then read the recommendations that follow.

Reading Skills Assessment: Answers and Skills Analysis

Item Answers	Correct ✓	Error X	Skipped O	I have this question.	I need instruction.	Refer to these lessons.	Reading Skill Categories*
1 C						4	2
2 D						2	4
3 B						4	1
4 D						5	4
5 A						3	5
6 C						6	5
7 C						4	2
8 D						2	3
9 C						2	3
10 C						2	3
11 C						6	5
12 C						4	2
13 D						2	3
14 A						2	4
15 D						2	3
16 C						4	2
17 D						5	4
18 C						2	3
19 B						6	5

Item Answers	Correct ✓	Error X	Skipped O	I have this question.	I need instruction.	Refer to these lessons.	Reading Skill Categories*
20 A						4	2
21 D						6	4
22 C						3	5
23 A						5	4
24 D						2	3
25 C						5	4
Totals	Correct	Errors	Skipped	Questions	Instruction	Lessons	Skills

* Key to Reading Skill Categories
1. Interpret Graphic Information
2. Words in Context
3. Recall Information
4. Construct Meaning
5. Evaluate/Extend Meaning

Note: These broad categories of reading skills are broken down into subskill categories. Question numbers are aligned with the subskill titles as well as the lesson to which you can return for a review.

Reading Skills Analysis

Interpret Graphic Information

Reference Sources

LIBRARY CATALOG CARD DISPLAY

Maps

Forms   3   (See Lesson 4)

WORDS IN CONTEXT

Same Meaning   1, 7, 12, 20   (See Lesson 4)

Opposite Meaning   16

RECALL INFORMATION

Details   8, 10, 13, 18, 24   (See Lesson 2)

Sequence   9   (See Lesson 2)

Stated Concepts   15   (See Lesson 2)

CONSTRUCT MEANING

Character Aspects		
Main Ideas	2, 14	(See Lesson 2)
Summary/Paraphrase		
Cause/Effect		
Compare/Contrast	21	(See Lesson 6)
Conclusion	4, 17, 23, 25	(See Lesson 5)
Supporting Evidence		

EVALUATE/EXTEND MEANING

Fact/Opinion	22	(See Lesson 3)
Predict Outcomes		
Apply Passage Element	5	(See Lesson 3)
Generalizations		
Effect/Intentions	11	(See Lesson 6)
Author Purpose	6, 19	(See Lesson 6)
Point of View		
Style Techniques		
Genre		

RECOMMENDATIONS

To discover your areas for skills improvement in the Reading Section, do three things:

1. Total your number of correct answers out of the 25 possible answers. To score a passing grade, you should have 90 to 95 percent correct (or 23 to 24 correct answers).
2. Total the correct answers in each subset of skills. For example, in the subset *Recall Information,* there are seven correct answers. To score a passing grade, you should have 95 percent correct (or 6 correct answers).
3. Wherever your score is below 95 percent, go back to that lesson (indicated in parentheses) and review the skill.

LESSON 2 First Steps

In Lesson 2, you will follow Mike through additional pre-employment steps at Ace Computer Chip Company. He has taken the TABE reading pretest—as you have. He has also participated in the self-study exercises you learned about in Section 1. You will see the results of Mike's work. Perhaps his experience will help you to evaluate your own self-study.

You will also have an opportunity to think about important reading skills: reading to understand the main idea and supporting details.

Words to Know

Alliance	An association
Distinguish	Tell one from another
Preferences	Favorites
Confirmed	Found correct

Down to Work

At his interview with Ms. Mendez, Mike learned that Ace Computer Chip Company had an ongoing training program. Training would increase his knowledge of computer programs. In addition, through the training program, Mike would also explore many different jobs in the company. As a matter of fact, all employees at Ace took six credits of training per year. Ace Computer Chip Company had good reasons for this. Ace hoped to promote employees from within the staff. The courses offered employees a chance to learn about all the departments. Each department required different education and training.

The company also had an alliance with a nearby community college. Mike would be encouraged to take advantage of the college's more advanced computer courses. Before he interviewed at Ace, Mike had not known about financial aid. He learned that taking the TABE was a way to qualify for Ability to Benefit federal financial aid. This was another reason to do as well as possible on the tests.

TARGET: Reading for Main Ideas and Reading for Details

Reading for Main Ideas: Why is this always one of the first reading skills taught in any reading improvement course? You are probably saying, "The answer to that question is simple: If I don't get the main idea of what I'm reading, what is the point of wasting my time?" And, of course, you would be right. That is why we will take the time to review this important skill.

Warming Up for the Event

A reader should prepare himself or herself for reading just as an athlete prepares for an athletic event. Athletes need to warm up before a practice session, and so does a reader before a reading session. Your warm-up involves getting your brain "warmed up" to the subject matter. How do you do that?

 STUDY TIP

- Look at the title of the article, or chapter, or other informational material. Does it give clues to the main idea?
- If you need more clues, read the first sentences of a few paragraphs. Then read the entire last paragraph, a summary of main ideas. Any of these may hold strong main idea clues.
- Ask yourself, before you read the entire article, whether you already know something about the topic. You may be able to predict what it is about.
- Ask yourself what you can expect to learn from the reading. After you finish reading, go back and check to see if you were right.
- Look for graphic information and pictures for clues to the main idea before you start reading.
- As you read, *actively* look for the main idea.

The authors hope that we can convince you that this warm-up will take very little time. The more often you practice this skill, the faster you will become. The time spent is well worth it. At the end of a reading, you won't hear yourself saying, "I just read two pages and I have no idea what they were about!"

When you read for a main idea, you actively look for the most important thought in the passage. You ask yourself what idea the writer wanted you to know after reading the passage. For example, in paragraph 1, under the title, "Down to Work," what is the main idea? Look for the sentence that tells what the paragraph is about.

Write your answer here: _____

If you said that the paragraph is about Ace Computer Chip Company's ongoing learning program, you were right. Notice that the main idea is in the first sentence. Writers often (but not always) place the main idea in the first sentence. In that way, the writer helps readers to quickly establish a new train of thought. The readers do not have to wait to know the most important idea. Their thinking is set in the correct direction to receive the details that follow.

If the main idea is not found in the first sentence, where might it be? Sometimes a writer starts a paragraph with a transitional sentence. A transitional sentence ties the first sentence to the previous paragraph. You will read more about that later. Or, the writer might want to build evidence in the paragraph. In that case, the writer might start with supporting ideas and work up to the main idea, placing it in the last sentence. For now, you should know that the main idea is most often found in the first sentence.

Try to distinguish between the main idea and supporting details. Start by asking yourself a question: Which sentence is the sum of all the supporting details? That is the main idea. Now you are ready to look at the details.

Reading for Supporting Details: Now go back to paragraph 1. How do sentences 2, 3, 4, and 5 add detail and support to the main idea?

Write your answer here: _____

_____

You probably said that sentences 2, 3, 4, and 5 add meaning to the main idea by

- Stating that Mike would increase his knowledge of computers
- Explaining that the training program encourages employees to explore other job possibilities at the Center
- Stating that all employees take six credits of training per year
- Specifying that the training program offered opportunities to learn about the job requirements of each department

Target Practice: More Reading for Main Ideas

Now you know that when you search for a main idea in a paragraph, there is a very good chance that you will find it in the first sentence. Are main ideas found in other kinds of writing? Absolutely. Charts, graphs, and worksheets, for example, all have a main idea or a controlling topic.

Look at Mike's Learner Preference Worksheet printed below. What would you say was the main idea or topic of the worksheet? Write your answer here. _____

You probably realized that the main idea or controlling topic of the worksheet is a person's learning preferences. How did you know that? The answer is simple, of course: You read the title and probably skimmed the worksheet to see if, in fact, preferences were explored. Reading the title and skimming the worksheet were good examples of a reading warm-up.

Read Mike's Learner Preference Worksheet carefully.

Learner Preference Worksheet
Name: Mike Rinaldi

1. *What time(s) of day or night do you feel better able to study/work/read/write?*
Early morning ____ Afternoon ✓ Early evening ____ Late night ____

2. *Do you prefer to study or learn by yourself or with others?*
I like learning about new things with a study group. ____
I like learning about new things by myself. ✓
I like learning something new with one other person to help me. ____
It depends on the subject matter. ✓

3. *Do you learn best by: (Check all that apply)*

   Reading about something? ✓

   Seeing a picture or graph? ✓

   Hearing someone explain something? ___

   Doing what I'm learning about? ___

   Writing it down? ✓

   Talking about it with or without someone else? ___

4. *What length of time do you prefer to spend studying?*

   I prefer to work for periods of two hours or more. ___

   I prefer to work for shorter periods of time (less than an hour). ___

   I can work whenever time permits. ✓

5. *How's your concentration? (Check all that apply)*

   I need complete quiet when I study or read. ___

   I can study or read with some background noise. ✓

   I can study or read in any environment, quiet or noisy. ___

Mike finished the Learner Preference Worksheet. He had another meeting with the Human Resources Manager, Sue Mendez. Together they reviewed the worksheet. Mike thought that he knew what it would reveal. He was right about one item: listening. He confirmed that he did prefer to learn or receive instructions by reading, not by listening. Mike told Ms. Mendez that when he took verbal instructions, he often made mistakes. In fact, Mike remembered many such experiences. He had failed or done poorly on tests because instructions had been given verbally instead of in print. Mike recalled, with some embarrassment, that he had actually been fired from one of his first part-time jobs because of this. He did not follow verbal directions on the use of a dangerous machine.

Before you look back at the supporting details revealed in the worksheet, remember what Mike already knew about himself as a learner. He knew that he did not prefer listening as a learning tool. However, the Learner Preference Worksheet gave Mike an opportunity to explore different aspects of his preferences.

STUDY TIP: SKIMMING AND SCANNING

When a question asks you to find a detail, decide specifically what you'll be looking for. Then scan all the material for that word or number or phrase. That means that you should run your eyes down the middle of the reading, looking only for the item in question. You are not reading for meaning; you are reading to find a specific number, word, or phrase. When you reach the detail, read the words around it to be absolutely sure you have the right one.

Now answer this detail question.

Find three supporting facts that Mike discovered by working on the Learner Preference Worksheet.

_____

_____

_____

Did you find the following facts?

1 There was one preference he had never thought about before. That was the fact that he liked to learn from graphs or pictures or other representations of instructions.

2 Mike had never thought about studying or learning with others. He thought that most often he would want to study alone. But, for the first time, he considered that he might work with others—depending upon the subject.

3 Mike had never considered the time of day he studied. He had never thought that his ability to concentrate was important.

After Mike finished working on his Learning Preference Worksheet, he talked it over with Ms. Mendez. More than ever, he was concerned about his listening ability. Sue agreed with his evaluation of himself. Mike should definitely try to get instructions in writing whenever possible. She took the opportunity to mention that one of the company's training courses, "Communication Skills: Listening, Speaking, and Writing," was an excellent course for Mike. By taking the course, he would work on both of his areas of concern: listening and writing.

More about Main Ideas

You will recall that a main idea can be found somewhere other than in the first sentence. The preceding text contains a good example. Look at the paragraph that follows right after details 1, 2, and 3. The paragraph begins, "After Mike finished looking at his Learner Preference Worksheet, he talked it over with Ms. Mendez." Look back at that paragraph. Do you think of the first sentence as the main idea sentence? Is the entire paragraph about Mike's finishing the worksheet?

Your answer is probably, "No." In fact, that sentence is the bridge between the worksheet and what Mike really wants to discuss. His real concern is his inability to take verbal instruction. The first sentence is a good example of a transitional sentence. It ties the Learner Preference Worksheet to the new topic, Mike's concern about his listening ability.

To be sure, apply the test of a main idea. If, in fact, the second sentence is the main idea sentence, then all sentences that follow should support the main idea. Sentences 3, 4, and 5 strongly support Mike's concern.

Sue Mendez agreed with Mike's evaluation of himself and suggested that he do two things:

1. When it is possible, ask for written instructions in the workplace.
2. At the same time, take the training course, "Communication Skills: Listening, Speaking and Writing."

Target Practice: Reading for Main Ideas and Supporting Details

The following is a paragraph from Ace Computer Chip Company's Drug Free Workplace Policy. All new employees must sign the statement. Read the paragraph and answer the question that follows.

> Employees and management of Ace Computer Chip Company wrote the Drug Free Workplace Policy together. The policy hopes to create and keep a healthy and productive work environment. We believe that this policy will ensure the good health of the new employee who signs it. The rest of our workforce is also positively affected by the policy. Without a doubt, one employee's use of drugs or alcohol affects the safety and security of our entire staff. We believe that substance abuse affects the workplace by increasing absenteeism. It also lowers productivity and undermines, or weakens, the safety of all employees.

1. What is the main idea of the paragraph?
   A The Drug Free Policy as established applies only to employees who have worked at the company for over a year.
   B The Drug Free Policy states that the use of drugs is more serious than the use of alcohol.
   C According to the Policy, substance abuse affects productivity but has no affect on safety.
   D The Drug Free Policy was created to keep a working environment healthy and productive.

The following is a portion of the Application for Employment that Mike filled out after his first interview with Ms Mendez. After you read it, answer supporting detail questions that follow.

Application for Employment

Date _____ Name: First _____ Middle _____ Last _____

Social Security Number _____

Date of Birth _____ (if under 18)

Present Address _____ Previous Address _____

City _____ State _____ Zip _____

Home Telephone _____ Business Telephone _____

When are you available? Days? Evenings? Both?

Have you any relatives employed at Ace Computer Chip Company? If yes, please list relative(s) name(s).

What were your relative's dates of employment?

How did you learn about the job at Ace?

What position are you applying for? Salary desired?

Do you have a legal right to work in the United States?

Have you ever been convicted of a criminal offense?

If yes, please describe, including dates.

---

2. Complete this statement: The applicant may have a relative who worked at Ace Computer
   A But only within the past five years.
   B At any time in the present or past.
   C Just prior to this application.
   D But the relative must have a different address.

3. True or False: The applicant has little or no choice in the time of day he will work. _____

4. This application asks a potential employee if he/she has thought about
   A Moving from the current address
   B The salary he/she wants
   C The salary the relative earned
   D Working overseas

Use Reading Skills to Comprehend Graphs and Tables

STUDY TIP: FINDING MAIN IDEAS

You can find main ideas and details in graphic—or picture—materials. Look at the bar graph that follows. Use the skills you learned on page 29 to warm up for reading the graph. The technique works with other materials as well. Try this with charts, graphs, maps, tables, diagrams, and so forth.

Study the graph below. Use the three questions that follow to start your thinking process.

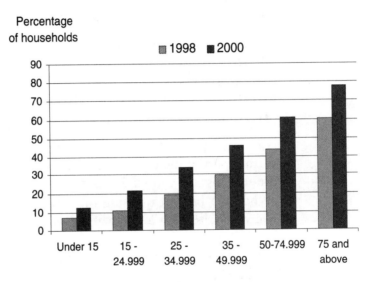

U.S. households with Internet access, by income: 1998 and 2000

Percentage of households

Household income (thousands of dollars)

Source: Science & Engineering Indicators - 2002, National Science Foundation
Graph based on Appendix table 8-6

The Warm-Up

5. Where did you find the main idea of the graph? _____

6. What one thing did you already know about the topic? _____

7. What can you expect to learn from reading the graph? _____

Answers to these questions will vary somewhat, but you should check the Answer Key to see if you are on the right track.

Now answer this question. Then check the Answer Key.

8. What is the main idea of the graph?
   A The years 1998 and 2000 in U.S. households
   B Internet access in the United States

C Internet access in U.S. households by income in 1998 and 2000
D Household income (thousands of dollars)

Warm-Up Continued

Supporting details are found in a number of places on a graph. To warm up, do this:

- Look at the left, right, and bottom margins of the graph.
- Say or write what you have found there, e.g., Household Income
- How do you think these details are related?
- Look inside the graph. Are there any distinctive ways the information is presented—for instance, different colors, heights, and so on.

Now review skimming and scanning skills above. Then answer this detail question. When you have finished, check the Answer Key.

9. A supporting detail in the graph states
  A Household income (hundreds of dollars)
  B Percentage of households
  C Only one family member's income
  D Answers B and C above

Look at a table whose main idea is the same as the graph's main idea. An important part of the title (main idea) is that the number of households with Internet access is expressed in percents.

What is a benefit of using the table form? Look at the table carefully before you write your answer below.

_____

The answer, of course, is that the reader can see the specific numbers behind the bar graph.

U.S. households with Internet access, by income: 1998 and 2000 (Percent)

Year	Household income (thousands of dollars)					
	Under 15	15–24.999	25–34.999	35–49.999	50–74.999	75 and above
1998	7.1	11.0	19.1	29.5	43.9	60.3
2000	12.4	21.3	34.0	46.2	60.9	77.7

Source: National Science Foundation.
http://www.nsf.gov/sbe/srs/seind02/c8/fig08-14.xls

10. What percentage of households earning under $15,000 had access to the Internet in 1998?
  A 12.4 percent
  B 11.0 percent
  C 34.0 percent
  D 7.1 percent

What reading skills did you use to answer this question? You probably used clue words from the question: *1998* and *Under 15*. You skimmed the table, looking for those clue words and numbers. There you found a number that was the percentage. Check your answer in the Answer Key.

Think about This

11. In your opinion is the table or the graph better for communicating the main idea? _____

12. Which one communicates specific details better? _____

Answers to these questions may vary. Look at the Answer Key for some ideas.

In the Math Section you will learn about working with the numbers in a table.

Answer Key: Section 2, Lesson 2

1. D

2. B

3. False

4. B

5. The main idea is found in the title, U.S. households with Internet access, by income: 1998 and 2000.

6. Answers will vary. You may have already known that Internet access increased with income.

7. Answers will vary. You may expect to learn how percentage of households at your income level increased over these years.

8. C, Answer C is the only answer that includes all parts of the main idea.

9. B. Answer B is the only correct answer: Answer A is an incorrect detail because income is stated in thousands; answer C is an incorrect detail because the graph deals with entire households; answer D is an incorrect answer because answer B is correct.

10. D.

11. You looked at the title in both the graph and the table in order to find the main idea. However, for many readers, there is a "picture" quality to the graph that gives meaning. The fact that the bars go from low to high suggests growth. Darker and lighter bars give a clear picture of the different years.

12. Clearly, the table communicates specific details better. The percentages of households, for instance, 7.1, 12.4, provide immediate knowledge of the numbers involved.

LESSON 3 Making Choices

In Lesson 3, Mike will learn much more about his choices for the future. The pre-employment steps helped him to think about what he really wanted of himself and the workplace. Follow Mike to the local Community College where he and other new students get involved in the admissions process.

Words to Know

Admissions process   Steps for getting into a program

Expand   Enlarge

Prerequisite   Requirement or precondition

Looking into the Future

Mike set some goals for himself when he graduated from high school. You probably recall that Mike said he wanted to (1) learn much more about the computer programs used in business and (2) make enough money to live on his own. Filling out the worksheet entitled Where Are You Headed? and going through the interviewing process at Ace Computer helped Mike to expand his thinking about his future. Read his worksheet below and think about where his answers might lead him.

Where Are You Headed?
Prospective Employee: Mike Rinaldi

I am studying to do well on the TABE to

(✓ all that apply):

✓ Qualify for "Ability to Benefit" federal financial aid

✓ Enroll in credit courses at a community college

✓ Enter a program of job training or career advancement

✓ Qualify for a promotion to the next level at my workplace

✓ Become more independent in handling my affairs

✓ Upgrade my basic skills for personal satisfaction

____ Enter a technical school

____ Help family members with their schooling

✓ Qualify for certification in Advanced WordPerfect, Microsoft Excel, Introduction to Freelance, Advanced Lotus

---

TARGET: Reading for Inferences

Have you ever thought about what it means to "read between the lines"? Obviously, there is nothing written between the lines, but there is *unwritten meaning* for the reader to construct. When you read to find an inference, you are *not* looking for stated facts. You are, instead, trying to figure out what the writer meant, but did not say. How do you do this? You look at the stated facts, but then you add your own knowledge to what you have just read. When you take these two steps, you are reading between the lines (reading for inferences).

One thing is notable about this reading skill: Inferences can be found in almost any kind of reading material. There are even ways to use the skill in reading worksheets. Later you will use the skill to read a nutrition label. But for now, look back to the worksheet, Where Are You Headed? Answer this question:

1. You can infer from the worksheet that
   A Mike will never qualify for a promotion at Ace Computer.
   B Mike thinks becoming more independent is the most important goal he can have.
   C Mike expanded his thinking about what he could accomplish at Ace Computer.
   D Mike decided that a technical school would provide him with the education he needed.

Write your answer here. _____

Did you choose answer C.? If you did, you were right. Answer A is not correct. You have no way of knowing if or when Mike will qualify for a promotion. What you do know is that he wants to learn more about the use of computers in business. Answer B is not a correct inference because the worksheet asks for "all that apply," not the most important goal. Answer C is correct. The goals that Mike talked about when you first met him were (1) to learn more about computer programs in business and (2) to earn enough money to live on his own. You can see from his choices on the worksheet that he's thinking about applying for financial aid, enrolling in a community college, and upgrading his skills both personally and at work. These choices imply that his knowledge of available resources has expanded and that his thinking has broadened to include many different choices.

Just ahead, you will have the opportunity to use this skill in a catalog of courses.

Going for the Goal

Mike was eager to find out what courses were offered at the community college. He went there to pick up a catalog of courses that would be given in the next semester. Mike found out that he could have accessed the courses just by going online. The community college had its own Web site. He sat in the lounge looking at the catalog. When he looked around, he saw a woman who was doing the same thing, but she looked very puzzled and worried. Mike asked her if she, too, was planning to take computer courses. She said, "Yes, I am, but I'm really nervous because I know nothing about computers."

Mike introduced himself and said, "Maybe I can help. Why do you need to use a computer?"

"I'm Michelle Gordon. I'm starting coursework to become a registered nurse. I haven't been in school since I became a Certified Nursing Assistant (CNA) years ago. I just found out that I must use a computer. Certain courses require that assignments be sent by e-mail. I don't know how to do that!"

Mike asked, "Can someone help you?"

"Well, my children have a computer, but they're young and they don't know anything about sending e-mail. I would love to be the one to show them how."

"It's not as hard as you might think. If you want me to, I'll look at the catalog with you and maybe we can figure out which course will help. I have to find a course, too, so I don't mind looking for both of us."

Mike opened the catalog to the section on computer courses. On page one he found the following:

Brightwater Community College
Catalog of Courses, Spring Semester

- **Introduction to Computers,** CT001, 4 credits, prerequisites: none, Professor Cabral, Tuesday, Thursday, 5 P.M.
  Description: Students will gain a basic understanding of computer equipment and procedures used in a work and/or study environment. Students will have hands-on experience with word processing, setting up e-mail accounts, and report writing and presentation.

- **Computer Business Applications,** CBA003 and IE005, 3 credits, prerequisites: CT001, Professor Mintz, Monday, Wednesday, 6 P.M.
  Description: This is a hands-on laboratory course using software for managing numerical, text, or graphic data in real-life business simulations.

- **Introduction to the Internet,** II002, 1 credit, prerequisite: CT001, Professor Santos, Saturday, 9 A.M.
  Description: This is for those who are inexperienced in using the Internet. You will learn the tools needed to navigate and search the Internet. Included is information on search engines, electronic mail, and access to many useful Internet resources.

- **Introduction to Microsoft Word,** IMW004, 3 credits, prerequisite: CT001 or permission of the instructor, Professor Davidson, Tuesday, Thursday, 6:30 P.M.

Description: This is a basic course for people with little computer experience, using a widely used word processing program. Participants will learn all of the main elements of the program, Word for Windows, toolbars, inserting and deleting text, scrolling, and much more.

- **Introduction to Excel,** IE005, 3 credits, prerequisite: CT001, Professor Cabral, Monday, Wednesday, 6 P.M.

    Description: If you need to use a spreadsheet for business, family expenses, or any other numerical data management, this is the course for you. Learn to move a mouse around a worksheet, enter text, edit cells, and produce clear reports.

- **Topics in Computers,** TC006, 2 credits, prerequisite: CT001, Professor David Dudley, Monday, 6 P.M. to 8 P.M.

    Description: Students will learn about computer equipment in the business environment. Students will gain practical knowledge of word processing, as well as learning about presentation software.

- **Introduction to Freelance,** IF008 3 credits, prerequisites: CT001 and IE005, Professor Cabral, Monday and Wednesday, 4 P.M.

Target Practice: More Reading for Inferences

2. From what you know about Michelle's educational needs, you can infer that she will choose which one of the following courses?
    A Introduction to Microsoft Word
    B Computer Business Applications
    C Introduction to Computers
    D Introduction to Excel

3. Considering what you know about Mike's goals for the future, what course would you say that Mike will choose?
    A Introduction to Computers
    B Topics in Computers
    C Help Desk Technology
    D Computer Business Applications

4. After reading the course information, you can infer that a new student with no background in computer use would be allowed to take which of the following courses?
    A Introduction to Excel
    B Computer Business Applications
    C All of the above
    D None of the above

Review Reading for Supporting Details (Important! Review the skimming and scanning skills presented in Lesson 2.)

5. A course that will teach Michelle how to use electronic mail (e-mail) is
  A Introduction to the Internet
  B Introduction to Excel
  C Introduction to Microsoft Word
  D Topics in Computers

6. Which one of the following courses does not require students to take a prerequisite?
  A Computer Business Applications
  B Introduction to Excel
  C Introduction to Computers
  D Introduction to Freelance

7. Which course teaches the use of a computer spreadsheet?
  A Introduction to Computers
  B Introduction to Excel
  C Introduction to the Internet
  D Introduction to Microsoft Word

8. Which course teaches the student how to use presentation software?
  A Introduction to Computers
  B Topics in Computers
  C Introduction to Freelance
  D Computer Business Applications

Reading for Inferences in Nutrition Labels

Study these two nutrition labels. Both are based on information from cereal boxes.

FRUIT AND BRAN CEREAL

Nutrition Facts

Serving Size 1¼ cups (55 g)
Servings Per Container About 8

Amount Per Serving	Cereal	Cereal with ½ cup Skim Milk
Calories	190	230
Calories from Fat	0	0
		% Daily Value**
Total Fat 0g*	0%	0%
Saturated Fat 0g	0%	0%
Cholesterol 0mg	0%	0%
Sodium 90mg	4%	7%
Total Carbohydrate 47g	16%	18%
Dietary Fiber 6g	24%	24%

Amount Per Serving	Cereal	Cereal with ½ cup Skim Milk
Sugars 13g		
Protein 5g		
Iron	6%	6%

Not a significant source of Vitamin A, Vitamin C, or Calcium.

* Amount in Cereal. One half cup skim milk contributes an additional 40 calories, 65mg sodium, 6g total carbohydrate (6g sugars), and 4g protein.

** Percent of daily Values are based on a 2,000-calorie diet. Your daily values may be higher or lower depending on your calorie needs:

	Calories	2,000	2,500
Total Fat	Less than	65g	80g
Saturated Fat	Less than	20g	25g
Cholesterol	Less than	300mg	300mg
Sodium	Less than	2,400mg	2,400mg
Total Carbohydrate		300g	375g
Dietary Fiber		25g	30g
Calories per gram:			
Fat 9	Carbohydrate 4	Protein 4	

NATURAL OAT CEREAL

Nutrition Facts

Serving Size: ½ cup dry (40g)
Servings Per Container 13
Amount Per Serving

Calories	150
Calories from Fat	25
	% Daily Value*
Total Fat 3g	5%
Saturated Fat 0.5g	2%
Polyunsaturated Fat 1g	
Monounsaturated Fat 1g	
Cholesterol 0mg	0%
Sodium 0mg	0%
Total Carbohydrate 27g	9%
Dietary Fiber 4g	15%
Soluble Fiber 4g	
Insoluble Fiber 2g	
Sugars 1g	
Protein 5g	
Vitamin A	0%
Vitamin C	0%

Calories	150		
Calcium	0%		
Iron	15%		

Percent Daily Values are based on a 2,000 calorie diet. Your daily values may be higher or lower depending on your calorie needs.

	Calories	2,000	2,500
Total Fat	Less than	65g	80g
Saturated Fat	Less than	20g	25g
Cholesterol	Less than	300g	300g
Sodium	Less than	2,400mg	2,400m
Total Carbohydrate		300g	
Dietary Fiber		25g	30g

Target Practice: Reading for Inferences

Now that you have read the nutrition facts on both labels, you can answer the inference questions that follow. Apply the two steps you have already learned to use in reading for inferences: (1) Look for the facts presented and (2) add *your* knowledge to the facts in order to read between the lines.

For example, suppose your doctor has advised you to lower your caloric intake to 2,000 calories per day. Dr. Wylie has also advised you to keep your sodium as close as possible to 0 mg per day.

9. You can infer from the nutrition facts in both cereals that your best choice is
   A No cereal at all
   B Either of these cereals
   C Fruit and Bran Cereal
   D Natural Oat Cereal

Suppose your doctor also wants you to lose weight. She advises that you select foods that are as low as possible in fat.

10. You can infer from the facts above that one of the cereals is a better choice. Which one is it?
    A Fruit and Bran Cereal
    B No cereal at all
    C Either of these cereals
    D Natural Oat Cereal

11. Another of Dr. Wylie's patients has been diagnosed with a mild case of diabetes. Which cereal should that patient avoid?
    A Either cereal
    B Fruit and Bran Cereal
    C Natural Oat Cereal
    D No cereal

Review Main Ideas and Details in Labels

12. The main idea of these labels is the following:
  A Every food contains certain nutrition and those facts are listed on the label.
  B Everyone should avoid all fat and calories.
  C It is possible to get large quantities of vitamins A and C from eating Fruit and Bran Cereal.
  D Every nutrition need we have is met by cereal.

13. A detail on the Fruit and Bran Cereal label tells the reader that calories are increased by
  A Increasing the amount of sodium
  B Increasing the amount of Vitamin C
  C Adding Vitamin A
  D Adding ½ cup skim milk

14. There are two kinds of dietary fiber:
  A Cholesterol and sodium
  B Insoluble and polyunsaturated
  C Soluble and insoluble
  D Soluble and saturated

Once again, you found that you needed to apply reading skills to fully understand the labels. You needed something else as well. You needed special math skills. Look for information on grams (*g,* as in *3 g*) and milligrams (*mg,* as in *300 mg*) on page 154 in Section 3, Lesson 6. In addition, you will study percents (%) in Section 3, Lesson 5.

Answer Key: Section 2, Lesson 3

1. C	**8.** B	**12.** A
2. C	**9.** D	**13.** D
3. D	**10.** A	**14.** C
4. D	**11.** B (To answer this question, you needed to know that	
5. A	people diagnosed with diabetes generally avoid foods	
6. C	that contain sugar.)	
7. B		

LESSON 4   Getting Information

In this lesson, Michelle and Mike pool their information and their resources. They have an opportunity to discuss their personal situations. You will have an opportunity to practice this skill: Understanding the meaning of words in context.

Words to Know

Literate	To be educated about, and skillful in using, something. For instance, if you are computer-literate, you know about computers and are skillful in using them.
User-friendly	An expression used to describe a computer program that is easy to use.
ISP (Internet Service Provider)	A company that connects you directly to the Internet

Networking

"Why does a nursing student have to take a computer class?" Mike asked Michelle.

"That's just what I asked!" Michelle exclaimed. "My very first nursing course requires me to get weekly assignments through the Internet. I also have to turn in my homework by e-mail. What a shock! Between raising a family and holding a part-time job, it took me eight years to complete the coursework I needed for acceptance into the Registered Nursing Program. Now I find out that I actually need another prerequisite—computer skills. I barely know how to turn on a computer, let alone use it for schoolwork. I never dreamed that it would be necessary for training as an RN.

"My advisor said not to worry because the computer program I need to learn is 'user-friendly.' She also informed me that being computer-literate is essential in today's workplace, no matter what your profession. Look here on top of the syllabus that outlines what we will study. She wrote down my username and password. I'm supposed to use these when I connect with the community college computer network. I'm not even sure which is which! Computer talk is like a foreign language to me."

"Whoa, slow down," Mike said. "Don't you have a friend who can help you?"

"Not really, my friends are as computer-challenged as I am. I did buy a second-hand computer for my kids, since they are starting to use one in school. They are way ahead of me but are too young to use the Internet. As a matter of fact, we're not even connected. Someone told me I had better choose an ISP and get connected quickly. What is an ISP and where do I get one?"

"Hey, I love computers; they are my world. Let me help. I can give you a couple of hands-on lessons using the computers in the library. You will be e-mailing in no time. Hands-on practice will help you so that computer talk like ISP is user-friendly and will start to make sense to you."

TARGET: Understanding Words in Context

We don't always know the exact meaning of all the words that we read (or hear). Of course, it is not practical to carry a dictionary all the time. However, there are techniques that good readers (and listeners) use to figure out what is being said. In fact, there is a helpful procedure to figure out the meaning of a word. That is, you examine the *context,* or situation, in which it is used. You check for clues in the words and sentences that surround the unknown word. Checking the main idea and tone of the whole article will also provide clues to word meanings.

STUDY TIP 1

Look at the word or words *immediately following* the word that you don't understand. Are commas or parentheses setting off those words? If so, the words within those punctuation marks may explain what the unknown word means. If not, look for clues in the sentences *just before or after* the word.

Example: Reread the paragraph that precedes the study tip. Find the word *context.* Now look at the words *or situation* that follow. What do you think? If you are thinking that *situation* is another way to say *context,* you are correct. These two words are synonyms, words that mean more or less the same thing. Writers will often place synonyms immediately before or after difficult words. Notice that the word *synonym* is defined, or explained, in the sixth sentence of the example.

Complete these sentences:

1. Synonyms are _____.
2. Another word for *defined* is _____.

You should have completed sentence 1 with *words that mean more or less the same thing.* The answer for sentence 2 is *explained.*

Now use Study Tip 1 to identify the meaning of the words in *italics* in the following sentences:

1. In response to the stress of tiring exercise, the human body produces chemicals called *endorphins,* the body's natural pain relievers. Endorphins are

   A A reaction to emotional stress

   B Safe medication for humans

   C Pain killers produced by the body

   D Chemicals known as dorphins

2. The professor wrote my user name and password on the top of my copy of the course *syllabus* that outlines topics she will cover in her class. A syllabus is

   A A list of books

   B A password to study materials

   C Related to the syllables of words

   D An outline of what will be studied

STUDY TIP 2

Look for patterns in the sentences that surround the unknown word. Do you see a group of words that are repeated two or more times? Are they also next to or near the unknown word? Writers sometimes structure the way they say things in order to help the reader get the message. They may purposely repeat groups of words in a sentence or paragraph for emphasis.

Example: Look back at the first paragraph under the heading, "Target: Understanding Words in Context." Locate and <u>underline</u> the group of words that is repeated in sentences three and four.

Did you underline the phrase *figure out* twice? Now circle the words that come before each of those phrases. Notice that these words—*technique* and *procedure*—have a similar meaning: They are both *a system, or a way,* to accomplish something—in this case, *a system to figure out the meaning* of words.

Now it's your turn to use Study Tip 2. In the sentences that follow, look for the similar word patterns that help define the words in *italics*.

3. Teaching about *morphemes* is an effective way to improve students' reading comprehension. Teaching about word parts that have meaning—prefixes, suffixes and roots—helps students improve their understanding of what they read.
   Morphemes are
   A Vocabulary definitions
   B Parts of words that have meaning
   C Form of an organism
   D Related to a student's reading speed

4. It took Michelle eight years to complete the coursework she needed before she could start the Registered Nursing Program. Then she discovered there was another kind of *prerequisite* she needed before she started: basic computer skills.
   Prerequisite means
   A A skill
   B A requirement for nurses
   C An exam
   D Something required ahead of time

5. *Consumption* of *legumes* in the U.S. is quite low. The average *per capita* consumption is about one pound per person each year. That means the average person eats just over one ounce of beans a month.

   From the context of these sentences, you can figure out that: (write your answers)
   A Legumes are _____
   B Consumption means _____
   C *Per capita* means _____

 STUDY TIP 3
Many words have more than one meaning. Sometimes you need to see a word used in a specific situation to know what it means. Often, the topic or the main idea of the passage will help you to interpret the meaning of individual words.

Example: (1) I was *down* for three days in bed with the flu. A friend unknowingly gave me the invisible *virus* when she sneezed.

(2) My computer system was *down* for three days after my friend unknowingly sent me e-mail that was infected by a *virus.*

In both sentences, the word *down* means "not working as usual." However, in the first sentence *down* means "in poor health." In the second sentence, it refers to "mechanical failure." Likewise, the word *virus* has two different meanings in the context of these sentences. In both cases, *virus* refers to something that has caused trouble. The system has stopped functioning normally. However, in the first sentence, *virus* means a biological organism that causes an illness. In the second sentence, *virus* means a piece of programming code that can cause damage to computer files.

Now it is your turn. Choose the meaning of the selected words in the context of these sentences.

6. The *mouse* rolled across the smooth top of the computer desk and fell with a crash on the tile floor.

Mouse means

A A small rodent with a long tail

B A small stuffed animal

C A small facial bruise, usually around the eyes

D A small device used to make selections on a computer screen

7. The suspect's testimony provided the detective with the missing *link* he needed to solve the crime.

Link means

A An association of detectives

B One of the connecting parts of a metal chain

C A word or icon connecting Web sites

D Information needed to uncover other information

Target Practice: Understanding Words in Context

Read the following selection. Pay special attention to the words in *italics.* Answer the questions that follow:

The World Wide Web (WWW) is a system that uses the Internet to link information to the world. The Web offers many different resources: Libraries, newspapers, shopping malls, telephone directories, and more exist on a *global* scale. As it continues to change and expand, the Web is becoming an enormous *repository* of human culture. The Web is a storage area for information about different ways of life.

Why has the Web become so popular? For the most part, it is a user-friendly information access tool. Also, it is fast and as easy as the nearest online computer. No wonder it is quickly becoming the research tool of choice. Experienced Web users can *readily* obtain information while saving time and energy. Indeed, young people today seem to know *intuitively* how to use the Web without having to ask. Learning opportunities are available to users of all ages, providing unlimited education at a distance. It is true that there are many irritatingly commercial, money-seeking sites. But there are many other sites that are wonderfully *altruistic.* Many sites offer information, services, and products for free.

Use the context clues in the preceding paragraphs to select the meaning of these words:

8. altruistic
   A Wonderful
   B Generous
   C Have an attitude
   D True to their word

9. global
   A On a small scale
   B Shaped like a globe
   C Worldwide
   D More than local

10. repository
   A A place for safe-keeping
   B A large container
   C A deposit box
   D A main storage area

11. readily
   A Gathering
   B Easily
   C Prepared
   D Steady flow

12. intuitively
   A Naturally
   B Bravely
   C Conclusively
   D Invitingly

More (or Less) about Michelle

Michelle wanted to stop talking about herself so she asked Mike, "How about you? Why are you looking at computer courses?"

He replied, "I can't wait to get my own place and get a better job that will pay my bills and more. After high school graduation, I just wanted to get into the workplace and leave school behind. Now, taking a job with Ace Computer Chip has opened my eyes to possibilities I hadn't considered. So here I am looking at how more education can improve my future. I know I want a career in computers. I know I want to make a good salary. I just don't know where to begin."

"Well, I do,' " Michelle offered. "I think the library is a great place to begin. My guidance counselor gave me some handouts today about job market trends for registered nurses. She told us to check out the reference section of the college library for more of the same. I'll bet you could find something like this for computer jobs."

Occupation Report

Occupation: Registered Nurses

State: (Your State)

Typical Educational Level: Associate degree

Licenses: This is a licensed occupation in (Your State). *Click here* to view licensing requirements.

Description: Administer nursing care to ill or injured persons. Licensing or registration required. Include administrative, public health, industrial, private duty, and surgical nurses.

Wages and Trends

	Registered Nurses Wages:			
Location	Median, 1998		Midrange, 1998	
	Hourly	Annual	Hourly	Annual
United States	$19.56	$40,700	$16.55–$23.59	$34,400–$49,100
(Your State)	$21.95	$45,700	$18.41–$26.36	$38,300–$54,800

Source: *Bureau of Labor Statistics, Occupational Employment Statistics Survey; Labor Market Information, Rhode Island Department of Labor and Training*

	Trends:			
Location	Employment		Percent Change	Average Annual Job Openings (due to growth and net replacement)
	1998	2008		
United States	2,078,800	2,529,700	22%	79,400
(Your State)	9,850	11,150	13%	290

http://www.acinet.org/acinet/occ_rep.htm?oescode=32502&stfips=44

Mike was excited, "This is good stuff. The future job market looks promising for you. Where did this data come from? Looks like a printout from the Web . . . oh yes, see these letters and symbols? (http://www.acinet.org/acinet/occ_rep.htm?oescode=32502&stfips=44/ . . .) That's the address of the Web site where your instructor found this chart.

"I will use this same address to search for data on computer jobs. Maybe the library is a good place to look for career information. I'm going to head for their computer lab right now. If you have time to come along, I can show you how easy it is to find this page on the Web."

When Mike and Michelle reached the library, Mike said, "It's amazing how getting information has changed." As they passed the library's card catalog, Mike couldn't resist pulling out a drawer to show Michelle an entry card. "Remember these?"

HF	
5600	Duffy, Malvern C.
W437	The Quality Revolution in Business / Malvern C. Duffy
1998	400 p
HF 5600 W425	1998
Library of Congress	

(The above is a model only.)

"Many people don't even use the card catalog in the library anymore. Now we can use the college library's Web site to see all of the titles in the library."

Michelle was amazed.

Mike continued, "But that's not all. You can use this computer to word process your college papers (or you could start using your kids' at home!). Look at this book," Mike said as he pointed to the reference shelf. He opened *Roget's Thesaurus* (a book of synonyms) and they looked at one example in it:

Encourage V. [Verb] cheer, hearten, reassure . . .

(Partial entry, *The New Roget's Thesaurus in Dictionary Form,* 6th edition, 1998.)

"Your word processing program has a thesaurus in it—and a spell check, too. As Ms. Santos said, we have no more excuses for spelling and word choice errors!"

"Actually, I should show you the library's home page first. Then it will only take a minute to show you how easily you can link, or connect, from the home page to the Web site you showed me. There are probably many other pages of information about registered nursing."

"That sounds good to me," said Michelle. "I have a couple hours before the school bus drops my children off. The sooner I get into this computer stuff, the better. Let's go."

Review: Reading for Main Ideas, Supporting Details, Inferences, and Conclusions

Look at the home page Mike accessed at the college library. Use the information to answer the questions that follow.

Bridgewater College Library
10 College Road
Anywhere, USA 00000
Phone: 000-000-0000 Fax: 000-000-0000

Library Online Catalog Library Hours & General Information

Online Research

Selected Web Sites

Reference Desk

Fiction

Local Newspaper

Newspapers Worldwide

Ask a Reference Question by E-Mail Help! I don't know which link to click.

Access other libraries in this state.

---

13. You can conclude that students use the library home page
  A To sign up for classes
  B Only to read the local newspapers
  C To link to the information they need
  D To write home for money

14. You can do more than access information; you can also
  A Find out what time it is
  B Ask a question via e-mail
  C Pay your bills
  D None of the above

15. If the book you need is not available at this library,
  A It is not available anywhere.
  B You should ask a reference question.

C Read a current newspaper instead.

D Click on Access other libraries in this state.

16. Michelle and Mike are likely most interested in which detail of this home page?

A The link to online research

B The library's address

C Fiction

D Newspapers Worldwide

Examine the Occupation Report that Michelle showed Mike. Use the information found there to answer the following questions:

17. What is the topic of this chart?

A Registered Nursing in Your State

B Median Wages for RNs

C Registered Nurses' Annual Wages

D Wages and Trends for the Occupation of Registered Nurses

18. In 1998, the median hourly wage for a registered nurse in the United States was

A $16.55–23.59

B $21.95

C $19.56

D $34,400

19. You can conclude from reading this chart that if you click on the words "click here"

A You can view licensing requirements

B You can view wages for the past 10 years

C You can register for the courses you'll need

D You can see the occupation trends for the 20th century

20. Look at the section of the chart on Wages. You can infer that *annual* means

A Hourly

B Yearly

C Weekly

D Monthly

21. True or False? A registered nurse does private duty only. _____

22. Looking at this chart, Michelle and her fellow nursing students can conclude that

A They should have chosen another profession

B The need for registered nurses is declining

C There is no further information available on their occupation

D The future for registered nurses is promising

Answer Key: Section 2, Lesson 4

1. C
2. D
3. B
4. D
5. beans, eating, per person
6. D
7. D
8. B
9. C
10. D
11. B
12. A
13. C
14. B
15. D
16. A
17. D
18. C
19. A
20. B
21. False
22. D

LESSON 5 A Continuing Search

In Lesson 5, Michelle continues her information search for college nursing courses. She was able to get lesson samples from Sally, another nursing student. Sally gave Michelle the following lesson samples from two of her first-year nursing classes. These were readings from patient treatment texts. Sally advised Michelle not to be concerned about the unfamiliar words used in the lesson samples. She should, however, definitely look at the Words to Know list first as a part of her reading warm-up. Michelle should read the lesson samples to see if she understood the content. In that way, Michelle will decide if she can handle these required courses.

Words to Know

Paraplegia	Complete inability to move the lower half of the body
Vena cava	A large vein that empties blood into the right atrium of the heart
Extremities	Bodily limbs (arms, legs)
Catheter	A flexible tube inserted into a vein or other hollow space

Intravenous   Within a vein or veins

Edema   Swelling of tissue

Read each of the following samples from a case study for a nursing student. Six of the medical terms used in the readings are defined above in Words to Know. Remember: Don't let the new and unfamiliar words get in your way. Read to get a general understanding of the case study.

Case Study for a Nursing Student, Sample I

Juan Pallo is a 23-year-old man who was injured in an automobile accident last spring. As a result of blood loss from the trauma, he suffered a spinal cord injury. The spinal cord injury led to paraplegia (i.e., paralysis of the lower extremities). Juan had a filter inserted in his inferior vena cava. It was placed there because of the high risk of complications from blood pooling in the lower extremities. The filter was to prevent blood clots from traveling to his lungs. However, approximately six months after his injury, he was readmitted to the hospital. He had developed blood clots in both legs.

Juan has been unable to work. Instead, he watches his three-year-old daughter while his spouse works. Juan and his family live in an apartment in his mother's home. Juan does not receive physical therapy in his home or at an outpatient facility. He does not have a whirlpool or a gym set up in his home, and finances are tight. During the admission history, the nurse learned that Juan does his own passive range of motion exercises. He lifts and lowers his thighs as he sits in his wheelchair.

Medical Procedure, Sample II
Medical Terminology and Its Use:

Adapted from *Taber's Cyclopedic Medical Dictionary,* 1954, PA Davis: Philadelphia

Parenteral Hyperalimentation:

Some patients are unable to take food orally. Part of their care is to provide the total caloric needs by intravenous route. Although this is extremely difficult, patients have been maintained in a healthy state for prolonged periods. Nutrients are provided through a catheter extending through the subclavian vein to the superior vena cava.

The daily feeding of 2,500–3,000 kcal for an adult includes the following:

- 2,500–3,000 ml of water, 100–130 gm
- Protein hydrolysate (amino acids).

- 525–625 gm dextrose; 125–150 mEq sodium, 75–120 mEq potassium; 4–8 mEq magnesium, plus
- Vitamins A, D, E, C, thiamine, riboflavin, niacin, and pantothenic acid. Calcium, phosphorus, and iron are given as required.
- Vitamin B12, folic acid, and vitamin K are given intramuscularly as needed.
- Trace elements are required after one month of continuous feeding.

Nursing Implications:

- Explain the procedure to the patient.
- Obtain a nutritional assessment of the patient.
- Monitor and record intake and output.
- Assist with the catheter insertion. Observe for adverse effects.
- Document procedure and initial fluid administration.
- Monitor fluid flow with mechanical device and frequent nursing observations.
- Inspect and redress catheter site every 24–48 hours using strict aseptic technique.
- Document condition of site and position of catheter. Evaluate for catheter leakage and report to a physician immediately.
- Monitor electrolytes. Administer (I.M.) weekly vitamin supplements as prescribed.
- Observe for presence of edema or dehydration.
- Provide discharge teaching for patient and those in the household who will be caring for the patient.

TARGET: Reading to Draw Conclusions

Both of the preceding readings are filled with words and information that are probably unfamiliar to you. However, key words and phrases help to explain the procedure. You can draw conclusions about the meanings of unknown words. That is, you can make a decision about their meaning by reading words and phrases near the unknown words. Go back to the case of Juan and answer the following questions by looking for key words and phrases in the text.

1. From which set of key words can you draw a conclusion about how Juan's injury occurred?
   A Automobile accident
   B Spinal cord
   C Blood loss
   D Blood pooling

If you answered A, *automobile accident,* you are correct. You knew the answer because the key words are familiar to you; they were used in the same sentence as the word *injury.* Sometimes, however, you must search for the key words embedded in the text. Go back to Juan's case again and answer Question 2.

2. What can you conclude about Juan's current situation?
  A Juan is fine and needs no further assistance.
  B Juan will be able to go back to his full time job.
  C Juan can afford to have a nurse come into his home for therapy.
  D Juan is on his own when it comes to his physical therapy.

If you answered D, you are correct. Look at key words and phrases, "finances are tight," "does not receive physical therapy," "does his own . . . exercises," and "does not have a whirlpool or gym." You are able to draw the conclusion from the facts. Juan is on his own when it comes to his physical therapy. None of these words or phrases would support the other ideas in answers A through C.

Michelle was nervous when she looked at the unfamiliar words in the cases. However, after trying the first two questions, she was feeling better about her ability to figure out what she was reading. The fact that she is a Certified Nursing Assistant made it a little easier for her to understand some of the words in the cases.

Use the key word and phrase technique when you draw conclusions, and you too will find it easier to read unfamiliar text. Try this technique now when answering questions about Case II above.

3. Parenteral Hyperalimentation refers to
  A Parental duties
  B Vitamin deficiency
  C Intravenous feeding of a patient
  D Documentation procedures

If you answered C, intravenous feeding of a patient, you are correct. Key words and phrases in the first paragraph, "unable to take food orally" and "daily feeding for an adult," help you draw the conclusion. *Parenteral hyperalimentation* refers to intravenous feeding of a patient. Even though the term may be unfamiliar, the key words and phrases in the paragraph assist you in drawing a conclusion about its meaning. Now try the next question.

4. What conclusion can you draw from reading the Nursing Implications?
  A Intravenous feeding of a patient is not a complicated procedure.
  B Once the patient is discharged, there is nothing left to be concerned about.
  C A patient who is being fed intravenously must be monitored regularly.
  D Patients can feed themselves intravenously.

If you answered C, you are correct. Keywords "assist," "observe," "document," "inspect," and "evaluate" all lead you to draw that conclusion. A patient being fed intravenously must be monitored regularly. None of the other statements can be made about the case in question.

Review: Reading for Details and Conclusions

5. According to Medical Procedure, Sample 2, nutrients flow through a catheter
   A Extending through the subclavian vein to the superior vena cava
   B Extending through the vena cava to the subclavian vein
   C Folic acid and vitamin K
   D Only if the patient is able to walk

6. You can infer from the information in Sample I that
   A Juan will return to full activity in one week.
   B Juan will not be able to work in the near future.
   C Juan's wife will give up work soon.
   D Juan's child will care for him.

7. One of the nursing implications in the Medical Procedure is
   A To keep Juan's wheelchair in excellent working order
   B To obtain a nutritional assessment of the patient
   C Explain the procedure to the doctor
   D Leave the room while the catheter is inserted

Drawing Conclusions from a Chart

When she was an assistant nurse, Michelle learned to take a patient's vital signs. Vital signs are the important signs of life. These signs show the health of the body in four main ways. The main vital signs include:

- Temperature—The measure of the balance between heat loss and heat produced
- Pulse—The pressure of the blood felt against the wall of an artery.
- Respiration—Breathing in and breathing out.
- Blood pressure—The force exerted by the heart against arterial walls when the heart contracts or relaxes

Reading a chart requires many skills. The chart that follows gives you many facts. You can also use those facts to draw conclusions. Start by reading the title; it tells you the main idea or topic of the chart. Go on to read the supporting details such as these: Day in Hospital, Date, Hour, and so forth.

Study this portion of a vital signs chart. Then answer the questions.

Chart of Vital Signs

Patient's Name: Doe, Felix/Doctor's Name: Dr. John Smith Room No. 206
Patient ID907.

Date:	12/1/03	12/2/03	12/3/03	12/4/03	12/5/03	12/6/03
Day in Hospital:	1	2	3	4	5	6
Hour:	AM PM 4 8 12 4 8 12	AM PM 4 8 12 4 8 12	AM PM 4 8 12 4 8 12	AM PM 4 8 12 4 8 12	AM PM 4 8 12 4 8 12	AM PM 4 8 12

T
E
M   A
P   D   102°
E   M   100° 101°
R   I   99.8° 99.6°
A   T   98.6° 98.6°
T   T
U   E
R   D
E

8. According to the chart, Felix's temperature became normal
   A On the second day after admission to the hospital
   B At the same time each day
   C Two days after Felix went home
   D In the morning only

9. After he was admitted, Felix remained in the hospital for a total of how many days?
   A One
   B Two
   C Three
   D Four

10. If normal temperature is just below 99°, Felix's temperature was normal on day

   A one

   B three

   C four

   D two

11. You can also conclude that Felix's temperature was higher in the

   A Evening

   B Admitting room

   C Morning

   D In the operating room

Michelle knew that all children were supposed to be immunized, or protected against diseases. She knew that the immunizations would keep her children safe from serious diseases. Her children were up-to-date on their immunizations and doses. But she had never seen a chart of immunizations until now. Read along with Michelle to see all the immunizations that children must have.

There are many facts in this chart and even a conclusion that you can draw. Warm up for the activity by reading the title and the explanation below it.

Recommended Childhood Immunization Schedule
United States, January–December 2001

Vaccines are listed under recommended ages. Bars indicate the range of recommended ages for immunization. Any dose not given at the recommended age should be given as a "catch-up" immunization at a later visit as shown. Ovals indicate vaccines to be given if the recommended doses were missed or given earlier than the recommended minimum age.

Vaccine	Birth	1 mo	2 mos	4 mos	6 mos	12 mos	15 mos	18 mos	24 mos	4–6 yrs	11–12 yrs	14–18 yrs
Hepatitis B		Hep B #1										
X			Hep B #2			Hep B #3					Hep B	
Diphtheria-tetanus toxoids-pertussis			DTaP	DTaP	DTaP		DTaP			DTaP	TD	
Haemophilus Influenzae type b			Hib	Hib	Hib	Hib						
Inactivated poliomyelitis			IPV	IPV		IPV			IPV			
Pneumococcal conjugate			PCV	PCV	PCV	PCV						
Measles-mumps-rubella						MMR			MMR		MMR	
Varicella						VAR					VAR	
Hepatitis A									Hep A in selected areas			

☐ Range of recommended ages for vaccination.

⬭ Vaccines to be given if previously recommened doses were missed or were given earlier than the recommended minimum age.

▨ Recommended in selected states and/or regions.

Source: Centers for Disease Control and Prevention.

http://www.cdc.gov/mmwr/preview/mmwrhtml/mm5001a3.htm

12. Bars and ovals are used to organize information in the chart. They indicate
 A Where and when the children were born
 B The names of two diseases only
 C Age ranges and missed doses
 D The names of doctors you need to see

13. The Hepatitis B #1 immunization is given
 A After Hepatitis B #2
 B Between birth and two months
 C After DTaP3
 D To adults only

14. You can conclude from information in the chart that
 A Immunizations are never given to people after age 18.
 B All children receive their shots and doses at exactly the same ages.
 C If an immunization is missed, it can be given later.
 D There is only one hepatitis vaccine.

LESSON 6 Back to School

In Lesson 6, you will follow Michelle as she experiences the pleasures and trials of going back to school as an adult. She has been to her first class and returned home, thinking about the commitment she has made.

In this lesson, you will have an opportunity to practice the reading skills associated with essays, autobiography, and fiction. You will consider the author's purpose, style, and technique.

Words to Know

Metaphor	A symbol
Empathizes	Identifies with
Eligible	Entitled

The First Class

Michelle drove home after her first class, amazed that she had not only learned and understood the Introduction to Computers first lesson, but also that she really enjoyed it. She couldn't wait to demonstrate her new skills to her children. She feared that the course would not continue to be this easily understood. Fortunately, she could add Mike Rinaldi to her list of supports. He would help her if she needed to ask him. She thought he was a very nice young man and that he would go far with his knowledge of computers.

Michelle also felt fortunate to have met another woman her age, maybe a little older, who was starting her second semester at the community college. She confided her worst fears of failure to Ruth.

When they walked to the bookstore together later that first day, Ruth said that a friend of hers had given her something to read. Ruth had placed it on her refrigerator door six months ago. Whenever Ruth felt unsure of herself, it helped to know that others had been through the same things and survived. She would reread the statements. She wanted Michelle to read them, so she promised to bring it to their next class.

True to her word, Ruth arrived the next time with the two personal statements, one written by a student and the other by a well-known comedian. Michelle read them and smiled. Here were two people who knew exactly how she felt.

Read the passages and answer the questions that follow.

Essay #1

I find that life can be compared to a gigantic roller coaster, with a never-ending track, boasting extremely dangerous curves. Sometimes you can be moving so fast that it feels like the brakes have been torn out from under you. I find that when you start in a downward motion, your roller coaster car can be hard to steer on your own.

But sometimes in the roller coaster nightmare you are going so fast that it becomes difficult to get off and you begin to feel like there is nobody who is willing or capable of helping you slow down that roller coaster car, or even help you negotiate those tight and narrow turns.

Sometimes there are other people's roller coaster cars that are more skilled at traveling that track, and they are so concerned to reach the end of their journey that they forget about other people's roller coaster cars. When you are traveling that track, your body and soul become worn down and eventually you end up falling off one of those tight and narrow turns.

Is there anybody on that track who is willing to slow down and help you travel that twisty, windy path?

I hope that type of individual exists on our track of life today, for you and me.

If this individual does exist, I hope I can find him or her before I hit the wall and end up burning in a ball of flames. I hope society is able to realize the importance of those types of people and the gifts they offer society, before society destroys all the tracks by traveling too rapidly.

—Cindy Hedrick, "The Roller Coaster," Voices: New
Writers for New Readers
Issue 10, Volume 4, Number 1, Fall 1991

Essay #2

Life is truly a ride. We're all strapped in and no one can stop it. When the doctor slaps your behind, he's ripping your ticket and away you go. As you make each passage from youth to adulthood to maturity, sometimes you put your arms up and scream; sometimes you just hang on to that bar in front of you. But the ride is the thing. I think the most you can hope for at the end of life is that your hair's messed, you're out of breath, and you didn't throw up.

—Jerry Seinfeld, excerpt from *SeinLanguage,* p. 153

TARGET: Reading to Recognize Literary Techniques

You can see that two very different people wrote the passages. A student wrote the first one. A well-known comedian wrote the second. Still, they both have used the same technique. Both used a metaphor, or symbol, for life. What is that symbol? Write your answer here. _____

You probably realized that both writers used a ride or roller coaster as a symbol for what happens in life. The reader easily empathizes with the picture of the rider hurled through space. You know or can vividly imagine the feeling of being flung through space (life) as you hang on with all your strength.

What else can you tell about the two writers from these passages? Can you tell something about their moods? What is the overall tone—that is, the outlook or feelings exhibited by each author?

Answer the following questions to explore the authors' motivations, tone, and meaning.

1. The conclusion that Jerry Seinfeld has reached is that
   A If you don't want to ride, just get off
   B Everyone knows exactly what life will bring to them
   C The ride is the important thing
   D You're a baby if you scream

2. The tone of the first passage tells you that the writer's life has
   A been really easy and predictable
   B been easily steered, especially the tight turns
   C been as frantic and scary as a roller coaster ride
   D all of the above

3. The student's essay ends
   A In complete despair
   B On a hopeful note
   C With no hope
   D In negotiation

4. In the Seinfeld article, what does the final sentence mean?
   A Don't go on the roller coaster if you don't like getting your hair messed up in the wind.
   B Don't go on the roller coaster if you're afraid of throwing up, and if you have a hard time breathing.
   C Don't go on the roller coaster if you do have a cold and have a hard time breathing.
   D If your hair's messed, you're out of breath, and you didn't throw up, you've probably taken part in and succeeded in life.

5. Cindy's second and third paragraphs express
   A A real cry for help
   B Her despair because she is worn down in body and soul

C The fear that she will fall off the track

D All of the above

6. What is Cindy's hope for society?

    A Society will realize the importance of people who help others.

    B Everyone will leave her alone so that she can get on with her life.

    C She can get her children to school on time with the help of others.

    D Answers A and B above.

7. Compare the two passages. Which of the following statements is true about the passages?

    A Seinfeld's is true for everyone, while Cindy's is true for no one.

    B Seinfeld's is resigned but positive, while Cindy's is fearful but willing to go forward.

    C Seinfeld's is without humor, while Cindy's is humorous throughout.

    D Cindy writes about other people's lives, while Seinfeld writes only about himself.

The Star Thrower Story

From the story by Joel Barker, inspired by Loren Eiseley. (*www.starthrower.com/aboutbody.html#4*)

There's a story I would like to share with you. It was inspired by the writing of Loren Eiseley. Eiseley was . . . a scientist and a poet. And from those two perspectives he wrote insightfully and beautifully about the world and our role in it.

Once upon a time, there was a wise man, much like Eiseley himself, who used to go to the ocean to do his writing. He had a habit of walking on the beach before he began his work. One day he was walking along the shore. As he looked down the beach, he saw a human figure moving like a dancer. He smiled to himself to think of someone who would dance to the day. So he began to walk faster to catch up. As he got closer, he saw that it was a young man and the young man wasn't dancing, but instead he was reaching down to the shore, picking up something and very gently throwing it into the ocean.

As he got closer, he called out, "Good morning! What are you doing?"

The young man paused, looked up and replied, "Throwing starfish into the ocean."

"I guess I should have asked, Why are you throwing starfish into the ocean?"

"The sun is up and the tide is going out. And if I don't throw them in they'll die."

"But young man, don't you realize that there are miles and miles of beach and starfish all along it. You can't possibly make a difference!"

The young man listened politely. Then bent down, picked up another starfish and threw it into the sea, past the breaking waves. "It made a difference for that one!"

His response surprised the man. He was upset. He didn't know how to reply. So instead, he turned away and walked back to the cottage to begin his writings. All day long as he wrote, the image of the young man haunted him . . .

8. The author's purpose in writing this story is to remind the reader that
   A The tide goes out once a day.
   B Eiseley was a poet and a scientist.
   C The beach is no place for serious work.
   D Each of us has the ability to make a difference in the world.

9. You can conclude that Eiseley used his writing ability as well as his knowledge of science to
   A Help people to better understand and live in their environment.
   B Make people understand that throwing one starfish in the ocean is no help at all.
   C Comment on the dancing ability of people who walk the beach.
   D Keep from taking a job.

10. How do you think this story ends?
   A The writer in the story goes home and spends the day being angry with the young man.
   B The young man stops throwing the starfish as soon as he meets the writer and realizes that he alone cannot make a difference.
   C When the writer in the story goes home, he realizes that the young man was someone who had decided to make a difference.
   D When the story ends, only two starfish have been saved.

Now let's look at the work of a writer, Maya Angelou, who turned a personal statement into an autobiography. The name of the book is *I Know Why the Caged Bird Sings*. The book, published in 1970, was nominated for the National Book Award.

When Maya and her brother were three and four years old, their father sent them to live with their grandmother. As you will see, Maya's name was Marguerite Johnson before she changed it. The following has been adapted from the original.

When I was three and Bailey four, we had arrived in the musty little town, wearing tags on our wrists which instructed—"To Whom It May Concern"—that we were Marguerite and Bailey Johnson Jr., from Long Beach California, en route to Stamps, Arkansas, c/o Mrs. Annie Henderson.

Our parents had decided to put an end to their calamitous marriage. Father shipped us home to his mother. A porter had been charged with our welfare—he got off the train the next day in Arizona—and our tickets were pinned to my brother's inside coat pocket.

I don't remember much of the trip. But after we reached the segregated southern part of the journey, things must have looked up. Negro passengers, who always traveled with loaded lunch boxes, felt sorry for "the poor little motherless darlings" and plied us with cold fried chicken and potato salad . . .

The town reacted to us as its inhabitants had reacted to all things new before our coming. It regarded us a while without curiosity but with caution. After that we were seen to be harmless (and children). The town closed in around us, as a real mother embraces a stranger's child. Warmly, but not too familiarly.

We lived with our grandmother and uncle in the rear of the Store (it was always spoken of with a capital s). She had owned it for some twenty-five years.

Early in the century, Momma (we soon stopped calling her Grandmother) sold lunches. She sold to the sawmen in the lumberyard (east Stamps) and the seedmen at the cotton gin (west Stamps). Her crisp meat pies and cool lemonade, when joined to her miraculous ability to be in two places at the same time, assured her business success. From being a mobile lunch counter, she set up a stand between the two points of fiscal interest. She supplied the workers' needs for a few years. Then she had the Store built in the heart of the Negro area. Over the years, it became the lay center of activities in town.

The formal name of the Store was the Wm. Johnson General Merchandise Store. Customers could find food staples, a good variety of thread, mash for hogs, corn for chickens, coal oil for lamps, light bulbs for the wealthy . . . Anything not visible had only to be ordered.

11. In the second paragraph, you can conclude that the word *calamitous* means
  A Loving
  B Disastrous
  C Enduring
  D Bright

12. According to the passage, Marguerite and Bailey did not go hungry on the train; they
  A Ordered all the food they could eat in the dining car; money was not a problem.
  B Carried enough food for a three-day trip.
  C Were fed very well by other Negro passengers once they reached the southern part of the trip.
  D Offered some of their very large food supply to other people on the trip.

13. After a while, the children referred to their grandmother as
  A Their best friend
  B Their aunt

C Their enemy

D Their mother

14. If you met Marguerite's grandmother today, you might think of her as

  A A very mean and unfeeling woman

  B A busybody

  C A person with no ambition

  D A very talented businesswoman

Review Reading Skills

Read the following paragraph adapted from a nonfiction book called *Coping with Difficult People*. Answer the questions that follow the paragraph.

Introduction to Coping with Difficult People, by Robert M. Bramson, Ph.D.

This is a book about impossible people and how to cope with them. Your life may be free from hostile customers and co-workers. You may not have an indecisive, vacillating boss. The people who work for you may not be overagreeable (but do-nothing). If you work with none of those who deserve to be called Difficult People, read no further. Consider yourself extraordinarily lucky and move on to pleasanter fare. If, however, those constant headaches have intruded, read on. The purpose of this book is to show you how to identify, understand, and cope with the Difficult People who come into your life. It is directed primarily to those who must work with others to accomplish common tasks. The methods described here, however, are applicable in many different settings . . .

15. You can see that the main idea of the paragraph

  A Tells the reader the main theme of the book

  B Is stated in the first sentence

  C Immediately prepares the reader for what is to come

  D All of the above

16. The paragraph talks about a serious subject, but the author

  A Does not expect many people to agree with him

  B Feels that all readers have all the answers to the problem

  C Has adopted a light tone

  D Knows that no one can help the reader to understand this topic

17. Read the word "vacillating" in its context. What other word helps you to understand it?

  A Indecisive

  B Hostile

  C Do-nothing

  D Subordinates

18. The writer says that those who are "free from hostile customers and coworkers . . ." should "read no further." You can conclude that

   A The author expects you to close the book immediately.

   B The author knows that everyone in the world needs to read this book.

   C The author himself has never had experiences with difficult people.

   D The author knows that many people have had experiences with difficult people in different settings

Answer Key: Section 2, Lesson 6

1. C	**5.** D	**9.** A	**13.** D	**17.** A
2. C	**6.** A	**10.** C	**14.** D	**18.** D
3. B	**7.** B	**11.** B	**15.** D	
4. D	**8.** D	**12.** C	**16.** C	

3 Mathematics

LESSON 1 Time for a Change

Kenneth Williams started working as soon as he turned 16. The world outside of high school interested him more than his studies. It offered him rewards for work that he enjoyed. After graduation, the thought of more schooling never entered Kenneth's mind.

Ken's forte is construction work. Employers find him to be dependable, hardworking, and congenial. He finds the work satisfying. But now, after 15 years, marriage, and three children, Ken wants more choices in his life. His search has brought him to the campus of Brightwater Community College, where he has an appointment to meet with Ray Stanton, Director of Career Services.

Words to Know

Forte	Specialty or strength
Congenial	Sociable; agreeable
Remedial instruction	Instruction needed to fill in the gaps in one's knowledge or skills in a certain subject in order to advance to a higher level

Investigating Options:

"Hello, Kenneth; I'm Ray Stanton. Welcome to Brightwater."

"Thank you," said Ken. He grinned and shook his head, "I must admit it feels odd being here instead of on the job. I guess I did it backwards—marrying, having kids, and working first. Now I'm starting what I was supposed to start 15 years ago."

"Don't sell yourself short," said Ray. "That kind of 'supposed to' thinking went out years ago. 32 isn't too old for starting out. These days, adults need to gear up for a lifetime of learning. Today's average worker needs to be prepared to change jobs, if not careers, four or five times. That often means going back to school. We have partnerships with several employers. They send their workers here for retraining and skills upgrading. Tell me, what do *you* hope to accomplish with more education?"

"I want a job I can still do if my back fails me—one that gives me more time with my family, and better pay. Basically, I'm a laborer in construction.

You name a type of construction, I'll bet I've done it. I enjoy the work, but I can see the time coming when my back won't let me keep going. I want to stay in construction and qualify for a different position. For that, I know I need more education."

"It seems you have given this a lot of thought. Have you figured out what position you'd like to qualify for? Do you know what courses you want to take?"

"No. I need advice on both those things. Right now, I want to take something that will help me advance above laborer. I also want to take just one course at first, to find out if I can keep up with college-level work. That way, too, I can keep my job."

"Sounds reasonable." agreed Ray. "With your years of experience, a small amount of formal training in the classroom may take you a long way. You may want to consider something like building inspection technology. Talk with an advisor in our Engineering Technology Department. Ask him if a class in blueprint reading or CAD—Computer Aided Drafting—might be a place to start."

Roadblock? "I'd like something like that," Ken said. Then his face fell. "I have a problem I haven't mentioned. My math skills are in the basement. I took the Assessment Tests after I registered and did not score well enough in the math to enroll in college credit classes. I know I can take Fundamentals of Math 101, but I don't want to spend money and time on that remedial class if I can help it. Is there some place I can get help with math now? I'm willing to put in as much study time as it takes to qualify for one of the courses you talked about by next semester. Any suggestions?"

"Definitely," said Ray. "The Academic Success Center should be your next stop. There you will find other students working on whatever basic skills they need to improve."

"Great. Thanks for your advice," said Ken as he stood up and shook hands with Ray.

"You're welcome, Ken. Good luck."

Next Step: André Brown, a Brightwater student, greeted Ken at the Success Center. Ken told him why he had come. "You just missed Connie Garcia, the Center Director. This is a great place to get help, but first things first." He handed Ken a Math Self-Assessment Packet. "Just follow the directions in this packet. If you can't stay now to do it, complete it at home. It contains what you need to get started. Then come meet Connie."

Getting Started: After he arrived home, Ken opened the Math Self-Assessment Packet and glanced through it. The first form to fill out was a survey about how he used math in his daily life. Ken sat down at the kitchen table, grabbed a pencil, and started writing.

Math in My Daily Life

I use math as a ✓ Consumer (buy food, household goods, and equipment)

    ✓ Renter or ___ Homeowner ✓ Car owner
    ✓ Bill-payer (✓ Cash ✓ Checkbook ___ Savings account)
    _?_ Athlete ___ Craftsperson ___ Hobbyist

I use math to ✓ Keep healthy ✓ Furnish/decorate my home ✓ Landscape yard/garden

    ✓ Plan for the future

I also use math to _figure my bowling average; Poker night with guys_
I use math to help these people in my life _kids – homework; mom – her bills; wife – budget_
I use math to figure out _how much I can spend on food & entertainment_
I use math on the job to _will use on future jobs I hope to get_
I want to get better at using math to _do well in tech classes— be confident_
I already know I need to learn more about _Fractions, percents, algebra & formulas_

Applied Mathematics

I am able to use math to understand these types of materials:

Advertisements	✓ Yes	___ No	___ Need practice	___ I don't know
Maps	✓ Yes	___ No	_?_ Need practice	___ I don't know
Graphs and diagrams	✓ Yes	___ No	✓ Need practice	___ I don't know
Tables and charts	___ Yes	___ No	✓ Need practice	___ I don't know
I can visualize, or draw pictures, to help me solve word problems.	___ Yes	___ No	___ Need practice	✓ I don't know
I use estimation to figure things out.	✓ Yes	___ No	✓ Need practice	___ I don't know
I can measure distances, weight, and time.	✓ Yes	___ No	✓ Need practice	___ I don't know
I can figure perimeter, area, and volume.	✓ Yes	___ No	✓ Need practice	___ I don't know

Math Computation

I know my basic number facts.	✓ Yes	___ No	___ Need practice	___ I don't know
I understand math symbols.	___ Yes	___ No	✓ Need practice *on lots of them*	___ I don't know
I am comfortable with math terminology.	___ Yes	___ No	___ Need practice	✓ I don't know
I use a calculator. *just the basics*	✓ Yes	___ No	___ Need practice	___ I don't know
I can do equations. *I REALLY Need this!*	___ Yes	___ No	✓ Need practice	___ I don't know

Now it's your turn. Follow Ken's example with your own information.

Math in My Daily Life

I use math as a ___ Consumer (buy food, household goods, and equipment)

     ___ Renter or ___ Homeowner ___ Car owner
     ___ Bill-payer (___ Cash ___ Checkbook ___ Savings account)
     ___ Athlete ___ Craftsperson ___ Hobbyist

I use math to ___ Keep healthy ___ Furnish/decorate my home ___ Landscape yard/garden

     ___ Plan for the future

I also use math to _____
I use math to help these people in my life _____
I use math to figure out _____
I use math on the job to _____
I want to get better at using math to _____
I already know I need to learn more about _____

Applied Mathematics

I am able to use math to understand these types of materials:

Advertisements	___ Yes	___ No	___ Need practice	___ I don't know
Maps	___ Yes	___ No	___ Need practice	___ I don't know
Graphs and diagrams	___ Yes	___ No	___ Need practice	___ I don't know
Tables and charts	___ Yes	___ No	___ Need practice	___ I don't know

I can visualize, or draw pictures, to help me solve word problems.	____Yes	____No	____Need practice	____I don't know
I use estimation to figure things out.	____Yes	____No	____Need practice	____I don't know
I can measure distances, weight, and time.	____Yes	____No	____Need practice	____I don't know
I can figure perimeter, area, and volume.	____Yes	____No	____Need practice	____I don't know

Math Computation

I know my basic number facts.	____Yes	____No	____Need practice	____I don't know
I understand math symbols.	____Yes	____No	____Need practice	____I don't know
I am comfortable with math terminology.	____Yes	____No	____Need practice	____I don't know
I use a calculator.	____Yes	____No	____Need practice	____I don't know
I can do equations.	____Yes	____No	____Need practice	____I don't know

Back at the kitchen table: The next thing Ken pulled out of the Math Packet looked suspiciously like a test. He groaned, "Well, I knew I'd have to do something like this, so I better get started." However, after Ken read the directions, he decided to wait until the next day. It was almost time for his kids to get home from school. He knew the house would explode with sound and motion. It would be hard to concentrate. He also knew that before he sat down to focus on a bunch of math problems, he would need some fresh air and exercise. **How about you?**

Math Skills Assessment

Choose Your Time and Place   Take this assessment when you have the time and the energy to focus on the questions. Take it in a place where you will be undisturbed. If you get interrupted, and cannot concentrate, finish it at another time.

Set Your Own Pace   This is _not_ a timed test. Its purpose is to help you sort out what you know and don't know. _If you don't know how to work a problem, put a ? beside it and move on._ You will have a chance to learn about that type of math question in the lessons that follow.

 FYI

This two-part assessment is the same length, and covers the same type of math, as the Survey Forms 7 and 8 of TABE Level A. The Posttest at the _end_ of this book will be timed in the same manner as the TABE. For now, make a note of your start and stop times in order to get an idea of how long it takes you to complete your math work _at this point in time._

Math Skills Assessment
Part I: Computation
Note: No calculator permitted.

Date: _____ Location: _____ Start time: _____

1 $5.065 + 25 + 1.3 =$
  A 31.365
  B 5.215
  C 5.315
  D 5,315
  E None of these

2 $44 \times 10.60 =$
  A 848.0
  B 4,664
  C 46.64
  D 466
  E None of these

3 $7.50 \div 2.5 =$
  A 3.0
  B 2.30
  C 0.34
  D 30.00
  E None of these

4 $2\frac{3}{4} \times \frac{1}{2} =$
  A $1\frac{3}{8}$
  B $5\frac{1}{2}$
  C $3\frac{5}{8}$
  D $1\frac{1}{2}$
  E None of these

5 $12\frac{1}{4} - 9\frac{3}{4}$
  A $3\frac{1}{2}$
  B $3\frac{1}{4}$
  C $21\frac{1}{4}$
  D $2\frac{1}{2}$
  E None of these

6 $|{-30}| + |8| =$
  A -22
  B 38
  C -24
  D 22
  E None of these

7 $(-7) + 3 =$
  A 10
  B -4
  C $+4$
  D 21
  E None of these

8 $6 + (-9) =$
  A -3
  B -15
  C 15
  D $+3$
  E None of these

9   25% of 40 =

    A   65

    B   ¼

    C   10

    D   15

    E   None of these

10 $6.00 is what percent of $8.00?

    A   50%

    B   0.75%

    C   48%

    D   75%

    E   None of these

11   5% of $100 =

    A $5.25

    B $20.25

    C $5

    D $52.25

    E   None of these

12 $80^2 + 8^2 =$

    A   176

    B   6,416

    C 640^2

    D   6,464

    E   None of these

13 $7a - 2a =$

    A   −5

    B $7a^2$

    C   5a

    D   5 + 2a

    E   None of these

14 $8a + a - 3b^2 =$

    A $9a^2 - 3b^2$

    B $6a^2b^2$

    C $9a - 3b^2$

    D $8a^2 - 3b^2$

    E   None of these

15 $10^6 \div 10^2 =$

    A 10^4

    B 1^4

    C 100^4

    D 100^3

    E   None of these

16 $\dfrac{3y^2 + 10y}{2y} =$

    A $8 y^3$

    B $3y^2 + 5y$

    C $1.5y + 5$

    D   6.5y

    E   None of these

Stop time: _____

Math Skills Assessment

Part II: Applied Math
Note: Calculator permitted.

You may use a calculator as you solve problems in Part II, but you may find that some questions are solved just as easily without one. Have scratch paper handy to help you work through the problems.

Date: _____ Location: _____ Start time: _____

Questions 1–3 refer to the following information.

> **Recycling**
>
> The Parent Group of the local Head Start promoted recycling in their neighborhood one Saturday in March by distributing sets of blue and green recycling bins to grocery shoppers at Central Marketplace. Out of the 248 shoppers who stopped by Head Start's Recycling Information Table, 168 took home a set of bins. "We are pleased," said Rosa Torres. "That's a pretty good percentage. Some of them said they had never recycled before."

1 What percentage of shoppers stopping by the table took home bins? Round your answer to the nearest whole percent.

 A   50%

 B   80%

 C   68%

 D   34%

 E   75%

2 The recycling bins came in sets of two: blue for paper; green for glass, plastics, and metal. Which expression can be used to find the total number of bins given out?

 A $2(168 + 248)$

 B 168×2

 C $2(248 - 168)$

 D $416/2$

 E   None of these

3 What is the ratio of the shoppers who took bins to the total number of shoppers who stopped at the Information Table? It is *approximately*

 A   1 out of 2

 B   2 out of 3

 C   3 out of 4

 D   5 out of 8

 E   None of the above

Questions 4 and 5 refer to the following information.

The U.S. Environmental Protection Agency collects data yearly on the estimated amounts and types of solid waste generated in this country. It also keeps records on the amount of waste that is recovered (reused) through recycling. The waste measured comes from residential, commercial, institutional, and industrial sources.

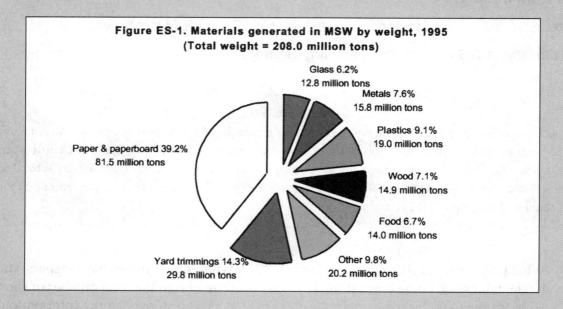

Figure ES-1. Materials generated in MSW by weight, 1995
(Total weight = 208.0 million tons)

Glass 6.2%
12.8 million tons

Metals 7.6%
15.8 million tons

Plastics 9.1%
19.0 million tons

Wood 7.1%
14.9 million tons

Food 6.7%
14.0 million tons

Other 9.8%
20.2 million tons

Yard trimmings 14.3%
29.8 million tons

Paper & paperboard 39.2%
81.5 million tons

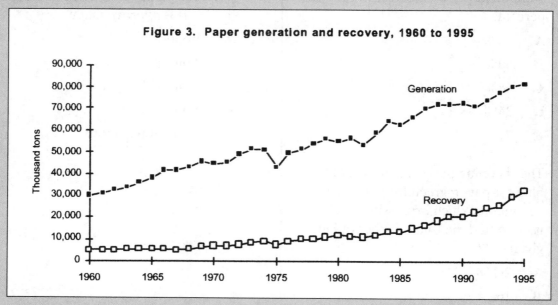

Figure 3. Paper generation and recovery, 1960 to 1995

Source: Environmental Protection Agency.
http://www.epa.gov/garbage/pubs/msw96rpt.pdf

4 How many tons of paper and paperboard waste were generated in 1995?

    A   81.5 tons

    B   39.2 tons

    C   81,500,000 tons

    D   81,500 tons

    E   None of the above

5 According to the line graph above, approximately what fraction of the paper and paperboard waste generated in 1995 was recovered?

    A   ¼

    B   ½

    C   ⅙

    D   ⅜

    E   None of the above

6 In 1995, the population of the United States was 262,755,000. It was estimated that the plastic waste per person per day was 0.40 lbs. Based on this estimated daily amount, how many lbs of plastic did the average person throw away that year?

    A   14.6 lbs

    B   146 lbs

    C   105,102,000 lbs

    D   105,102 lbs

    E   None of the above

7 Two straight roads intersect at point A. The highway surveyor measured the angles formed at that intersection. If the measurement of ∠WAX is 120°, what is the measurement in degrees of ∠YAX?

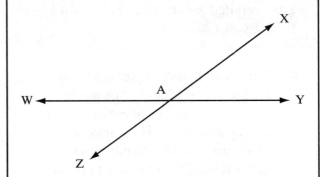

    A   90°

    B   45°

    C   240°

    D   30°

    E   60°

Prices at the Pump

Premium: 1.659; Super: 1.599; Regular: 1.499

Carol had just begun her drive to work when the dashboard's warning light flashed. It signaled an almost-empty tank. She knew she would run out of gas before she reached work, so she pulled into the nearest gas station. Her wallet held a $5 bill. Under the floor mats, she discovered 6 quarters. She estimated that amount of money would buy her enough of the regular gas to last for her driving needs for that day.

8 Carol watched the numbers fly by on the gas pump window. She put in exactly the number of gallons that her money would buy. How many gallons of gas was she able to put into her gas tank? Round your answer to the nearest tenth of a gallon.

   A   9.7 gallons

   B   17 gallons

   C   4.3 gallons

   D   4.16 gallons

   E   Not enough information

9 Her car traveled an average of 28 miles per gallon. At that rate, *approximately* how many miles could she travel on the gas she bought that morning?

   A   A little over 100 miles

   B   A little under 100 miles

   C   Between 130 and 150 miles

   D   Between 150 and 200 miles

   E   Not enough information

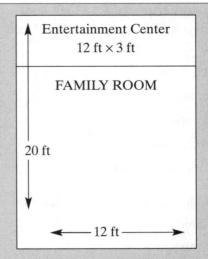

Was $2.91 SALE! $1.89 / SF

Laminate Blowout!
RED OAK
Price: $ Was 70.08 SALE: 45.56
Per Carton (24.11 SF)

Installation Type: Click Together
Dimensions: 7.75″ × 50.5″
Board Thickness: .25″
Pieces per Unit: 9
Unit Weight: 38 lbs
(SF = sq. ft.)

Home Remodeling

The Greens decided to rip up the worn wall-to-wall carpeting in their family room and replace it with oak laminate flooring. The local building supply store was running a special on do-it-yourself flooring. Diana and Rob looked at the samples of laminate. They preferred the Red Oak. The final choice would be made on the basis of what they could afford. They agreed that $500.00 was their limit for this purchase. Above is a diagram of their family room, and the sales information for the Red Oak laminate.

---

10 The family room is in the shape of a:

   A   Quadrilateral

   B   Polygon

   C   Parallelogram

   D   None of the above

   E   All of the above

11 According to the specifications mentioned in the sales ad above, approximately how much will each board of Red Oak laminate weigh?

   A   4 lb

   B   7 lb

   C   9 lb

   D   38 lb

   E   42 oz

12 The space taken up by the built-in entertainment center in the family room does not require new flooring. Which of the expressions below answers the question, "How many square feet of Red Oak laminate will be needed for the family room?"

   A $2(20) + 2(12)$

   B 12×20

   C $12(20 - 3)$

   D $[2(20) + 2(12)] - (3 \times 12)$

   E $(20 \times 12) + (3 \times 12)$

13 How many cartons of Red Oak laminate will the Greens need to purchase for their flooring project?

    A   8 cartons

    B   9 cartons

    C   10 cartons

    D   9½ cartons

    E   None of the above

14 What is the price for each carton during this sale?

    A $1.89

    B $24.11

    C $70.08

    D $45.56

    E $2.91

15 Diana put all the figures into her calculator and found that the flooring would cost them $410.04 before the sales tax was added.

On that basis, Diana and Rob decided:

    A   They could buy what they needed for the family room and have enough money left over to buy 3 additional cartons to redo their 8 × 12-ft kitchen floor.

    B   They could afford to the buy the flooring itself, but not the added 7% sales tax.

    C   They could not afford the Red Oak at the discounted sale price.

    D   They could afford to cover their family room floor with the Red Oak.

    E   Not enough information is provided.

16 Which of these number sentences is true?

    A $-6 < -4 + 1$

    B $4 - 1 < -6$

    C $-6 > -4 + 1$

    D $6 - 2 = -4$

    E $4 + 1 < -6 + 1$

Questions 17–19 refer to the following table and text:

U.S. Postal Rates Rising Again
New Rates Recommended by Postal Rate Commission

	Current	Recommended	% Increase
First-class letter (1 oz.)	34¢	37¢	8.8%
Additional ounce	23¢	23¢	
Priority Mail (1 lb.)	$3.50	$3.85	?
Express Mail (½ lb.)	$12.45	$13.65	9.6%

Rates effective June 30, 2002.
http://www.prc.gov

The cost of mail delivery and postal operations has risen. People are using the U.S. mail service less. These trends and others have caused economic problems for the agency. Postal Service officials say the higher rates could raise an extra $4 billion each year.

17 After the new postal rates went into effect, Marilyn went to the post office to mail a 1-lb package to her sister. She wanted the package to go by Priority Mail. Marilyn also purchased a book of 20 first-class stamps. How much was her change from a $20 bill?

- **A** $11.25
- **B** $9.70
- **C** $8.75
- **D** $10.30
- **E** None of the above

18 By what percent did the cost of Priority Mail (1 lb) rise?

- **A** 10%
- **B** 12%
- **C** 3.5%
- **D** 9.1%
- **E** 0.1%

19 Which of the following notations is another way to express the 4 billion dollars that might be raised each year by the higher rates?

- **A** $4,000,000,000,000
- **B** 4×10^9
- **C** $4,000,000
- **D** 4×10^6
- **E** $4 \times 100,000,000$

20 While on a vacation in Australia, Bob spiked a fever. By the time he got to the Emergency Room, the nurse told him he had a temperature of 40°C (Celsius.) How high was Bob's temperature as measured in degrees Fahrenheit (F)? Use this formula to find the equivalent: $F = 1.8C + 32$

- **A** 102.8°F
- **B** 104°F
- **C** 103.8°F
- **D** 105°F
- **E** None of the above

Questions 21 to 23 refer to the following situation:

Marta picked up a part-time job working the sandwich counter at Sam's Deli. Her 3-hour shift covered the lunch hour, 5 days a week. Marta made delicious sandwiches quickly and always had a smile for her customers. There was a tip cup on the counter. Several of her regular customers added to it daily. At the end of each shift, Marta counted her tips and recorded them in a small notebook. Starting with last week's tips, Marta decided to save her tip money to buy her son inline skates for his birthday. She found a nice pair for $139.79 plus 7% tax, and put them on lay-away.

21 How much will it cost Marta to purchase the inline skates she has put on lay-away?

- **A** $149.79
- **B** $139.79
- **C** $149.58
- **D** $140.77
- **E** $97.859

Marta wondered if she would be able to earn enough tip money to pay for the skates by her son's birthday. She had 14 more working days to earn tips. She realized she could predict the answer to her question by finding her average daily tip total. Marta got out her notebook and looked at the daily totals for last week's tips: $10.90, $9.25, $8.10, $11.75, $9.55. She found the average by dividing the sum of the tips by the number of days it took to earn them.

22 Choose the expression that shows what Marta did to calculate her average daily tip:

- **A** 10.90 + 9.25 + 8.10 + 11.75 + 9.55 ÷ 5
- **B** 0.07 (10.90 + 9.25 + 8.10 + 11.75 + 9.55)
- **C** 139.70 − (10.90 + 9.25 + 8.10 + 11.75 + 9.55) ÷ 5
- **D** (10.90 + 9.25 + 8.10 + 11.75 + 9.55) ÷ 5
- **E** 0.07 ($139.79) − (10.90 + 9.25 + 8.10 + 11.75 + 9.55)

23 If Marta continues to get similar tips for the next 14 days, and adds them to her tips from last week, which of the following statements is correct?

- **A** Her tip money will more than cover the total cost of the skates.
- **B** Her tip money will cover the cost of the skates, but not the 7% tax.
- **C** Her son will be happy to receive inline skates for his birthday.
- **D** Her tip money will not be enough to purchase the skates in time for his birthday.
- **E** Not enough information.

Questions 24 and 25 refer to the following table of information:

TABE 7 & 8 Levels E, M, D, and A: Item Counts and Time Limits

Subtest	Complete Battery		Survey	
	No. Items	Testing Time (minutes)	No. Items	Testing Time (minutes)
Reading	50	:50	25	:25
Math Computation	25	:15	15	:09
Applied Math	50	:50	25	:25
Language	55	:39	25	:18
Spelling	20	:10	20	:10
Total				

24 To answer the questions on the Applied Math Subtest of the Complete Battery of the TABE, examinees

    A Are given 9 minutes to complete their work

    B Have an average of one-half minute to spend on each question

    C Can use a calculator to solve the problems

    D Are given 25 minutes to complete their work

    E Have an average of one minute to spend on each question

25 What is the total testing time of the Complete Battery Form of the TABE?

    A 156 minutes

    B 1 hour and 64 minutes

    C 2 hours and 44 minutes

    D 200 minutes

    E 127 minutes

Stop time: _____

Answer Key to Math Skills Assessment Part I: Computation

To the Student: Check your answers, and record your results in this chart. Use the three columns next to the Item Answers to mark your responses as *Correct, Error,* or *Skipped.* Use the other columns to record information you may want to remember about the individual math problems. Total the number of your responses in each column at the bottom of the chart.

Answer Key and Skills Analysis Chart

Item Answers	Correct ✓	Error X	Skipped O	I have this question.	I need instruction.	Refer to these lessons.	Math Skill Objectives*
1 A						5	1
2 E						5	1
3 A						5	1
4 A						5	2
5 D						5	2
6 B						7	3
7 B						7	3
8 A						7	3
9 C						5	4
10 D						5	4
11 C						5	4
12 D						3	5
13 C						8	5
14 C						8	5
15 A						3	5
16 C						8	5
TOTALS	Correct	Errors	Skipped	Questions	Instruction	Lessons	Skills

*KEY to Math Skill Objectives

1 Decimals   2 Fractions   3 Integers   4 Percents   5 Algebraic Operations

Answer Key to Math Skills Assessment
Part II: Applied Math

To the Student: As you check your answers, record the results in this chart. Use the three columns next to the Item Answers to mark your answers as *Correct, Error,* or *Skipped.* Use the other columns to record additional information you want to remember about the individual math problems. Total the number of responses you marked in each column. Read the recommendations that follow

Answer Key and Skills Analysis Chart

Item Answers	Correct ✓	Error X	Skipped O	I have this question.	I need instruction.	Refer to these lessons.	Math Skill Objectives*
1 C						5, 2	7
2 B						3	4
3 B						5	2
4 C						2, 3	1, 3
5 D						5, 3	3
6 B						2, 5	7
7 E						4	6, 3
8 C						6	7, 3
9 A						6	8, 5
10 E						4	6
11 A						2	3, 8
12 C						3, 4	5, 4
13 B						4	5
14 D						2	3, 7
15 D						5	7
16 A						7	1
17 C						5	3, 5
18 A						5	2
19 B						3	1
20 B						8, 6	4, 5
21 C						5	1, 7
22 D						3	4
23 A						2, 5	7, 8
24 E						6	3, 5
25 C						6	3, 5
TOTALS Correct	Errors	Skipped	Questions	Instruction	Lessons		Skills

*KEY to Math Skill Objectives

1-Numeration   2-Number Theory   3-Data Interpretation   4-Pre-Algebra/ Algebra
5-Measurement   6-Geometry   7-Computation in Context   8-Estimation

Analyze Your Results

Write the number of items you answered correctly for Parts I and II in the spaces provided below.

Divide your score for each part by the total number of questions asked. The result of each division will be a decimal fraction, such as 0.875 or 0.72. Record it.

Move the decimal point two spaces to the right and add the % sign. Record your percentage.

Math Assessment, Part I—*Correct Answers* ÷ **16** = _____ = _____ %

Math Assessment, Part II—*Correct Answers* ÷ **25** = _____ = _____ %

Plan Your Course of Study

This assessment gives you a good idea of the types of items you will find on Math Part I and II of the TABE, Level A. To be confident of doing well on the math section of the exam, a score of 90 percent or better is recommended. That means answering 15 or 16 items correctly on Part I, and 23 or more on Part II.

Recommendation:

For each item you answered incorrectly, skipped, or did correctly but still have questions about, work through the pages of the lessons indicated. At this point, don't worry if it seems you have a long way to go. The lessons that follow are designed to boost your skills and your confidence. For best results, complete the lessons in order.

 FYI

The TABE math test will have items you have not directly prepared for. This will be true as well for other tests that cover content similar to the TABE.

If you do these things:

- Work through all the lessons in order
- Complete the exercises and take time to understand the explanations

you will build the foundation skills you need to be a successful problem-solver.

LESSON 2 Common Sense to Number Sense

> "Common sense is the knack of seeing things as they are, and doing things as they ought to be done." *Josh Billings*

Getting Started

Ken returned to the Academic Success Center with his Math Packet in hand. Connie Garcia, Center Director, welcomed him. "I hear you are eager to improve your math skills before next semester," she said. "That's right," Ken replied. "I've never connected with higher math. Now I'd like to connect quickly."

Connie looked at Ken's Math Packet. "I see by your check marks that you use math quite often." Ken nodded, "I don't think of it as using *math*. I think of it as using my common sense. The math I'm worried about gives me a headache—special rules, special words, and formulas to memorize."

"Getting comfortable with that kind of math can be a challenge," said Connie, "but since you already use 'common sense' math, you probably have the foundation skills to meet that challenge."

"I hope you're right," said Ken. "I've worked in construction for 15 years. I know what can happen when a foundation has cracks."

"Good point, Ken. Actually, that *is* your first job here: Inspect your math foundation before you start to build on it."

> **Learner Profile**
>
> *Kenneth Williams*
> **Age:** 32
> **Education:** High School Diploma
> **Background Information:**
> • Works in construction
> • Married with 3 children
> **Scenario:** Looking for education that will qualify him for a different job within the construction industry
> • Concerned with his math ability
> • Hopes to qualify for college-credit coursework

Activity 1: What Is Sensible?

Many daily activities involve using numbers to make decisions and get jobs done. Experience gives us a *feel* for what numbers make sense in different situations.

Target Practice: Number Sense

Use your common sense about these numbers. Place them in the blanks next to the things they describe or measure in these situations.

1 3   7½   42   Tony painted his kitchen. He paid _____ dollars to buy _____ gallons of paint and spent _____ hours painting.

2 750   48   2½   She works _____ hours a week, earns a weekly salary of $_____, and gets _____ weeks of vacation time a year.

3 16   7   601   Jack lives in the _____ area code, has a _____ digit phone number. He makes about _____ long-distance calls a month.

Circle the quantity that makes sense:

4 5.250 52.50 525.0   Elisa's family of four spends about $_____ per month on food.

5 0.137^9 1.37^9 13.79^2 Last week, a gallon of gas at the pump cost $_____.

6 19.33 1.933 1,933   The U.S.-Mexican border is approximately _____ miles long.

TARGET: Estimation and Basic Operations

Words to Know

Calculate	To count; compute; work with number data
Digit	One of the 10 *symbols* used to write number values: 0 1 2 3 4 5 6 7 8 9
Operation	Addition, subtraction, multiplication, and division are the 4 basic mathematical operations
$\cong$	Is *approximately* equal to, or *about* the same as; for example, $\$25.89 \cong \$26.00$

Activity 2: Get Comfortable with Calculating—Two Ways

Whether a situation calls for estimation, or exact calculation, *mastery* of basic arithmetic facts and procedures will make your job easier.

Target Practice 1: Know Your Basic Facts

Complete this cross-number puzzle using your memory of math basics. If you get different numbers for the same square, redo both calculations and self-correct. Goal: 100%

Across
1. 19×37
3. $575 \div 25$
4. $84 + 361 + 486$
6. $2 \times 2 \times 2 \times 2 \times 2 + 17$
7. 29×21
9. $30 \times 12 + 7$
10. $89 - 72$

Down
1. $4{,}284 \div 6$
2. $702 \div 18$
3. $3 \times 3 \times 3 - 6$
5. $1{,}246 - 896$
7. 6×113
8. $675 + 244$
9. $992 \div 31$

STUDY TIP

Calculators are tools of the math trade. Learn to use them with accuracy. Calculators are used routinely in the workplace. You will use one as you work through this math section. Calculator use is often permitted on sections of math exams. These exams include the TABE, in its Applied Math Section, and the GED Math Test, Part I.

Target Practice 2: Know Your Calculator, Test Your Accuracy

Key numbers, signs, and symbols into your calculator to compute the answers to the following number sentences. Watch those decimal points.

1 A $12.9 + 62 + 8.09 =$
  B $9 \times 8 \times 7 \times 6 \times 5 \times 4 \times 3 \times 2 \times 1 =$

2 A $3{,}390 \div 5 =$
  B $5.40 - 1.88 =$

3 A $25 \times 0.025 =$
  B $144 \div 12 =$

4 A $\$2{,}500 \times 0.07 =$
  B $\$2{,}500 \times 1.07 =$

5 A $62.8 \text{ feet} \div 3.14 =$
  B $3.14 \times 20 \text{ feet} =$

Caution: Calculator use can be harmful to your math skill health when it is used as a crutch to

- *Avoid extra effort,* even though basic math facts are known
- *Avoid learning* basic math facts in the first place

Result: Chronic calculation weakness and poor estimation skills

Words to Know

Approximate	Close to; about the same as
Estimate	To use round numbers to calculate an answer (verb); an answer *close enough* to the exact answer to be helpful (noun)
Round	To change an *exact* number to a number that is *close* to it in value and easier to work with

Activity 3: When Is Close Enough Good Enough?

You make statements and decisions every day using your powers of estimation. Each time you find yourself saying the words *about* or *approximately,* you are estimating. "I will need *about* 3 gallons of paint to finish this job" or "It will take me *approximately* 15 minutes to get there." It is not always necessary to know the exact measure of something in order to plan or make a decision. Some people call this process "making a guesstimate."

Target Practice 1: Estimate with Easier Numbers

1 Cheryl made 6 payments of $195 when she bought a new computer system. The total she paid was *approximately:*

    A $1,500

    B $1,200

    C $600

    D $2,000

2 The *North Shore Times* has 8,065 subscribers. The *Independent Press* has 9,987 subscribers. *About* how many more people subscribe to the Press than the Times?

    A 2,000

    B 200

    C 1,000

    D 2,500

Make It Round. Did you find yourself trying to remember how to round off numbers when you answered the two questions above? Here's how:

Step 1. Locate the digit that is in the *place* you want to round off *to:* 8264 <u>Underlining it helps.</u>

Step 2. Look at the digit to its right.
If it is 5 or more (8264) <u>round up</u> to the next larger number 8264 → 8300
and change the digits that follow to zeros

If it is less than 5 (8234), <u>leave it alone.</u>   8234 → 8200
and change the digits that follow to zeros

Target Practice 2: Rounding

Round these dollars to:

the nearest ten $	the nearest hundred $	the nearest thousand $
$28,463 → $28,460	$28,463 → $28,500	$28,463 → $28,000
1 $80,729 → _____	$80,729 → _____	$80,729 → _____
2 $5,864 → _____	$5,864 → _____	$5,864 → _____
3 $25,093 → _____	$25,093 → _____	$25,093 → _____
4 $17,605 → _____	$17,605 → _____	$17,605 → _____

Moving on, let's look at numbers in picture form.

Target: Bar Graphs and Tables

It's All in the Presentation

Words to Know

Consecutive	Following each other; in a row
Data	Known facts and figures; information base
Bar graph	A display of data in bars of different lengths; bars show how quantities of things *compare*
Statistics	The science of collecting and analyzing numerical data
Table	An organization of data in columns and rows

Activity 4: Main Ideas and Details in Bar Graphs and Tables

Graphs show the main ideas and details of numerical data "at a glance" in picture form. Tables communicate that information by organizing the data in columns and rows.

Bar graphs are used primarily to make comparisons. This bar graph uses double bars to compare two things at once: (1) the sales levels of three departments, and (2) department sales records from two consecutive years. The bars in the graph end at *approximate* numbers. They show you *estimates* of the specific numbers involved. In round numbers, Building Materials sales totaled *about* $125,000 last year. (Refer to Reading, Lesson 2, pages 35 and 36 for more information on reading bar graphs.)

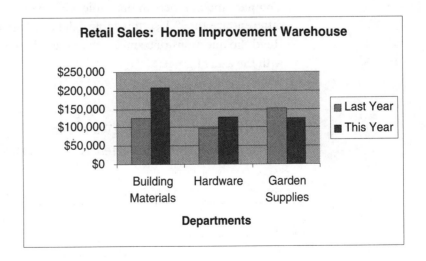

Target Practice 1: First, the Bars—Main Ideas and Details

Read the bar graph to answer these questions about retail sales at the Home Improvement Warehouse.

1 A Which department had the *greatest change* in sales from one year to the next? _____

B List the approximate sales for this department Last year: _____ This year: _____

C Approximately how much *greater* were the sales this year? _____

2 By *about* what amount did Garden Supplies sales *decrease* this year?

_____

3 Choose the best *estimate* of total sales for last year (all departments):
A $300,000
B $325,000
C $350,000
D $375,000

4 Choose the best *estimate* of total sales for the <u>two-year period</u> shown in the graph:
A $750,000
B $800,000
C $825,000
D $850,000

Target Practice 2: Now, the Table—Detailed Details

While graphs are effective for illustrating main ideas of statistics, tables are better for displaying details. They list specific numerical information in columns and rows. Any table of statistics can be transformed into a graph.

The information in this table was used to create the bar graph above.

However, the *specific* numbers that appear here do not appear in the graph. **Compare** the numbers in this table with the bars that represent them. How different are they? Use this table's data to answer questions 1 to 4 above. Read the questions once more, then record your answers below—this time with the *exact* figures:

The Numbers behind the Bars:

Retail Sales: Home Improvement Warehouse

Department	Building Materials	Hardware	Garden Supplies
Last Year	$124,568	$99,650	$152,138
This Year	$207,135	$126,878	$125,030

1 A _____
B _____ _____
C _____

2 _____

3 _____

4 _____

Question: Which is the best way to present statistics, with a graph or in a table? *Answer:* It depends on *who* is asking for the facts, *why* they need them, and *what* decisions they will make on the basis of the facts. Sometimes close enough is good enough; sometimes it is not.

 FYI: THE PROS AND CONS OF GRAPHS

Pros: Graphs catch people's attention. News can be communicated quickly to a lot of people. Graphs can make statistics easier to understand. They can help make complex number details and relationships easier to grasp. *Cons:* Graphs can be misunderstood if they are glanced at too quickly. A wrong conclusion may be drawn if labels or number details are skipped, and only the "big picture" is read. Graphs can mislead if they are based on inadequate data or if the person constructing the graph designs it to be misleading.

What are the *facts* behind this graph about Brand X? How many people were actually surveyed? 4,000, 400, 40, or 4? Notice the numbers given are percentages, so the actual number of people surveyed is "hidden information" here. What was the wording of the question they were asked? The title of the graph does not tell us "what" 3 out of 4 people chose Brand X "for." Maybe they voted never to use it again!

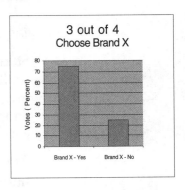

STUDY TIP

Look for graphs in newspapers, advertisements, and magazines. Examine them for main ideas and details. For each one, ask yourself, "If this graph was on a math exam, what question might be asked? How would I answer it?" Test your question on someone else.

TARGET: Solving Problems

Solving a word problem in math is not very different from solving questions of daily living: Some questions are easy to answer. Other questions are not. Sometimes, figuring out solutions requires us to consider several facts—one step at a time.

Word Problems $\cong$ Life Problems

Activity 5: Driving Cross-Country

Make a movie in your mind's eye as you place yourself in the following situation.

Target Practice 1: Be a Back-Seat Driver

Situation: Your friend plans to drive from Miami, Florida, to San Francisco, California. A grid on a map of the United States shows it to be a distance of 3,106 miles. She wants you to help her figure out how much she should budget for gas for this car trip. She estimates her car gets 26 miles to the gallon.

Ask: "How much will gas for this trip cost?"

Information: Here is what you know: Trip distance is 3,106 mile. Gas mileage is 26 mpg (miles per gallon).

Setup Operation: What is the *relationship* of miles traveled to gallons of gas? Think of it this way: For each 26-mile section of the trip, your friend will need to buy a gallon of gas. Picture that each gallon gets her closer to her destination, 26 miles at a time. What is the *action?* You are *splitting up* the distance—*that's division.*

Setup: Miles to travel ÷ Miles per gallon = Gallons needed for the trip

Operation: Division

Wait a minute. Will this setup answer her original question? Knowing the number of gallons needed gets her (and you) only halfway there. More information is needed to determine her gas expenses. What is the current price of gasoline? Let's say it is $1.52⁹. Your friend will spend approximately that amount *for each* of the gallons used during the trip. *What's the action to find the total cost? Multiplication.* You need a second setup.

Setup II: Gallons needed × Price per gallon of gas = $ Total gas expenses

Operation: Multiplication

Estimate ≅ Use numbers that are easier to work with:

Travel distance:	3,106 miles	*Round* to 3,000 miles
Miles per gallon:	26 miles	*Round* to 25 miles
Price of 1 gallon of gas	$1.52^9	*Round* to $1.50

Target Practice 2: Write It Up

Insert the <u>rounded</u> figures here, then calculate.

1 Setup, Part I _____ miles ÷ _____ miles per gallon ≅ _____ gallons of gas needed

2 Setup, Part II _____ gallons needed × $_____ per gallon ≅ $_____ fuel cost estimated

Evaluate = Insert the original numbers, then calculate.
  Use: 3,106 miles, $1.52^9, 26 mpg

3 Setup Part I _____ ÷ _____ = _____ (Round to two places after the decimal point)

4 Setup Part II _____ × $_____ = $_____ fuel cost detailed (Round to the nearest penny)

Check your results. Cost estimated and cost detailed should be close. If not, calculate both again.

5 Cost estimated: _____ Cost detailed: _____

Reflect: Is *close enough good enough* in this situation? Common sense answers, "Yes. The estimated results are close enough to figure out a gas budget." Common sense also says your friend should budget *more* than the estimate, especially for a long trip with many unknowns.

Calculators can't do it all. If you used a calculator to do the math above, and the results were $1826.54 or $18.26 or $1.82, what happened? The decimal points were entered incorrectly. *If you do not estimate first, you may accept what a calculator tells you, even if it's an error.*

TEST TIP: SAVE TIME AND PREVENT MISTAKES—ESTIMATE, THEN CALCULATE

- Estimating may be all you *need* to do to choose the correct answer among the four or five choices in front of you. That saves time.
- An estimate can be a *reality check* on your calculations. It can prevent error. Multiple-choice answers often include one or two choices that are the results you will get if you make a calculation error, or fail to work through all the steps.

Activity 6: Estimate to Answer

Discover if estimation will give you the answers that you need.

Target Practice: Expenses

Use rounded numbers to estimate costs for the trips below. On the basis of your estimates, answer the multiple-choice questions. *Then* calculate fuel expenses with the exact number data.

Trip 1: St. Louis, Missouri to Denver, Colorado

Information: Distance—860 miles; mpg—21; Price of gas—$1.399/gal.

1 Estimated cost: $_____

2 About how much money will you spend on gas for this trip?
   A Between $45 and $55
   B Between $55 and $65
   C Between $65 and $75
   D Between $70 and $80

3 Detailed cost: $_____

Trip 2: Chicago, Illinois to Salt Lake City, Utah

Information: Trip distance— 1,382 miles; mpg—28; Price of gas—$1.489/gal.

1 Estimated cost:
   $_____

2 About how much money will you need to spend on gas for this trip?
   A $40.00
   B $50.00
   C $700.0
   D $70.00

3 Detailed cost: $_____

Problem-Solving Template: Take Five
Read about the situation. Read it twice. Then:
1 ASK: _____?
2   Information_____
_____
_____
3   SET UP
Operations _____
_____
4   Estimate ≈ _____
Evaluate = _____
_____
5 ANSWER _____
Check and Reflect

Words to Know

Template   A blank form to be filled in with details; a model to follow for getting certain jobs done.

STUDY TIP
Give the template a try. Refer to it when you are setting up calculations in your math notebook. Use it to organize your data and your thinking.

Practice Unlimited. Look for more word problems to solve. Check out workbooks at your library or adult learning center. Look for specialized math texts in an area that interests you, such as business, nutrition, or ecology. Several Web sites provide interactive problem-solving opportunities.

Let common sense and estimation be your guides.

Answer Key: Section 3, Lesson 2

Activity 1: What Is Sensible?

TARGET PRACTICE: NUMBER SENSE

1. 42 dollars, 3 gallons, 7½ hours
2. 48 hours, $750, 2½ weeks
3. 601 area code, 7 digit, 16 long-distance calls
4. $525.0
5. $1.37^9
6. 1,933 miles

Activity 2: Get Comfortable with Calculating

TARGET PRACTICE 1: KNOW YOUR BASIC FACTS

Across		Down	
1	703	**1**	714
3	23	**2**	39
4	931	**3**	21
6	49	**5**	350
7	609	**7**	678
9	367	**8**	919
10	17	**9**	32

TARGET PRACTICE 2: KNOW YOUR CALCULATOR

1. **A** 82.99
   B 362,880
2. **A** 678
   B 3.52
3. **A** 0.625
   B 12
4. **A** $175
   B $2,675
5. **A** 20 feet
   B 62.8 feet

Activity 3: When Is Close Enough Good Enough?

TARGET PRACTICE 1: ESTIMATE WITH EASIER NUMBERS

1. **B** $1,200
2. **A** 2,000

1. $80,730 $80,700 $81,000

2. $5,860 $5,900 $6,000

3. $25,090 $25,100 $25,000

4. $17,610 $17,600 $18,000

Activity 4: Main Ideas and Details in Bar Graphs and Tables

TARGET PRACTICE 1: FIRST, THE BARS

1. A Building Materials
   B Last Year: about $125,000   This Year: about $210,000
   C About $85,000

2. About $25,000

3. D: $375,000

4. C: $825,000

TARGET PRACTICE 2: NOW, THE TABLE

1. A Building Materials
   B Last Year: $124,568   This Year: $207,135
   C $82,567

2. $27,108

3. $376,356

4. $835,399

Activity 5: Solving Word Problems

TARGET PRACTICE: WRITE IT UP

1. 3,000 miles; 25 mpg; 120 gallons

2. 120 gallons; $1.50; $180

3. $3,106 \div 26 = 119.46$

4. $119.46 \times \$1.52^9 = \$182.65$

5. Cost estimated: $180; Cost detailed: $182.65

Activity 6: Estimate to Answer

TARGET PRACTICE: EXPENSES

Trip 1

1. Estimated cost: About $60

2. B; between $55 and $65

3. Detailed cost: $57.29

Trip 2

1. Estimated cost: About $75

2. D; $70.00

3. Detailed cost: $73.49

"Not everything that can be counted counts, and not everything
that counts can be counted."
Albert Einstein

24 Is Not Enough

"You look exhausted," Ken said to André. "You should take more breaks
from that computer screen." "That's not it," sighed André. "Besides studying
and working the night shift this week, I've spent every spare moment helping out my mom. Dad ended up in the hospital a week ago. Since then, I have
been going nonstop, 24/7."

"Sorry, André, I didn't realize," Ken apologized. "How is your dad doing?"

Numbers Talk André used numbers to emphasize why he looked so exhausted.
Ken understood him because the expression "24/7" has become a popular way
to say "all the time." It is common knowledge there are 24 (only 24) hours in a
day, and 7 (only 7) days in a week. Ken understood André felt as if he had been
working around the clock: *24 hours* a day for all *7 days* of the week.

The <u>value</u> of the phrase *twenty-four, seven* can be expressed with numbers
and symbols in any one of these ways: 24×7, $24\,(7)$, or $24 * 7$. Whichever way it
is expressed, the result is 168 hours of continuous work. Now that is exhaustion.

The language of mathematics is our second language. It expands our
ability to communicate.

Do You Speak Math?

Do you think and speak in numbers? You may do it more than you realize.
The language of math is part of our everyday language. Like Ken in Lesson
2, many people are not conscious of how often they use math language and
math skills to perform daily tasks and make decisions.

There are rules and standards for speaking and writing the languages of
the world. Mathematics is a language, and it has standards and rules as well.
Because mathematics is an *international* language, the rules for speaking and
writing it are especially important to know and understand.

Language = Communication

English:	Math:
Words and Symbols in Phrases and Sentences	Numbers, Symbols, and Signs in Expressions and Equations
Words **name** living things, spaces, objects, and ideas: *Nouns and adjectives*	Numbers and symbols **name** quantities and sizes of living things, spaces, objects, and ideas: $0.0009\,n^3 \bullet \$\,'\,''\,\angle\,87,654,321.$

Words and Symbols in Phrases and Sentences	Numbers, Symbols, and Signs in Expressions and Equations
Words communicate **what is happening:** Verbs and adverbs	Signs communicate **what is happening:** $+ - \times * () \div / -$
Words describe **relationships** between, people, places, things, and ideas: Adjectives	Symbols describe **relationships** of quantities, sizes, and things: $= \neq \cong > < + - : \% \frac{1}{2} \perp$
Symbols **clarify** meaning and **direct** how to read and work with words in phrases and sentences: . ? ! . . . , : ; - " . . . "	Symbols **clarify** meaning, and **direct** how to read and work with numbers and letters in expressions and equations: , . () [] —
English Language Rules: Grammar	**Math Language Rules:** Order of operations

Our Second Language

We act and *react* to information involving numbers. We act, and react, according to what we *think* is being said. Being able to understand others when they talk or write mathematically is not a luxury; it is a survival skill. Without it, we risk making poor decisions, getting confused, or being cheated.

Speaking math and writing math are two sides of the language coin. How does the language of math look written down? Can you translate its meaning?

Math Language, Part I

TARGET Place Value: Naming Values with Notation

Words and Symbols to Know

Exponent	A raised number that indicates how many times to use its base number in repeated multiplication. Expressed as: base ^{exponent}. For example: $7^4 = 7 \times 7 \times 7 \times 7$
Notation	The way something is written or recorded; *mathematical notation* uses digits, letters, signs, and symbols
Root	A number that is "at the base" of a higher value when it multiplies itself. For example: 8 is the *root* of $64 \rightarrow 8 \times 8 = 64$
Scientific notation	Mathematical shorthand for writing very large and very small values. For example, using *the powers of 10:* $7.2 \times 10^8 = 720,000,000$.
$\sqrt{}$	Symbol for *the square root of* a number. For example: $\sqrt{25}$ means *the square root of 25.*

Activity 1: Warm Up to Numbers Large and Small

Numbers can name any extreme in quantity or size you can imagine. Make a connection to some extremes with the help of these practice exercises.

Target Practice 1: Imagine Large and Larger— Count Dollars, Days, and People

LARGE: You are given one million dollars ($1,000,000) in $100 bills. You must spend or give away one of these bills each day, 365 days a year, until the million dollars are gone.

1. How many days will you be handing out those $100 bills? _____
2. How many years will it take until the money is gone? _____
3. If you start today, how old will you be when you hand out your last $100 bill? _____
4. What is the meaning of one million to you? _____

LARGER: The total population of the world in July of 2002 was projected to be 6,234,250,387. That's *six billion, two hundred thirty-four million, two hundred fifty thousand, three hundred eighty-seven* people.[1]

This estimate of world population, rounded to the nearest billion, amounts to 6 billion people. That count is *6,000 times larger* than 1 million: $6,000 \times 1,000,000 = 6,000,000,000$

CONNECT: The thickness of a paper dollar bill is 0.44 millimeters. Stacked on top of each other, 6 billion bills would stretch 1,628.4 miles into space.[2]

Target Practice 2: Imagine Small and Smaller—Scope-it to Micro-scopic

SMALL: This line measures one inch in length |_____|.

SMALLER: "A single drop of blood contains millions of red blood cells which are constantly traveling through your body delivering oxygen and removing waste. If they weren't, your body would slowly die."[3]

CONNECT: The approximate size of a single red blood cell is 0.0003 inch. If you divide the 1-inch line above by the size of one red blood cell (1 ÷ 0.0003), the result is 3,333. Can you visualize 3,333 whole red blood cells lined up end to end on that line? How can millions of cells fit in a single drop of blood? If they measure *three ten-thousandths* of an inch in diameter, they can.

---

[1] Source: **International Data Base;** U.S. Bureau of the Census.
[2] Reference: Purkey, William W. & Stanley, Paula H. "Blue Leader One: A Metaphor For Invitational Education." *Journal of Invitational Theory and Practice.* 3, 1 (Winter 1994).
[3] From the Franklin Institute at http://sln.fi.edu/biosci/blood/red.html.

Activity 2: Number Names and Notation—Location, Location, Location

In review: We speak of size and quantity using 10 symbols called digits: 0 1 2 3 4 5 6 7 8 9. Digits take their value from the *place* they occupy in a specific number. Our number system is called a *decimal* number system because it is based on the number 10 (*deci* is the Latin root meaning *10.*) A digit in *any* place is worth *10 times more than* the digit to its right and *10 times less than* the digit to its left. Value differs place to place by *a magnitude of* 10.

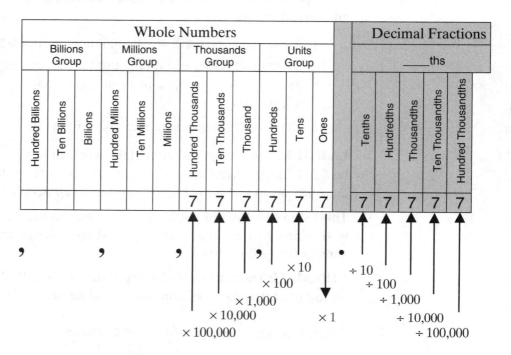

The decimal point separates *whole* number values from values that are *parts* of a whole.

Target Practice: On Both Sides of the Point

Identify and write the *value* of the digits underlined in the numbers below. Follow the examples:

Number	Digit	Place Name	Value Written Two Ways
9̲6,525	9	*ten thousands*	9 × 10,000 or 90,000
79.6109̲	9	*ten-thousandths*	9 ÷ 10,000 or 0.0009

1 1,3̲06,111 _____

2 4.0561̲3 _____

3 217̲,608 _____

4 1.647̲0 _____

Activity 3: Powers in Addition to Places Raise Number Values

A number "raised to a power of itself" is represented this way: number$^{\text{raised number}}$. The number on the bottom is called the *base*. The raised number on top is called the *exponent*. The <u>exponent counts how many times to use the base</u> in repeated multiplication. For example:

Base$^{\underline{\text{Exponent}}}$ $7^3 = 7 \times 7 \times 7$ $2^5 = 2 \times 2 \times 2 \times 2 \times 2$

7^3 is the *exponential form* of the value 343. 2^5 is the *exponential form* of the value 32.

Target Practice 1: The Raised Power Pattern

Read each line out loud, left to right, to *hear* as well as *see* the pattern. Fill in the blanks of the last three lines to complete the pattern.

5^1 "5 raised to the power of 1" $= 5$ $= 5$

5^2 "5 raised to the power of 2" $= 5 \times 5$ $= 25$

5^3 "5 _____" $= 5 \times 5 \times 5$ $= 125$

5^4 "5 raised to the power of 4" $= 5 \times 5 \times 5 \times 5$ $=$ _____

5^5 "_____" $=$ _____ $=$ _____

Target Practice 2: Value Written Three Ways

Exponent	Repeated Multiplication	Value
4^5	$= 4 \times 4 \times 4 \times 4 \times 4$	$= 1024$
1. 6^3	$=$ _____	$=$ _____
2. 2^-	$= 2 \times 2 \times 2 \times 2 \times 2 \times 2 \times 2 \times 2$	$=$ _____
3. 8^4	$=$ _____	$=$ _____
4. 3^7	$=$ _____	$=$ _____

FYI

These two rules hold true: $n^1 = n$ $n^0 = 1$ (n = a number)

$n^1 = n$. Any number raised to 1 equals the number itself. The exponent 1 counts how many times to use the base in multiplication. A number raised to 1 *stands alone*. Alone, its value is the same.

$n^0 = 1$. The value of any number raised to 0 equals 1.

Activity 4: Squares and Roots

A number raised to the power of two (or the second power) is also known as that number *squared*. It is easy to see why:

$2 \times 2 = 4$

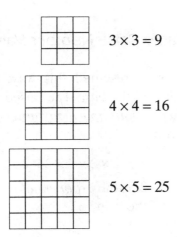

$3 \times 3 = 9$

$4 \times 4 = 16$

$5 \times 5 = 25$

Each of these perfect squares *is based on* a number: the number of units of its sides. The number that measures the units of each square's side is known as the *root* of the square.

A number placed *inside* this symbol $\sqrt{}$ is the *result*, or *product* of, another number multiplied by itself. A square measuring 4 units by 4 units has 16 square units inside it. When you see a number inside this symbol: $\sqrt{}$, ask yourself, "What number multiplied by itself is equal to this value?"

Target Practice: Table These Squares and Roots

Squared numbers and their roots are used frequently in math, especially in geometric formulas. Get acquainted with the facts. Complete this table of squares and roots. Speak it as you write it. For example, say "11 squared is 121; the square root of 121 is 11."

$4^2 = 16 \ldots \sqrt{16} = 4$	$7^2 =$	$\ldots \sqrt{} =$	$10^2 =$	$\ldots \sqrt{} =$	$13^2 =$	$\ldots \sqrt{} =$
$5^2 = \ldots \sqrt{} = 2$	$8^2 =$	$\ldots \sqrt{} =$	$11^2 =$	$\ldots \sqrt{} =$	$14^2 =$	$\ldots \sqrt{} =$
$6^2 = \ldots \sqrt{} = 3$	$9^2 =$	$\ldots \sqrt{} =$	$12^2 =$	$\ldots \sqrt{} =$	$15^2 =$	$\ldots \sqrt{} =$

Activity 5: Scientifically Speaking

Scientists and others who deal with very large and very small numbers have a special way to write them down. This method of *noting* values is called scientific notation. Values are written as the *product* of a number [between 1 and 10] and a *power* of 10.

276,000 written in scientific notation = 2.76×10^5 ◄— exponent

a number between 1 and 10   ➤ a power of 10

Target Practice 1: Chart the Powers of 10

Follow the patterns in the rows and columns of this chart. Fill in the missing numbers.

Repeated Multiplication of 10		Value	How many zeros?
10^0	any number raised to the power of 0 equals 1	1	0
10^1	any number raised to the power of 1 equals itself	10	___
10^2	10×10	___	2
10^3	$10 \times 10 \times 10$	1,000	___
___	$10 \times 10 \times 10 \times 10$	10,000	___
10^5	_____	_____	5
10^6	$10 \times 10 \times 10 \times 10 \times 10 \times 10$	1,000,000	___
10^7	_____	_____	___
___	_____	100,000,000	___
___	$10 \times 10 \times 10 \times 10 \times 10 \times 10 \times 10 \times 10 \times 10$	_____	___
10^{10}	$10 \times 10 \times 10 \times 10 \times 10 \times 10 \times 10 \times 10 \times 10 \times 10$	_____	___
___	$10 \times 10 \times 10 \times 10 \times 10 \times 10 \times 10 \times 10 \times 10 \times 10 \times 10$	100,000,000,000	___
___	$10 \times 10 \times 10 \times 10 \times 10 \times 10 \times 10 \times 10 \times 10 \times 10 \times 10 \times 10$	_____	___

FYI

Look at the count of zeros you charted in the last column above. Did you notice this pattern appear as you wrote it down? A reliable pattern is a rule to remember: The value of a power of 10 is written with the same number of zeros as the exponent that raises it.

Target Practice 2: Note These Values Three Different Ways

Follow the example at the head of each column as you practice different ways of writing down values . . .

Scientific Notation	Standard Notation	In Numbers and Words
5×10^6	5,000,000	5 million
2×10^5	_____	2 _____
8×10^7	_____	80 _____
___ $\times 10^{...}$	40,000,000,000	40 _____
$6 \times 10^{...}$	600,000	6 _____

Short-hand instruction for noting values great and small:

1 Place a decimal point *after the first digit* of the large value: 741,612,321

2 Count how many digits are to the right of that decimal point
7.41612321 ⟶ 8 digits

3 Raise 10 to that power: 10^8 (8 digits to the right, raise 10 to the *eighth*)

4 Round off to one or two places after the decimal point: 7.4

5 Now show it as being multiplied by the power of 10 from Step 3.
Result: 741,612,321 is expressed in scientific notation as 7.4×10^8

Target Practice 3: Express It Scientifically

1 The distance from the earth to the sun is *about* 93,000,000 miles. In scientific notation, that mileage can be expressed as:

A 9.3×10^8

B 9.3×10^7

C 9.3×10^6

2 Rounded to the nearest trillion, the national debt in May 2002 was calculated to be $6,000,000,000,000 or _____. (Write it in shorthand.)

3 The speed of light is 300,000,000 meters/second or

A 3×10^8

B 3.0×10^9

C 3×10^{10}

4 An average pint of blood contains 2,500,000,000,000 red blood cells. In scientific notation, that many cells are expressed as _____.

TARGET: Line Graphs

Activity 6: Lines Tell a Story of Change

Words to Know

Projection   An estimate of *future change* based on past data

Trend   The general direction of change, or "how something is going"

Line graphs show how number values change over time

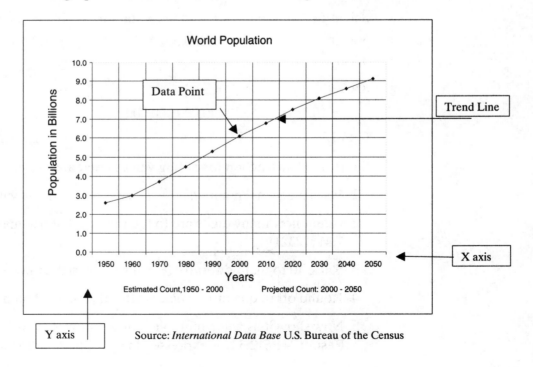

Source: *International Data Base* U.S. Bureau of the Census

Data points plotted on a grid mark the value of what is being measured. Data points are connected with line segments. The line displays a trend. *The story of change is in the line*. When people read a line graph, they look for patterns in the way the line rises and falls. If they see a consistent pattern of change, they may use that information to make predictions.

Target Practice 1: Orient Yourself to the Line

1 The *title* tells you this graph displays changes in the size of _____.

2 The *categories* labeled along the bottom horizontal line of the graph (the *x-axis*) tell you that the data being shown is for a _____ year period, 1950 to _____.

3 The years along the x-axis are spaced at regular intervals. The line *midway* between 1950 and 1960 marks the year 1955. The line between 2010 and 2020 marks the year _____.

4 The vertical line that forms the left side of the graph (the *y-axis*) is a scale of number *values*. The label tells you these numbers represent _____ of people.

5 Locate the point for 1975 along the x-axis. Move up until you reach the trend line. Place a straightedge (a ruler, a 3×5 card, a piece of paper) at this point so it is parallel with the horizontal scale and crosses the vertical scale. Read the value there. World population in 1975 was estimated to be _____.

6 The source of information for this graph is _____.

 FYI
A good graph will always tell you where to find the statistics *behind* the picture. Don't be in doubt, find out: Discover data details through research, contact the source.

Target Practice 2: Review—Place Value, Scientific Notation, Graph Reading

Use the information presented in the line graph to answer these questions:

1 The world population in 1950 was approximately
  A 2.0
  B 20 billion
  C 2,600,000,000
  D 2,600,000

2 In the first decade shown on this graph, the population of the world increased about
  A 4 million
  B 400 million
  C 40 million
  D 4 billion

3 In the year 2050, it is projected the population of the world will reach a little more than nine billion people. Written with scientific notation, that number is
  A 9×10^8
  B 9.0×9.0
  C 9×10^9
  D 9×10^6

4 What happened to the world's population in the last half of the twentieth century?
  A It grew from 2.6 to 3.4 billion
  B It more than doubled
  C It increased by almost 6 billion

5 From the way the trend line curves, the projected *rate* of growth in the twenty-first century will
  A Speed up
  B Remain the same as in the twentieth century
  C Slow down

6 Although the total population of the world is projected to keep increasing in the future, the number of people added each *decade* starting with *2010* is approximately the same. It is
  A A little more than one billion
  B A little less than one million
  C About half a billion

Activity 7: PS

Scientific notation is also used to express values less than 1.

Target Practice 1: Shorthand for Small

Powers of 10 can be used to write values *less* than one whole. If the exponent has a *minus* sign in front of it, it refers to a value that is to the *right* of the decimal point and is *a decimal fraction*. A negative exponent to the base 10 means to *divide* by that power of 10. *Look twice* at these three ways to represent a small value:

$$7 \times 10^{-4} = 7 \div 10,000 = 0.0007$$

Do you see the pattern?

Hint, Hint, and Hint:
  1 The exponent is _____.

  2 The number of zeros in the divisor (10,000) is _____.

  3 The number of digits to the *right* of the decimal point in the decimal fraction is _____.

STUDY TIP: THE MORE PATTERNS YOU SEE, THE EASIER MATH WILL BE

The language and operations of math are filled with patterns. When you discover a pattern, learn from it and use it.

Target Practice 2: On the Right Side of the Point

1 A dust particle has a mass of approximately 0.0000000007 kilograms. Count the number of digits to the right of the decimal point: _____. That is the number to use as the exponent to the base 10. Remember to make it a *negative* exponent.

2 The mass of a dust particle, 0.0000000007 kg, can be written in scientific notation as:

   A 7×10^8 kg
   B 7×10^{-9} kg
   C 7×10^{10} kg
   D 7×10^{-10} kg

3 0.0003 inch is the approximate size of one red blood cell. That can also be represented as

   A 3×10^{-3} inch
   B 3×10^4 inch
   C 3×10^{-4} inch
   D 3.0×10^{-5} inch

4 Another way to express 6×10^{-3} is

   A 0.0006
   B 0.600
   C 0.006
   D 6,000

5 9×10^{-2} has the same value as

   A 9.00
   B 0.90
   C 0.09
   D 90,000

 FYI

Several industries require workers *to read and write decimal fraction values correctly*. Misreading decimal fractions can cause serious errors in financial transactions, production details, construction stability, doses of medicine, travel safety, and more.

Math Language, Part II

TARGET Operations: Notation for Action

Words and Symbols to Know

Evaluate	To find the value of; to solve by doing the mathematical operations.
Expression	Value represented by numbers and one or more operations. For example:

$$24 \div 6 \qquad 5^2 \times 5^4 \qquad \frac{345 + 1,050}{5} \qquad (5 \times 25) - 65$$

Order of operations	Rules for the order in which to perform multiple operations in expressions.
Setup	An expression that is a plan to solve a problem.
Simplify	To rewrite a numerical expression as simply as possible.
( ) parentheses	(1) Enclose number work that must be kept together; for example, $2 + (8 - 3)$; (2) are a sign for multiplication; for example, $2\,(3)$.
————	A long division bar separates number work into two groups.

Activity 1: What Action Is This? Get Your Signs and Signals Straight

Several signs signal multiplication and division. Do you recognize these commands?

Multiply: $\quad 4 \times 25 \qquad 2(50) \qquad (20)(5) \qquad 10 * 10 \qquad 25 \cdot 4 \qquad 10^2$

Divide: $\qquad 24 \div 6 \qquad 24/6 \qquad 6\overline{)24} \qquad \dfrac{24}{6}$

Split up the action. Two symbols do the job:

1. Division bars tell you how to divide and conquer.

$$\frac{\text{Complete the operations on top}}{\text{Complete the operations on bottom}} \qquad \frac{6 * 4 = 24}{3 - 1 = 2}$$

Divide the results $\qquad \dfrac{24}{2} = 12$

2. Parentheses pull things together. They enclose number work that must be calculated before you move on to complete the rest of the operations. The same sequence of numbers and operations can have different results when parentheses group the action differently. For example: Parentheses can change the value of $7 + 5 \times 4$.

$$7 + (5 \times 4) = 7 + (20) = \mathbf{27} \qquad \text{HOWEVER,} \qquad (7 + 5) \times 4 = (12) \times 4 = \mathbf{48}.$$

Target Practice: Act According to Signs and Symbols

Watch out for grouped action.

1 A $144/12 = $ _____

  B $(4)(3)(2) = $ _____

  C $\dfrac{4 * 50}{25} = $ _____

2 A $3 \cdot 10^5 = $ _____

  B $\dfrac{144/12}{6(2)} = $ _____

  C $10^{-2}\,(5) = $ _____

3 A $8 \times (4 + 5) = $ _____ However, $(8 \times 4) + 5 = $ _____

  B $3\,(2 + 6) = $ _____ However, $(3 \times 2) + 6 = $ _____

4 A $14 \times (3 + 2) = $ _____ However, $(14 \times 3) + 2 = $ _____

  B $(40 - 10) - 2 = $ _____ However, $40 - (10 - 2) = $ _____

Activity 2: Operate with Exponents to the Same Base

It is business as usual when you add and subtract powers of the same base:

ADD: $6^3 + 6^2 = $ SUBTRACT: $6^3 - 6^2 = $

    $(6 \times 6 \times 6) + (6 \times 6) = $ $(6 \times 6 \times 6) - (6 \times 6) = $

        $216 + 36 = 252$ $216 - 36 = 180$

There are shortcuts for multiplying and dividing powers of the same base:

MULTIPLY: $6^3 \times 6^2 = $

              $(6 \times 6 \times 6) \times (6 \times 6) = (216) \times (36) = 7776$

Shortcut: Add the exponents of the bases, then evaluate:

$6^3 \times 6^2 = 6^{3+2} = 6^5 = 7776$

Why? The operation of multiplication between same-base exponents *continues* the *repeated multiplication* of the base.

DIVIDE: $6^3/6^2 = (6 \times 6 \times 6) / (6 \times 6) = 216/36 = 6$

Shortcut: Subtract the exponents of the bases, then evaluate

$6^3/6^2 = 6^{3-2} = 6^1 = 6$

Why? Division is the opposite of multiplication. Division between same-base exponents involves the repeated division of the base number by itself.

Target Practice: Show the Shortcut

Write out the shortcuts you can use for multiplying and dividing powers of the same base. Refer to the instructions above. Use a calculator to compute the final answers.

Follow this example:

- $7^4 \times 7^2 = 7^{4+2}$ $= 7^6$ $= 117,649$

1. $3^6/3^2 =$ _____ $=$ _____ $=$ _____
2. $5^4 \times 5^3 =$ _____ $=$ _____ $=$ _____
3. $2^4/2^2 =$ _____ $=$ _____ $=$ _____
4. $8^3 \times 8^2 =$ _____ $=$ _____ $=$ _____

Activity 3: Follow These Orders—It's The Law.

Mathematicians worldwide follow a standard sequence of steps when they evaluate expressions that contain several operations. It is called the *Order of Operations.* Remember it with this phrase: **P**lease **E**xcuse **M**y **D**ear **A**unt **S**ally. (Look at the steps below. Do you see where this phrase comes from?)

> Step 1. Look for number work enclosed in **P**arentheses. Do it.
> Step 2. Look for numbers with **E**xponents or Roots. Calculate their value.
> Step 3. Perform all **M**ultiplication *and* **D**ivision from left to right *in the order they occur.*
> Step 4. Perform all **A**ddition *and* **S**ubtraction from left to right *in the order they occur.*

For example, for the following equation:

$$7 + 5 \times 4$$

you would perform multiplication before addition, even though it *looks like* multiplication should be done second. See Steps 3 and 4 above. This is the correct order:

$$7 + 5 \times 4 = 7 + 20 = 27$$

In the following equation:

$$(7 + 5) \times 4$$

Addition comes first, and the calculations work in this order:

$$(7 + 5) \times 4 = (12) \times 4 = 48$$

Why? Because of the Parentheses rule. See Step 1 above.

It pays to keep things orderly when following orders. Use this format when evaluating complex expressions. Each time you perform an operation, rewrite the simplified expression on the next line, directly underneath. Structure is a mistake-prevention strategy in math.

For example, evaluate the following:

$$4^2 \div (2 + 6) \times 5 - 2$$

Parentheses:

Exponents:

Multiply and **D**ivide: (left to right, in the order they occur)

Add and **S**ubtract: (left to right, in the order they occur)

Re-Write Column Format

$4^2 \div (2 + 6) \times 5 - 2$
$4^2 \div 8 \times 5 - 2$
$16 \div 8 \times 5 - 2$
$2 \times 5 - 2$
$10 - 2$
8

Target Practice: Operate Politely with
Dear Aunt Sally

Try using the rewrite column format as you simplify these expressions in your math notebook. Record your answers below.

1 $30 + 8 \div 4 - 5 \times 3$ _____

2 $\$50.00 - 6\ (\$8.75 - \$1.25)$ _____

3 $8 + 4 \times 3^3$ _____

4 $(6 - 2)/(3 + 1)$ _____

5 $30 - 120/4$ _____

6 $21 - 3\ (7) + 22/11$ _____

Math Language, Part III

TARGET Expressions: Notation for Solutions

Words to Know

Expression   A combination of numbers and one or more operations
            Examples:

            $24 \div 6$ $5^2 \times 5^4$ $345 + 1{,}050/5$ $(5 \times 25) - 65$

Setup   An expression that is *a plan to answer a question*

Take Time to *Take Five:*

As you work through the next three Activities, refer to the *Take Five* template on page 100. The problem-solving process you worked through in Lesson 2 is being followed here. Activity 1 reviews Steps 1 and 2. Activity 2 reviews Steps 2 and 3. Activity 3 reviews Steps 3, 4, and 5.

Activity 1: What Is the Story?

Shawn entered the grocery store at 9 P.M. with two 20-dollar bills to spend on party food for his nephew's birthday. He scooped up 4 cartons of ice cream @ $3.50 each, 5 jars of chocolate sauce @ $1.99, 1 jumbo roll of paper towels @ $.99, 1 box of chocolate sugar cones @ $2.49, 3 jars of cherries @ $1.50 a jar, and 2 cans of pressurized whipped cream @ $1.99. At the checkout, the cashier handed Shawn a Buy-3-Get-1-Free coupon for the brand of ice cream he was purchasing. Shawn left the store at 9:35 P.M. a happy man.

Target Practice: Match Expressions to Words

Match these expressions of value with the words that identify them.

1	$3(1.50) + 2(1.99) + 5(1.99)$	**A**	Amount saved by using the coupon
2	$2(20)$	**B**	Cost of cherries, whipped cream, chocolate sauce
3	$9:35 - 9:00$	**C**	Money in Shawn's hand before checkout
4	$4(3.50) - 3(3.50)$	**D**	Cost of the food
5	$3(3.50) + 5(1.99) + 2.49$ $+ 3(1.50) + 2(1.99)$	**E**	Time it took Shawn to shop

6 How many of the five expressions above will you need to use to solve a word problem about this situation? _____

Resist the grab-the-numbers-and-run approach to word problems. Focus on the question; then look for what you need.

 TEST TIP: CHOOSE THE SETUP, NOT THE SOLUTION
Math tests often include setup questions. You are asked to choose the *plan*, or *expression*, that will result in the correct answer.

Activity 2: What Is the Plan?

Remember helping your friend figure out a budget for gas money as she made plans for a car trip across the United States (Lesson 2, page 98)? You were asked to write up a mathematical *plan* that would get you to the solution. You *set it up* and thought about it before taking action. A "setup" is a mathematical expression that is *a plan to answer a question. It gives instructions* by its arrangement of numbers, symbols, and signs.

Target Practice: Choose the Plan

1 Carmella gets paid every two weeks. Last pay period, she worked her regular 40 hours per week at $12 an hour. How much was her paycheck, before taxes and withholding? <u>Underline</u> three expressions that will result in the correct answer.

A 40×12
B $2(40 + 12)$
C $12(40 + 40)$
D $2(40 + 12)$
E $(40)(2)(12)$
F $(40 \times 2)(12)$

Check with the Answer Key before moving on.

Note: As a reminder, when adding or multiplying numbers, it does not matter which number comes first. Match facts carefully with the parts of set-up expression choices.

2 During one 2-week pay period, Carmella (from Question 1) worked her regular hours plus 16 hours of overtime. She gets $18 an hour for overtime. Which expression is set up to figure her gross pay for that period?

A $12(40 + 2) + 18(16)$
B $12(40 \times 2) - 18(16)$
C $12(40 \times 2) + 18(16)$

3 Leo's job pays him a salary of $42,000 a year. His benefit package is valued at $9,600. Which expression represents the total value of Leo's compensation for this job?

A $42,000($9,600)$
B $9,600 + $42,000$
C $42,000/$9,600$
D $46,000 + $9,200$

4 The Community College awarded 245 certificates and 1,700 associate degrees to students this spring. Of the students receiving certificates and associate degrees, 238 were unable to attend the graduation ceremony. Which expression represents the graduates who did attend?

A $1,700 - (245 + 328)$
B $(238 + 1,700) - 245$
C $(1,700 + 245) - 238$
D $1,700 - 238$

5 Danielle purchased a used car selling for $7,800. She put $1,000 down and agreed to pay $350 a month for 22 months. Which expression shows the total she will pay for the car?

A $7,800 - 1,000/350 \times 22$

B $350 \times 22 \times 1,000$

C $1,000 + 350 \times 22$

D $7,800 + 22(350)$

Activity 3: How Does It End?

Now that you have made careful plans, calculating the solutions will be the easy part. In this Target Practice, refer back to the plans just made in Activity 2 as you fill in the blanks below. Use the answers to 1 as an example.

Target Practice: Evaluate the Plans to Find the Solutions

Value asked for	Set-up	Solution
1 Carmella's regular paycheck	(40)(2)(12)	$960
2 Carmella's wages this pay period	_____	
3 Leo's compensation package	_____	
4 Graduates who attended	_____	
5 Final cost of Danielle's car	_____	

STUDY TIP

Consider choosing one of these sayings for your motto as you work *smarter, not harder:*

"Think like a woman of action; act like a woman of thought."

"Think like a man of action; act like a man of thought."

Answer Key: Section 3, Lesson 3

Math Language, Part I

Activity 1: Warm Up to Numbers

TARGET PRACTICE 1: IMAGINE LARGE AND LARGER

1. 10,000 days

2. about 27.5 years (27.397)

3. Answers will vary

4. Answers will vary

TARGET PRACTICE 2: IMAGINE SMALL AND SMALLER

This target practice is a test of your ability to visualize the invisible. How did you do?

Activity 2: Number Names and Notation

TARGET PRACTICE: ON BOTH SIDES OF THE POINT
1. 3 hundred thousands $3 \times 100{,}000$ or $300{,}000$
2. 3 hundred thousand**ths** $3 \div 100{,}000$ or 0.00003
3. 7 thousands $7 \times 1{,}000$ or $7{,}000$
4. 7 thousand**ths** $7 \div 1000$ or 0.007

Activity 3: Powers in Addition to Places Raise Number Values

TARGET PRACTICE 1: THE RAISED POWER PATTERN

5^3 "5 raised to the power of 3" $= 5 \times 5 \times 5$ $= 125$

5^4 "5 raised to the power of 4" $= 5 \times 5 \times 5 \times 5$ $= 625$

5^5 "5 raised to the power of 5" $= 5 \times 5 \times 5 \times 5 \times 5$ $= 3125$

TARGET PRACTICE 2: VALUE WRITTEN THREE WAYS
1. $6 \times 6 \times 6 = 216$
2. $2^8 = 256$
3. $8 \times 8 \times 8 \times 8 = 4096$
4. $3 \times 3 \times 3 \times 3 \times 3 \times 3 \times 3 = 2187$

Activity 4: Squares and Roots

TARGET PRACTICE: TABLE THESE SQUARES AND ROOTS

$4^2 = 16$	$\sqrt{16} = 4$	$7^2 = 49$	$\sqrt{49} = 7$	$10^2 = 100$	$\sqrt{100} = 10$	$13^2 = 169$	$\sqrt{169} = 13$
$5^2 = 25$	$\sqrt{25} = 5$	$8^2 = 64$	$\sqrt{64} = 8$	$11^2 = 121$	$\sqrt{121} = 11$	$14^2 = 196$	$\sqrt{196} = 14$
$6^2 = 36$	$\sqrt{36} = 6$	$9^2 = 81$	$\sqrt{81} = 9$	$12^2 = 144$	$\sqrt{144} = 12$	$15^2 = 225$	$\sqrt{225} = 15$

Activity 5: Scientifically Speaking

TARGET PRACTICE 1: CHART THE POWERS OF 10

10^0	any number raised to the power of 0 equals 1	1	0
10^1	any number raised to the power of 1 equals itself	10	1
10^2	10×10	100	2
10^3	$10 \times 10 \times 10$	1,000	3
10^4	$10 \times 10 \times 10 \times 10$	10,000	4
10^5	$10 \times 10 \times 10 \times 10 \times 10$	100,000	5
10^6	$10 \times 10 \times 10 \times 10 \times 10 \times 10$	1,000,000	6
10^7	$10 \times 10 \times 10 \times 10 \times 10 \times 10 \times 10$	10,000,000	7
10^8	$10 \times 10 \times 10 \times 10 \times 10 \times 10 \times 10 \times 10$	100,000,000	8
10^9	$10 \times 10 \times 10 \times 10 \times 10 \times 10 \times 10 \times 10 \times 10$	1,000,000,000	9
10^{10}	$10 \times 10 \times 10 \times 10 \times 10 \times 10 \times 10 \times 10 \times 10 \times 10$	10,000,000,000	10
10^{11}	$10 \times 10 \times 10 \times 10 \times 10 \times 10 \times 10 \times 10 \times 10 \times 10 \times 10$	100,000,000,000	11
10^{12}	$10 \times 10 \times 10 \times 10 \times 10 \times 10 \times 10 \times 10 \times 10 \times 10 \times 10$	1,000,000,000,000	12

TARGET PRACTICE 2: NOTE THESE VALUES THREE DIFFERENT WAYS
1. 200,000   2 <u>hundred thousand</u>
2. 80,000,000   80 <u>million</u>

3. 4×10^{10} 40 <u>billion</u>

4. 6×10^5 6 <u>hundred thousand</u>

TARGET PRACTICE 3: EXPRESS IT SCIENTIFICALLY

1. B

2. 6×10^{12}

3. A

4. 2.5×10^{12}

Activity 6: Lines Tell a Story of Change

TARGET PRACTICE 1: ORIENT YOURSELF TO THE LINE

1. World Population

2. 100 year period; 2050

3. 2015

4. billions

5. 4 billion

6. <u>International Data Base</u> U.S. Bureau of the Census

TARGET PRACTICE 2: USE YOUR SKILLS

1. C

2. B

3. C

4. B (last half of the twentieth century 1950 to 2000)

5. C

6. C

Activity 7: PS

TARGET PRACTICE 1: SHORTHAND FOR SMALL

1. −4

2. 4

3. 4

TARGET PRACTICE 2: ON THE RIGHT SIDE OF THE POINT

1. 10

2. D

3. C

4. C

5. C

Math Language, Part II

Activity 1: What Action Is This?

TARGET PRACTICE: ACT ACCORDING TO SIGNS AND SYMBOLS

1. **A** 12

   B 24

   C 8

2. **A** 300,000
   B 1
   C 0.05
3. **A** 72 However, 37
   B 24 However, 12
4. **A** 70 However, 44
   B 28 However, 32

Activity 2: Operate with Exponents to the Same Base

TARGET PRACTICE: SHOW THE SHORTCUT

1. $3^{6-2} = 3^4 = 81$
2. $5^{4+3} = 5^7 = 78,125$
3. $2^{4-2} = 2^2 = 4$
4. $8^{3+2} = 8^5 = 32,768$

Activity 3: Operate Politely with Aunt Sally

TARGET PRACTICE

1. 17
2. $5.00
3. 116 (Did you remember to calculate the exponent first?)
4. 1
5. 0
6. 2

Math Language, Part III

Activity 1: What Is the Story?

TARGET PRACTICE: MATCH EXPRESSIONS TO WORDS

1. B
2. C
3. E
4. A
5. D (Did you notice the roll of paper towels is not included?)
6. You won't know until you read the question being asked.

Activity 2: What Is the Plan?

TARGET PRACTICE

1. C; E; F
2. C
3. B
4. C
5. C

Activity 3: How Does It End?

TARGET PRACTICE: EVALUATE THE PLANS TO FIND THE SOLUTIONS

1. example given
2. $12(40 \times 2) + 18(16)$ \$1248
3. $\$9,600 + \$42,000$ \$51,600
4. $(1,700 + 245) - 238$ 1707
5. $1,000 + 350 \times 22$ \$8700

LESSON 4   *Geometry*

Getting Started

In Section 1, we met Alice, who had seen a job posting in her department for a supervisory position. Alice knows she does her job well but was nervous when she saw how much math was involved in the supervisor's job. Read about Alice and then follow her through her journey as she learns Geometry:

During the first geometry class, the instructor explained that the first part of the lesson would focus on lines and angles. The second, she explained, would focus on shapes and geometric measurement. She began the lesson with an introduction to words and symbols that would be used in the lesson.

Learner Profile

Alice
Age: 50
Education: GED at age 34

Background Information:
- Single mom; 2 grown children
- Employed for the past 18 years in a small safety products manufacturing plant as an assembler.

Scenario:
- Concerned about her poor math skills; wants to apply for a supervisor job that requires math competence in geometry, fractions, and so on
- Sought help at the Hensen Adult Learning Center; worked with Education Counselor Gayle Richards to develop a learning plan that fit her needs

TARGET Lines and Angles: Connect with Your World

Words and Symbols to Know

●	Point	One position in space
●——→	Ray	A straight line of points that begins with one point and goes in one direction
←——→	Line	A straight path of points that goes in two directions

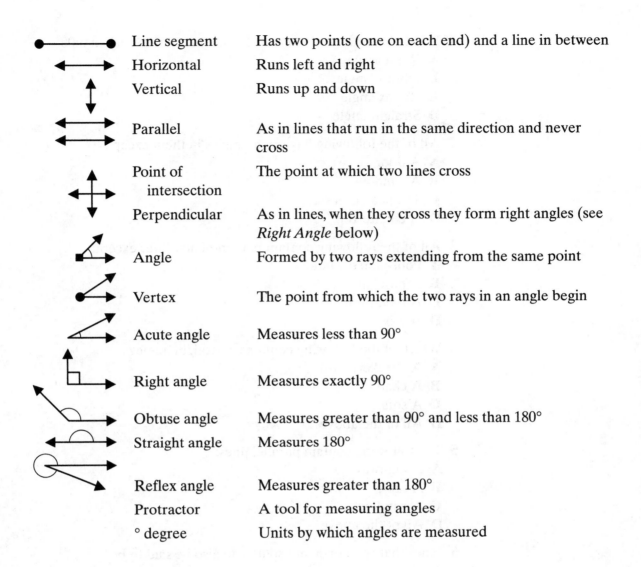

	Line segment	Has two points (one on each end) and a line in between
	Horizontal	Runs left and right
	Vertical	Runs up and down
	Parallel	As in lines that run in the same direction and never cross
	Point of intersection	The point at which two lines cross
	Perpendicular	As in lines, when they cross they form right angles (see *Right Angle* below)
	Angle	Formed by two rays extending from the same point
	Vertex	The point from which the two rays in an angle begin
	Acute angle	Measures less than 90°
	Right angle	Measures exactly 90°
	Obtuse angle	Measures greater than 90° and less than 180°
	Straight angle	Measures 180°
	Reflex angle	Measures greater than 180°
	Protractor	A tool for measuring angles
	° degree	Units by which angles are measured

Activity 1: Getting Comfortable

In the first two sections of this lesson, you will become familiar with, or revisit, some of the basics in geometry, such as shapes, lines, angles, and terminology. Then we'll move on to more advanced geometric applications, such as finding area, perimeter, and volume, and measuring angles and lines.

STUDY TIP: CONNECT WITH YOUR WORLD

As you learn new figures and concepts, make it a habit to look for these things around the house, in your backyard, or at work. Examine them and try to understand how they are used in their current form. You will find they make more sense when you see them "in action."

Target Practice: What's Your Angle? What's My Line?

The following common household items have lines and angles in them. Try to figure out what they represent:

1 What kind of angle is formed by the hands of a clock at 3:00?

   A Right angle

   B Obtuse angle

   C Reflex angle

   D Straight angle

2 All of the following have right angles in them except:

   A A door

   B A window

   C The peak of a steeple

   D A countertop

3 All of the following contain perpendicular lines except:

   A Four-paned window

   B A baseball

   C A tiled floor

   D A cross

4 Which of the following contains a straight angle?

   A A checkerboard

   B A chair

   C A sofa

   D All of the above

5 The following contain parallel lines:

   A A highway

   B A table

   C A window

   D All of the above

6 Lines that run north and south can also be said to be

   A Horizontal lines

   B Vertical lines

   C Line segments

   D Parallel lines

7 Lines that run east and west can also be said to be

   A Horizontal lines

   B Vertical lines

   C Line segments

   D Parallel lines

Turn to the Answer Key on page 138 to check your answers. Again, you may want to bookmark this page so you can check future work. How did you do? Do you see that the lines and angles you are learning about are familiar to you already? Although you may be putting the proper names to them for the first time, the important thing to remember is how they are used in your everyday world.

Activity 2: Angle Relationships

Now, let's see how lines and angles work together as we look at *angle relationships*. They are called angle relationships because they consist of more than one angle put together.

Words and Symbols to Know

Supplementary angles — Two angles that add up to 180 degrees (180°). For example: $\angle A + \angle B = \angle 180°$

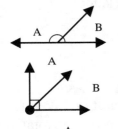

Complementary Angles — Two angles that add up to 90 degrees (90°). For example: $\angle A + \angle B = 90°$

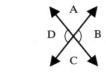

Adjacent angles — Two angles that share a side. For example: $\angle A$ and $\angle B$ are adjacent angles.

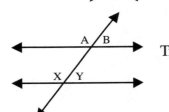

Vertical angles — Two angles that are across from each other (opposite) when two lines intersect (cut across each other). Vertical angles are equal to each other. For example: $\angle B$ and $\angle D$ are vertical angles.

Transversal line — A line that cuts across parallel lines, intersecting them. Note: The angles this line forms as it intersects each of the parallel lines are *congruent,* or equal. For example: $\angle A$ and $\angle X$ are *congruent.* $\angle B$ and $\angle Y$ are *congruent.* Congruent angles contain the same number of degrees.

STUDY TIP: GET TO THE ROOT!

More strange words to know! But, if you really look at some of these words, you will see that they may be somewhat familiar to you. For instance, look at the root word in supplementary—supplement. What does that word mean to you? To supplement means to *add* something. As you see from the definition above, supplementary angles are two angles that *add* up to 180°. Looking at the root word will often help you make sense of a concept or new term you are learning.

Target Practice: It Takes Two to Angle

When you are using both supplementary and complementary angles, it is important to note that by knowing the measurement of one of the angles, you can find the measurement of the other angle. For example, as you know, a supplementary angle is made up of two angles that add up to 180°. You can use a measuring device called a protractor to measure one angle, then subtract that number from 180° to find the measurement of the other angle. Or, if you are given only one angle measurement, you can find the other in the same way. The same concept applies to complementary angles. If you know or measure one angle, subtract that amount from 90° to find the measurement of the other angle. Try it for yourself:

1 A ladder leans against a house at a 45° angle from the ground. What is the value of the supplementary angle or the angle formed by the space between the ladder and the ground away from the ladder?

   A 135°

   B 45°

   C 90°

   D All of the above

If you answered 135°, you are correct. Because the question asked for the value of the supplementary angle, you are clued in to the fact the total measurement of the two angles is 180°. You also know the measurement of one of the two angles is 45°. Therefore, by simply subtracting 45 from 180, you arrived at a measurement of 135° for the other or supplementary angle. Now try a few more problems that deal with complementary, adjacent, and vertical angles.

2 Complementary angles

   A Are two or more angles that add up to 180°

   B Consist of three angles

   C Consist of two angles that add up to 90°

   D All of the above

3 The name supplementary angles comes from

   A The fact that they are supple

   B One angle is added to another

   C Greek mythology

   D Their measurements

4 You can tell when two angles are adjacent if

   A They are near each other

   B They add to each other

   C They share a side

   D All of the above

Please refer to the Answer Key on page 139 for the correct responses to the above questions.

At the Hensen Adult Learning Center, Alice's instructor suggested she begin looking for signs of geometry around her house. When Alice looked around, she found that everything in her house was made up of lines and angles. She spent the first night after class going around to different rooms in her house looking for examples of what she had learned in class that day. Now is a good time for you to try that too!

TARGET Basic Shapes: What's the Shape You're In?

Activity 3: Basic Geometric Shapes

As mentioned earlier, the next part of this lesson will cover basic geometric shapes. Some of the shapes in this section are considered flat, or two-dimensional. That is, they have length and width but no height. These consist of squares, rectangles, triangles, and circles.

Words and Symbols to Know

	Rectangle	A shape that contains four right angles. The sides opposite each other are equal in length and are parallel (they will never cross).
	Square	Like a rectangle, a square also contains four right angles, but its four sides are equal in length. The sides that are opposite each other are also parallel.
	Triangle	A figure with three sides.
	Right triangle	A triangle that has one right angle.
	Hypotenuse	On a right triangle, the side that is across from the right angle.
	Legs	On a right triangle, the sides that form the right angle.
	Circumference	The distance around the circle.
	Radius	The distance from the *center* to any point on the circle.
	Diameter	The distance across the circle that cuts through the center, forming two equal halves.

The points that make up a circle are all exactly the same distance from the center of the circle. As mentioned above, the distance around the circle is the circumference and the distance from the center to any point on the circle is the radius. The distance across the circle that cuts through the center is the diameter. Therefore, if you double the radius of a circle, you will know the diameter of the circle.

Target Practice: What Shape Are You In?

Again, just by looking around the house, you can find the basic geometric shapes we are looking at in this section.

1 A 6-inch-×-6-inch piece of floor tile is a
  A Square
  B Rectangle

   C Triangle
   D Circle

2 Your backyard is 25 feet wide and 30 feet long. You put up a fence around your yard. What shape does your fence form?
   A A square
   B A rectangle
   C A triangle
   D A circle

3 The tires on your car have a diameter of 16 inches. What is their radius?
   A 4 inches
   B 8 inches
   C 10 inches
   D None of the above

4 Which items may contain a triangle(s)?
   A A sandwich cut in half diagonally
   B A piece of cheese
   C A slice of pizza
   D All of the above

Activity 4: Pythagorean Theorem

A Greek mathematician named Pythagoras developed a formula over 2000 years ago for finding the lengths of the sides of any **right triangle.** (Refer to Activity 3: Basic Geometric Shapes for a picture.) It is called the Pythagorean Theorem and states that

> The square of the hypotenuse is equal to the sum of the squares of the other two sides. Or

$$c^2 = a^2 + b^2$$

The formula of the Pythagorean Theorem is used today by carpenters, architects, engineers, and graphic artists, among others. They use it in their construction, drawing, and design work. Let's walk through an example of how this formula works using this right triangle with sides of 3 ft and 4 ft and a hypotenuse of 5 ft.

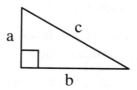

Hypotenuse c = 5

Side b = 4

Side a = 3

If these amounts are substituted in the formula, you can see that

$$c^2 = a^2 + b^2$$
$$5^2 = 3^2 + 4^2$$
$$25 = 9 + 16$$
$$25 = 25$$

Now let's put it to work to find the missing measure of the hypotenuse (c) of a triangle whose sides measure 12 feet and 16 feet. Substitute these values into the formula and do the calculations like this:

$$c^2 = a^2 + b^2$$
$$c^2 = 12^2 + 16^2$$
$$c^2 = 144 + 256$$
$$c^2 = 400$$
$$c = \sqrt{400} = 20$$

STUDY TIP

GET TO THE ROOT, AGAIN. When you use the formula of the Pythagorean Theorem to find the measure of one of the sides of a right triangle, **do not stop at the squared value** (a^2 or b^2 or c^2). Get to its root.

Simple! Now try a few of your own. Refer to Lesson 3 for a refresher on squares and square roots if you need to.

Target Practice: Two Sides Are Better than One

Find the hypotenuse (side c) of the following right triangles:

1 Side a = 9, Side b = 12, Side c = _____

2 Side a = 15, Side b = 20, Side c = _____

3 Side a = 18, Side b = 24, Side c = _____

Now we will move on to some shapes that you may not see in your everyday world.

Words and Symbols to Know

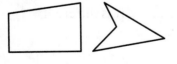

Closed figure	A figure where all segments meet
Polygon	A shape composed of three or more line segments and all line segments meet; a polygon is therefore considered a closed figure.
Rhombus	A shape with four equal sides where the opposite sides are parallel. It looks like a square that's about to tip over.

	Parallelogram	A shape that has two pairs of sides that are equal in length and are parallel. It looks like a rectangle that's about to tip over.
	Trapezoid	A shape that has four sides but only one set of opposite sides are parallel.
	Quadrilateral	A polygon with four sides. A rhombus, parallelogram, and trapezoid are all quadrilaterals, as are squares and rectangles.

STUDY TIP

When learning new or unfamiliar information or symbols, try to relate it to something familiar. Go back to something you already know, or look at the root word (the main part of a larger word) to give you a clue. For example, when trying to learn what a parallelogram is, look at the root word (parallel) and relate back to what you learned that it means. That way, you have a better chance of remembering what it looks like.

Activity 5: Polygons/Quadrilaterals

These shapes may look a bit odd to you. You probably don't normally see them or use them on a daily basis. We can understand simple shapes like squares and circles and what they represent, but when was the last time you saw a rhombus hanging around the house? The word quadrilateral is probably not in your daily vocabulary, as in, "Please pass the quadrilateral" or "Wow, that's a heck of a quadrilateral you've got out back!" Learning these shapes will take a little bit more work.

Target Practice: Out-of-Shape Shapes

Use what you already know, what you've learned in previous activities in this chapter, and/or look for clues in the words to answer the following:

1 A quadrilateral
  A Is a polygon
  B Has four sides
  C May look like a square
  D All of the above

2 Fill in the blanks: A rhombus is like a square because it has _____ sides that are _____ and the opposite sides are _____. It is different than a square because it looks like it is _____ (more than one word here).

3 Fill in the blanks: A parallelogram is similar to a rectangle because it has two _____ of sides that are _____ in length and are _____. It is different from a rectangle because it looks like it is _____ (more than one word here).

4 A trapezoid is a quadrilateral because it has _____ _____.

5 A polygon has _____ or more closed line segments. One that has four closed line segments is called a _____.

6 What does the root word of the figure "parallelogram" tell you about it _____?

7 How might you use part of the word "trapezoid" to help you remember something about what it looks like _____?

8 Can you tell something about a "quadrilateral" from its root word "quad" _____?

Check Your Skills

Did you find yourself going back to what you already knew about certain shapes like a square and a rectangle to answer some of these questions? Were some of the meanings of root words that you already knew or just learned helpful in remembering something about the new shapes you just saw? Use these strategies whenever you are learning something that may be totally unfamiliar to you.

TARGET Geometric Measurement: Perimeter, Area, and Volume

In this section we will bring together concepts from the sections on lines, angles, and shapes to look at measurement in geometry. Understanding this kind of measurement can be very useful when doing projects around the house or in the workplace. You may have figured out the perimeter, area, or volume of things without even knowing it. For example, have you ever measured a room for wall-to-wall carpeting? Ever measured walls before buying wallpaper? Measured your windows to put up blinds? If you have, then you have measured area. What about perimeter? Have you ever measured your yard for a fence? Have you ever had to figure out how much molding to put around a window? That's measuring perimeter.

Words and Formulas to Know

Perimeter — The measure of the distance around a plane (flat) figure such as a square, rectangle, or triangle. Think of it as measuring the distance around your backyard or a window. Perimeter is measured in units like inches, feet, yards, miles, meters, and centimeters. When looking for the measure around a circle, the term used is *circumference*.

Area — A measure of the surface area within the perimeter of a flat figure such as a square, rectangle, triangle, and circle. Think of it as measuring the space of a floor or wall in your home. Area is measured in *square units,* such as square inches, square feet, and square meters.

Area Formulas

To figure area, put the actual measurements of the figures into these formulas in place of the words:

Side, Length, Width, Base, and Radius.

Square: Side^2 or (Side $\times$ Side) = A
Rectangle: Length $\times$ Width = A
Triangle: $\frac{1}{2} \times$ base $\times$ height = A
Circle: π (pi) $\times \text{radius}^2$ = A (π (pi) is equal to approximately 3.14, or 22/7).

Volume — A measure of the space inside a three-dimensional (not flat) or solid figure (think of the space inside an aluminum can or a box). Volume is measured in cubic units, like cubic inches or cubic meters.

Cube — A cube is a three-dimensional figure that is a square, but it also has height as well as length and width.

Rectangular solid — A rectangular solid is a rectangle that also has height as well as length and width.

To figure volume, put the actual measure of the figures into these formulas in place of the words:

Side, Length, Width, Height, and Radius

You may be unfamiliar with some of them, so pictures have been provided.

Cube: $Side^3 = V$
Rectangular Solid: Length × Width × Height = V.
Cylinder: π (pi) × $Radius^2$ × Height = V (π = 3.14 or 22/7)
Cone: $\frac{1}{3}$ × π × $radius^2$ × height = V (π = 3.14).

Cylinder   A circle that also has height.

Cone $\frac{1}{3}$ × π × $Radius^2$ × Height (π = 3.14)

You can determine the distance around a flat surface, the space within the perimeter of a flat surface, and the space inside a three-dimensional figure by using actual measurements and the formulas provided. Let's try some examples.

Activity 6: Measure Your World

Target Practice 1: In the Garden

Scenario: You have a garden in your backyard that is rectangular in shape. It is 5 feet long and 4 feet wide. You want to condition the garden soil by mixing in some peat moss before planting your summer vegetables and flowers. At the garden store, you see that peat moss is sold by the cubic foot (cu ft). Directions on the bag recommend spreading a 2-inch layer of peat on top of the soil before mixing it in. You need to figure how much to buy.

1 From the information provided, you can tell that the type of measurement you will be figuring is
   A Perimeter
   B Volume
   C Area
   D None of the above

2 The formula you need to use is
   A $Side^3 = V$
   B Length × Width = V

C Length × Width × Height = V

D π (pi) × Radius² × Height = V

3 The clerk at the garden store reminds you that you need to convert inches to feet when you use the formula. You know that 2 inches is equal to ⅙ foot. You round that figure off to 0.2 ft. The *approximate* amount of peat moss you will need for your garden is

    A 3.5 cu ft

    B 4 cu ft

    C 5 cu ft

    D 4.5 cu ft

STUDY TIP

To make sure you understand the examples so far, go to the Answer Key now on page 137 to check your work. This will help you determine if you need more help with this concept.

Target Practice 2: Drill a Bit

1 Scenario: You work in a machine shop and are asked to find the correct drill bit to drill a hole that has a circumference of 9.42 millimeters. You know the diameter for each bit because they are individually labeled. From the information given, which measurement will you need to know to find the correct tool?

    A Radius

    B Length

    C Diameter

    D Volume

2 The formula you need to use to calculate this measurement is

    A 4 × S = P

    B 2 × Length + 2 × Width = P

    C Side 1 + Side 2 + Side 3 = P

    D π (pi) × diameter = C

3 The correct drill bit will have a diameter of approximately

    A 3 millimeters

    B 4 millimeters

    C 5 millimeters

    D 18 millimeters

Check your answers with the Answer Key on page 139 to make sure you understand so far. Were you able to use the clues in the scenario to help you?

Target Practice 3: Cover the Top

Scenario: Mary decides to give jars of strawberry preserves to her friends as holiday presents. She wants to dress up the jars, so she buys some festive fabric to glue onto the tops of the jars.

1 The festive fabric Mary bought measures 18 inches by 36 inches. The area of that fabric, measured in square inches (sq in), is

A 54 sq in

B 72 sq in

C 108 sq in

D 648 sq in

2 The diameter of each jar top is 3 inches. What is the area of each top? Round your answer to the nearest square inch.

A 7 sq in

B 8 sq in

C 9 sq in

D 10 sq in

3 She plans to cut the fabric into 3-inch squares. From each square, she will cut a circle. How many circles of fabric will that be?

A 92

B 81

C 72

D 18

Review with This Old House

One of Alice's classmates brought in a picture that she had drawn of the outside of her house to help her identify some of the concepts she had learned in class. The teacher decided to add some measurements to it. She wrote questions to go with it and handed it out to the class. Use the drawing and questions below to help you review what you have learned in this lesson. As you do so, you may want to refer to *Words and Symbols to Know* on pages 124, 127, 129, and 131.

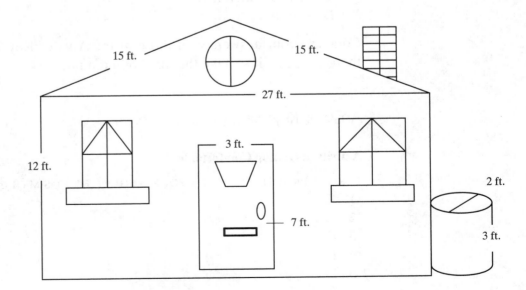

1 Make a list of seven shapes used in the drawing.

_____

2 If the window in the peak of the house has a radius of 1 foot, *approximately* (≈) how many square feet of glass will it contain?
   A ≈ 1 sq ft
   B ≈ 2 sq ft
   C ≈ 3 sq ft
   D None of the above

3 List five *types* of angles you see.

_____

Now mark and label these angles on the drawing itself.

4 Look at the windows beside the front door. Find and list four types of angle *relationships* seen in those windows.

_____

Mark and label the angle relationships on the drawing.

5 The perimeter of the triangle that forms the peak and roof of the house is _____.

6 What is the formula to use to find the area of the door? _____

7 The area of the door is _____

8 Which formula will find the volume of the rain barrel beside the house? _____

9 *Approximately* how many cubic feet (cu ft) of water will the barrel hold?
   A ≈ 6 cu ft
   B ≈ 9 cu ft
   C ≈ 24 cu ft meters
   D ≈ 36 cu ft

Compare your answers with those in the Answer Key. Did you miss anything? _____ If so, take the time to find it now.

Answer Key: Section 3, Lesson 4

Activity 1: Getting Comfortable

TARGET PRACTICE: WHAT'S YOUR ANGLE? WHAT'S MY LINE?
   1. A
   2. C
   3. B
   4. D
   5. D

6. B

7. A

Activity 2: Angle Relationships

TARGET PRACTICE: IT TAKES TWO TO ANGLE

1. A

2. C

3. B

4. C

Activity 3: Basic Geometric Shapes

TARGET PRACTICE: WHAT SHAPE ARE YOU IN?

1. A

2. B

3. B

4. D

Activity 4: Pythagorean Theorem

TARGET PRACTICE: TWO SIDES ARE BETTER THAN NONE

1. Side c = 15

2. Side c = 25

3. Side c = 30

Activity 5: Polygons/Quadrilaterals

TARGET PRACTICE: OUT-OF-SHAPE SHAPES

1. D

2. 4, Equal, parallel, tipping over

3. Pairs, equal, parallel, tipping over

4. 4 sides

5. 3, quadrilateral

6. It has parallel lines.

7. It looks like a trapeze.

8. Quad means 4.

Activity 6: Measure Your World

TARGET PRACTICE 1: IN THE GARDEN

1. B

2. C

3. B

TARGET PRACTICE 2: DRILL A BIT

1. C

2. D

3. A

TARGET PRACTICE 3: COVER THE TOP
1. D
2. A
3. C

Lesson 4 Review with This Old House
1. Shapes: Circle, oval, square, rectangle, triangle, trapezoid, cylinder
2. C
3. Angles: Right, straight, acute, obtuse, reflex
4. Angle relationships: Supplementary, complementary, adjacent, vertical
5. 57 feet
6. A = length × width (A = 7 × 3)
7. 21 sq ft
8. $V = \pi \times radius^2 \times height$ (V = 3.14 × 1² × 3)
9. B; V ≈ 9 cu ft

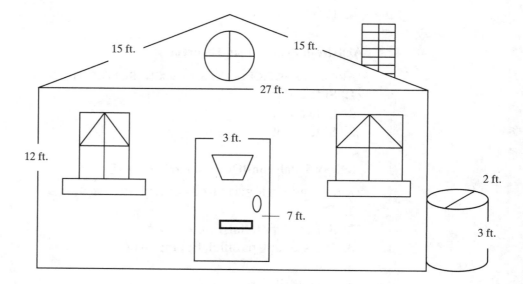

_____ **LESSON 5** **That's Just Part of It**

Getting Started

Alice finished her classes in geometry and is looking forward to learning more about fractions, decimals, and percents. She likes the way her instructor connects the mechanics of math to its practical real-life uses. Alice is getting better at making those kinds of connections for herself as well.

Learner Update: Alice
Success is encouraging:

- Alice was successful learning basic geometry. Now she is ready to improve her skills with fractions, decimals, and percents.

- She is seeing the connection between math and her everyday world more than before.

- She is more confident the math skills she needs to qualify for the supervisor's job are within her reach.

Make your own connections as you work through the activities and examples in this lesson.

TARGET Fractions: Divide and Conquer

You already know that a fraction is a part of something: A quarter is a fraction of a dollar, an inch is a fraction of a foot, a slice of pie is a fraction of a whole pie, and so on. If you need to, take time to review the basics of adding and subtracting fractions with the *same* denominators. In Activity 1, we begin with a review of a more complex process.

Activity 1: Working with Fractions with Different Denominators

When adding or subtracting fractions with different denominators, you must change the problem so that the denominators are the same. No magic involved, just a simple method called finding *the lowest common denominator,* or *LCD.* Remember that the LCD is the smallest number that can be divided *evenly* by all the denominators in the problem. To find the LCD, you must look at the denominators in the problem and raise at least one of them to a higher number. For example:

If the problem asks you to add

$$\begin{array}{r} \dfrac{2}{5} \\[4pt] \dfrac{3}{15} \\[2pt] \hline \end{array}$$

- **Step 1.** Look at the denominators. Can one of them be equally divided by the other? Yes. 15 is the LCD because 5 divides evenly into 15 (three times) and 15 divides evenly into itself one time.
- **Step 2.** Raise $\frac{2}{5}$ to 15ths. Write out your fractions like this first.

  To figure out how many 15ths $\frac{2}{5}$ is, multiply both the numerator and denominator by 3 (the amount of times 15 is divided evenly by 5). You should get <u>6.</u>
- **Step 3.** Now you can add $\frac{6}{15}$ and $\frac{3}{15}$ for an answer of $\frac{9}{15}$

Now let's try a few more.

Target Practice 1: Raise the Floor?

Follow the steps above to find the LCD and add or subtract the following:

1 $\dfrac{1}{2} + \dfrac{3}{4} =$ _____

2 $\dfrac{1}{3} + \dfrac{5}{6} =$ _____

3 $\dfrac{2}{3} + \dfrac{5}{9} = $ _____

4 $\dfrac{5}{6} - \dfrac{2}{3} = $ _____

Sometimes you need to find a common denominator other than one of those in the problem. For instance, take $\frac{2}{5} + \frac{2}{4}$. Neither denominator 5 or 4 can be equally divided by the other. In order to add these two fractions together, you must find another denominator that can be equally divided by the denominators 5 and 4. Follow these steps:

1 Multiply the denominators: $5 \times 4 = 20$. 20 is the LCD

2 Raise each fraction to 20ths (see Step 2 in Activity 1 above).

3 Add as usual.

Target Practice 2: Finding Higher Ground

1 $\dfrac{2}{3} + \dfrac{3}{5} = $ _____

2 $\dfrac{1}{3} + \dfrac{3}{7} = $ _____

3 $\dfrac{6}{7} + \dfrac{2}{6} = $ _____

4 $\dfrac{3}{4} + \dfrac{5}{6} = $ _____

Review: Reducing Fractions

Now that you've mastered *raising*, let's review *reducing*. You've heard the old adage what goes up, must come down, right? Well, it's the same principle here. The amount of the fraction doesn't change. When you reduce a fraction, you bring it to its *lowest terms*. That is, it can't be reduced any lower. To reduce a fraction, follow the steps that follow:

Example: Reduce $\dfrac{15}{20}$

1 Find a number that goes evenly into both the numerator and denominator. In this case, 5 is the largest number that goes evenly into both 15 and 20. Divide the numerator and denominator by 5.

$$\frac{15 \div 5}{20 \div 5} = \frac{3}{4}$$

2 Check to see if another number goes evenly into both 3 and 4. If not, you have reduced the fraction to its lowest terms.

STUDY TIP: REDUCING MADE EASIER, 3 WAYS

- In the case of a fraction like $\frac{30}{50}$, simply cross out both zeros and then you are left with $\frac{3}{5}$. Go to Step 2 to make sure no other number divides evenly into 3 and 5.

- If both the numerator and denominator are even numbers, reduce by 2 in Step 1.
- When reducing an improper fraction, simply divide the numerator by the denominator and list as a mixed number. For example: $\frac{12}{8}$ 12 divided by 8 is $1\frac{4}{8}$, which can be further reduced to $1\frac{1}{2}$.

Note: Before moving to Activity 2, read this next review:

Review: Mixed Numbers

Another important skill to review when dealing with fractions is changing mixed numbers (a whole number next to a proper fraction like $3\frac{1}{3}$) to improper fractions (remember, *improper* means it's not a true fraction). This will be important when we begin multiplying and dividing fractions. Follow these steps:

Example: Change $3\frac{1}{3}$ to an improper fraction.

1 Multiply the denominator by the whole number: $3 \times 3 = 9$

2 Add the result to the numerator: $9 + 1 = 10$

3 Place that result over the denominator: $\dfrac{10}{3}$

Activity 2: Multiplying Fractions

The denominators do not have to be the same when you multiply fractions as when you add and subtract fractions. Follow these steps to multiply the fractions in the example.

Example: $\dfrac{4}{7} \times \dfrac{3}{4} = $ _____

1 Multiply the numerators: $4 \times 3 = 12$

2 Multiply the denominators: $7 \times 4 = 28$

3 Reduce the fraction if possible: $\dfrac{12}{28} = \dfrac{3}{7}$ (both numbers are equally divisible by 4)

NOTE

If multiplying three fractions, multiply the first 2, then multiply the product of that by the third fraction. For example, in $\frac{3}{5} \times \frac{1}{2} \times \frac{3}{4}$, you would multiply $3 \times 1 = 3$, then multiply $5 \times 2 = 10$. Then you take $\frac{3}{10}$ and multiply it by $\frac{3}{4}$ and reduce.

Target Practice: Go Forth and Multiply!

1 $\dfrac{1}{3} \times \dfrac{1}{5} = $ _____

2 $\dfrac{5}{6} \times \dfrac{5}{8} = $ _____

3 $\dfrac{1}{6} \times \dfrac{5}{6} =$ _____

4 $\dfrac{3}{8} \times \dfrac{7}{8} =$ _____

NOTE

If multiplying a fraction by a whole number, change the whole number to a fraction by giving it a denominator of 1. For example, $8 = \frac{8}{1}$. If multiplying $8 \times \frac{2}{3}$, you would multiply $\frac{8}{1} \times \frac{2}{3}$.

Activity 3: Dividing Fractions by Fractions

To divide a fraction by a fraction, you actually multiply! But first you have to change the problem a bit. To divide fractions by fractions, whole numbers or mixed numbers follow these:

Example: $4 \div \dfrac{3}{4}$

1 Write each number in fraction form: 4 becomes $\dfrac{4}{1}$

2 Invert (flip over) the divisor $\left(\dfrac{3}{4}\right)$ and change the ÷ sign to a × sign: $\dfrac{4}{1} \times \dfrac{4}{3}$

3 Follow the rules (Activity 2) for multiplication of fractions: $\dfrac{16}{3}$

NOTE

If dividing with a mixed number, first change it to an improper fraction and follow Steps 2 and 3.

Target Practice: Divide and Conquer

Try these examples using Steps 1 through 3.

1 $\dfrac{1}{3} \div \dfrac{1}{6} =$ _____

2 $\dfrac{1}{3} \div \dfrac{2}{4} =$ _____

3 $\dfrac{2}{4} \div \dfrac{3}{6} =$ _____

4 $5 \div \dfrac{1}{5} =$ _____

Activity 4: Fraction Section Checkup

Before moving on to decimals, Alice's teacher provided the class with exercises that put their understanding about fractions to work.

Target Practice: Fractions at Work

1 Sherri works five days per week. She took two days off last week. Write a fraction to represent the part of the week Sherri worked. _____

2 Bryan usually works $32\frac{1}{2}$ hours per week. Last week, he worked an extra $1\frac{3}{4}$ hours. How many hours did Bryan work last week? _____

3 When Jenna arrived at the airport, she was told that her two bags could weigh no more than a total of 75 pounds. Her first bag weighed in at $42\frac{3}{4}$ pounds. Her second bag weighed in at $35\frac{1}{3}$ pounds. Her bags were _____ pounds over the weight limit.

4 Change $3\frac{4}{9}$ to an improper fraction. _____

5 If one yard of fabric costs $8.00, how much will $5\frac{1}{2}$ yards cost? _____

6 If it takes $3\frac{1}{2}$ yards of lumber to build an end table, how many end tables can be built out of 24 yards of lumber? _____

TARGET Decimals: Get to the Point

Decimals in Your Life

Decimals are types of fractions because they show parts of whole numbers. You are already very familiar with decimals because of their place in using money. But decimals are not only used when we talk about money. Have you ever been weighed on a digital scale? Say your weight is 132.5 pounds, or $132\frac{1}{2}$. You are using decimals. What about at the gas pump? You fill up your car and it takes 13.7 gallons. Right, decimals again. As you can see, understanding how decimals are used is very important in your everyday life. Let's review adding decimals first.

Activity 1: Review Adding and Subtracting

Adding? Line Them Up
When adding numbers that contain decimals, you must make sure to line them up, decimal under decimal. For example, if you were to add 3.57 + .16 you would line these numbers up as follows

$$
\begin{array}{r}
3.57 \\
+\ .16 \\
\hline
3.73
\end{array}
$$

As you can see, all the decimal points are lined up, one on top of the other.

Target Practice 1: Towing the Line

Try adding these decimals by first lining up the decimals one over the other.

1 Terri weighed 128.6 pounds at the beginning of the year. When she weighed herself three months later she had gained 7.5 pounds. How much does Terri weigh now?

A 135 pounds

B 136.1 pounds

C 131.1 pounds

2 Ronald drove 115.5 miles on the first day of his trip, 120.3 miles on the second day, and 110.8 on the third day. How many miles did he drive over a three-day period?

A 350.5

B 320.2

C 346.6

Subtracting? Line Them Up Again

As with addition of decimals, when subtracting decimals you must be sure to line up the numbers, decimal point under decimal point:

Target Practice 2: Get to the Point!

1 $4.5 - 3.26 = $ _____

2 $0.620 - 0.1592 = $ _____

3 $12 - 0.943 = $ _____

Activity 2: Multiplying Decimals

Multiplying decimals takes a little bit more work than adding and subtracting them. You don't need to worry about lining up decimals, but you do need to count decimal places so that you put the decimal in the right place in the *product* (*product* is the result of multiplication of numbers). Follow these:

Example: $3.56 \times .4$

1 Place the number with the most digits on top.

$$
\begin{array}{rl}
3.56 & \text{2 places} \\
\times\ .4 & \text{1 place} \\
\hline
1.424 & \text{3 places}
\end{array}
$$

2 Multiply

3 Start counting from the right in the answer, and place the decimal point so that you have the total amount of decimal points you counted in the two numbers you multiplied. In this example, you counted a total of three places to the right of the decimal points in 3.56 and .4. Therefore, you placed the decimal point three places in from the right in the answer. The best way to learn this method is to try a few examples yourself using the three-step process above.

Target Practice: The More the Merrier!

1 $.7 \times .6 =$ _____

2 $14 \times .03 =$ _____

3 It takes 3.5 hours for Jesse to manufacture 1 window. How many hours will he have to work to make 7 windows?

    A 25

    B 34

    C 24.5

4 At $3.00 per yard, how much will 4.5 yards of lumber cost?

    A $13.50

    B $12.50

    C $20.00

Activity 3: Dividing Decimals

There are two ways to look at dividing decimals: (1) dividing a decimal by a whole number and (2) dividing a decimal by a decimal. Let's look at the steps involved in both examples.

Dividing Decimals by Whole Numbers

Example: .8562 divided by 16.

1 Set up the example using a division bracket: $16\overline{).8562}$

2 Divide as you would any numbers, but remember to place the decimal in the answer or quotient exactly above where it appears in the dividend.

$$
\begin{array}{r}
.0535 \text{ remainder } 2 \\
16\overline{)0.8562} \\
\underline{8000} \\
562 \\
\underline{480} \\
82 \\
\underline{80} \\
2
\end{array}
$$

Dividing Decimals by Decimals

Example: .4127 divided by .14

1 Make the divisor (.14 in this case) a whole number by moving the decimal two places to the right. You must do this to the dividend (.4127) as well. Once you do this you will be left with 41.27 divided by 14.

2 Refer to *Dividing a Decimal by a Whole Number* above and proceed to the answer.

Target Practice: Move It or Lose It

1 .5525 divided by 19 = _____

2 .6842 divided by .38 = _____

3 .98 divided by 6 = _____

4 .35 divided by .7 = _____

TARGET Percents: What You Don't Know Can Hurt You

A percent is yet another way to describe a fraction or part of a whole. However, unlike the fractions we looked at earlier, percents can only have a denominator of 100. The denominator is not written out; it is shown as a percent sign (%). For example, 25 parts out of 100 ($\frac{25}{100}$) can also be written as 25 hundredths, or 25%. Additionally, you can write it in decimal form as 0.25. This example shows you how fractions, decimals, and percents are all related. They are all different ways to look at parts of a whole. Let's begin by looking at *changing decimals to percents* and *changing percents to decimals.*

Activity 1: Changing Decimals to Percents

To change decimals to percents, move the decimal two places to the right and write the percent sign. There is no need to write the decimal sign if it will go at the end of a number. You will need to add a zero as a placeholder if there are not two places to move.

Decimal	Move Two Places to the Right	Percent
.75	.75	75%
.6	.60	60%
.0005	.0005	.05%
.155	.155	$15\frac{1}{2}$%

Target Practice: Time for a Change

Practice changing these decimals to percents using the process above. Don't forget to add the percent sign at the right of the number.

1 .53 = _____

2 .0075 = _____

3 .455 = _____

4 .025 = _____

Activity 2: Changing Percents to Decimals

To change percents to decimals, drop the percent sign and move the decimal two places over to the left. You may have to add zeros in places where you would be unable to move two places without them. For example:

Percent	Drop % Sign: Move Two Places to the Left	Decimal
4%	.04	.04
50%	.50	.50
125%	125	1.25
.8%	.8	.008
$25\frac{1}{2}$%	$25\frac{1}{2}$	.255

Target Practice: The Old Switcheroo

Practice changing these percents to decimals.

1 25% = _____

2 4.5% = _____

3 .6% = _____

4 6% = _____

STUDY TIP
When learning the next few skills, try to come up with examples from your own life to use as practice. Do you lease a car, pay a mortgage, work a certain number of hours, make a certain dollar amount per hour, pay taxes, and so on?

Activity 3: Finding a Percent of a Number

Being able to find a percent of a number is a very useful skill. One use is to find the price of something when it is offered for sale at a certain percent off. Follow the steps below to find the percent of the number in the example:

Example: Find 30% of 80

Change 30% to a decimal: 30% = .3

Multiply the two numbers: 80 × .3 = <u>24</u>

By changing the percent to a decimal and multiplying the two numbers, you have found that 30% of 80 is 24. Now try a few on your own using this two-step method.

Target Practice: What's in a Number?

1 5% of 125 = _____

2 23% of 75 = _____

3 If the sales tax in your state is 6%, how much will the tax be on your purchase of $7.50? _____

4 Your gross salary is $400.00 per week. If you want to put 25% per week in a savings account, how much will you have to deposit? _____

5 You invited 80 people to your party. You got responses from 25% of them. How many people have you received responses from? _____

6 Sam works in a store where he gets a 15% discount on any of his purchases. If he were to buy something for $45.00, how much would his discount be? _____

Check your answers in the Answer Key to make sure you understand how to find the percent of a number

Activity 4: Finding What Percent One Number Is of Another

To find what percent one number is of another, you must first change the way the numbers look. Follow these steps:

Example: 8 is what % of 64?

Make a fraction by putting the first number over the second number, then reduce: $\frac{8}{64} = \frac{1}{8}$

Divide the numerator by the denominator (the line in the fraction means "divided by") .125.

Change the decimal to a percent: 12.5%

Try a few of these on your own.

Target Practice: For What It's Worth

1 14 is what % of 35? _____

2 15 is what % of 60? _____

3 16 is what % of 20? _____

4 On a loan of $500.00, the interest charged was $42.00. What percent of the loan amount is the interest? _____

How well did you do? Check your answers in the Answer Key before going on to the next activity.

Activity 5: Finding a Number When a Percent of It Is Given

When you find a number when a percent is given, you are performing the opposite activity of finding a percent of another. Follow these steps:

Example: 40% of what number is 60?

1 Change the percent to a decimal: .40

2 Divide the number by the decimal: 60 divided by .40 = 150

Therefore, 40% of 150 is 60. You can check your work by finding the percent of 150 to make sure 60 is right. To do so, multiply .40 × 150. Now you are ready to try some on your own.

Target Practice: What You Don't Know Can Hurt You

1 15% of what number is 12? _____

2 60% of what number is 75? _____

3 A family spends about $125.00 per week on food. If this is 30% of their weekly budget, what is their weekly budget amount? _____

4 The Dooley's saved $2,000.00 toward the purchase of a house. If this represents 5% of the cost of the house, what is the cost of the house?

_____

Activity 6: Reading Pictured Percents

This nation-wide company has customers in four major cities. As part of their quality assurance process, they periodically poll their customers regarding the degree to which they are satisfied with company services. Note that the bars in this graph do *not* measure the actual number of people polled. They show what *percent* of all responders were highly satisfied.

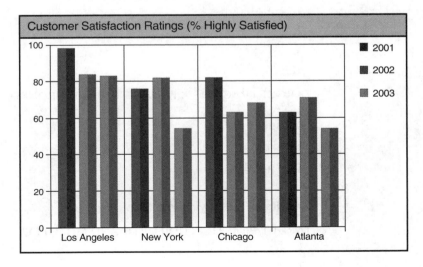

1 *Approximately* ($\cong$) what percent of customers were highly satisfied in New York and in Atlanta in the year 2003?

A $\cong 45\%$

B $\cong 50\%$

C $\cong 55\%$

D $\cong 60\%$

2 Were Los Angeles customers more highly satisfied than those in New York in the year 2002? If so, by how much?

A Yes; by $\cong 10\%$

B Yes; by $\cong 1\%$

C No.

3 By how much did customer satisfaction decrease in Los Angeles from 2001 to 2002?

A $\cong 8\%$

B $\cong 12\%$

C $\cong 14\%$

D $\cong 18\%$

4 Which city showed the greatest decrease in customer satisfaction between 2002 and 2003?

A New York

B Chicago

C Atlanta

D Los Angeles

Answer Key: Section 3, Lesson 5

TARGET Fractions: Divide and Conquer

Activity 1: Fractions with Different Denominators

TARGET PRACTICE 1: RAISE THE FLOOR?

1. $\frac{5}{4}$

2. $\frac{7}{6}$

3. $\frac{11}{9}$

4. $\frac{1}{6}$

TARGET PRACTICE 2: FINDING HIGHER GROUND

1. $\frac{19}{15}$

2. $\frac{16}{21}$

3. $\frac{36}{42} + \frac{14}{42} = \frac{50}{42}$

4. $\frac{9}{12} + \frac{10}{12} = \frac{19}{12}$

Activity 2: Multiplying Fractions

TARGET PRACTICE: GO FORTH AND MULTIPLY!

1. $\frac{1}{15}$

2. $\frac{25}{48}$

3. $\frac{5}{36}$

4. $\frac{21}{64}$

Activity 3: Dividing Fractions by Fractions

TARGET PRACTICE: DIVIDE AND CONQUER

  1. 2

  2. $\frac{2}{3}$

  3. 1

  4. 25

Activity 4: Fraction Section Checkup

  1. $\frac{3}{5}$

  2. $34\frac{1}{4}$ hours ($32\frac{2}{4} + 1\frac{3}{4} = 33\frac{5}{4} =$)

  3. $3\frac{1}{12}$ pounds ($42\frac{9}{12} + 35\frac{4}{12} = 77\frac{13}{12} = 78\frac{1}{12}; 78\frac{1}{12} - 75 =$)

  4. $\frac{31}{9}$ ($3 = \frac{27}{9}; \frac{27}{9} + \frac{4}{9} =$)

  5. \$44.00 ($\frac{8}{1} \times \frac{11}{2} = \frac{88}{2} =$)

  6. 6 end tables ($\frac{6}{7}$ yards of lumber will be left over)

Target Decimals: Get to the Point

Activity 1: Review Adding and Subtracting

TARGET PRACTICE 1: TOWING THE LINE

  1. B

  2. C

TARGET PRACTICE 2: GET TO THE POINT!

  1. 1.24

  2. 0.4608

  3. 11.057

Activity 2: Multiplying Decimals

TARGET PRACTICE: THE MORE THE MERRIER!

  1. .42

  2. 0.42

  3. C 24.5 hours

  4. A \$13.50

Activity 3: Dividing Decimals

TARGET PRACTICE: MOVE IT OR LOSE IT

  1. 0.0290 r 15

  2. 1.80 r 2

  3. 0.16 r 2

  4. 0.5

Activity 1: Changing Decimals to Percents

TARGET PRACTICE: TIME FOR A CHANGE
  1. 53%
  2. 0.75%
  3. 45.5%
  4. 2.5%

Activity 2: Changing Percents to Decimals

TARGET PRACTICE: THE OLD SWITCHEROO
  1. 0.25
  2. 0.045
  3. 0.006
  4. 0.06

Activity 3: Finding a Percent of a Number

TARGET PRACTICE: WHAT'S IN A NUMBER?
  1. 6.25
  2. 17.25
  3. $0.45
  4. $100.00
  5. 20
  6. $6.75

Activity 4: Find What Percent One Number Is of Another

TARGET PRACTICE: FOR WHAT IT'S WORTH
  1. 40%
  2. 25%
  3. 80%
  4. 8.4%

Activity 5: Find a Number When a Percent of It Is Given

TARGET PRACTICE: WHAT YOU DON'T KNOW CAN HURT YOU
  1. 80
  2. 125
  3. $416.67
  4. $40,000

Activity 6: Reading Pictured Percents

TARGET PRACTICE: COMPARE CUSTOMER SATISFACTION
  1. C
  2. B
  3. C
  4. A

<u>**LESSON 6**</u> **Measure It**

"To us Europeans it's very strange that water freezes at
+32 degrees . . . +32 with us is a very balmy day.
Vive la petite difference!!!"
http://www2.dicom.se/fuchsias/cf.html

Warming Up

In the United States, it is customary to measure temperature in degrees
Fahrenheit (°F). For Europeans, and people in most other countries of the
world, temperature is measured in degrees Celsius (°C). This graphic shows
how these two systems relate:

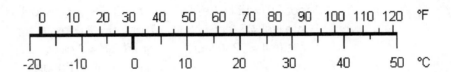

32 degrees Celsius is *approximately equal* to how many degrees Fahrenheit?

_____

Did you write a number between 88°F and 90°F? That's a balmy day, indeed!

TARGET Systems of Measurement: Metric and Customary

Which measurement system are you most comfortable using? _____
Both are used in the United States today, but the metric system still seems
like a foreign language to many Americans.

In the rest of world, metric prevails. Why? The metric system is a decimal
system of weights and measures. Because it is based on 10, it is simple to use.
Its basic units are related to larger and smaller ones by powers of 10 (and you
know how easy it is to multiply and divide by 10). There are just three basic
units of weight, length, and volume to remember: gram, meter, and liter. In
this lesson, you will get acquainted with them, and a handful of prefixes.
Together, these few roots and prefixes do the job of naming most of the common units in the metric system.

Activity 1: How Cold Is That?

Warmth can be the same by a different name when measured by different
scales. Refer to the Celsius/Fahrenheit graphic to answer Questions 1–3.

Target Practice

1 A European would say, "Water freezes at _____ degrees." (That's Celsius)

2 In the United States, most people would say they are comfortable in a room with the thermostat set at 70°F. Approximately how many degrees is that in °C? _____

3 True or False? You do <u>not</u> have to worry about frostbite when it is 5°C. _____

Words to Know

Equivalent   Of equal value

Customary Units of Measure

Length	Volume (liquid)	Weight
1 foot (ft) = 12 inches (in)	1 cup (C) = 8 ounces (oz)	1 pound (lb) = 16 ounces (oz)
1 yard (yd) = 3 feet	1 pint (pt) = 2 cups	1 ton = 2000 pounds
1 mile (mi) = 5280 feet	1 quart (qt) = 2 pints	
	1 gallon (gal) = 4 quarts	

Metric Units of Measure

	Length	Volume	Weight
Basic Unit	meter (m)	liter (l)	gram (g)
× 10	*deca*meter (dkm)	*deca*liter (dkl)	*deca*gram (dkg)
× 100	*hecto*meter (hm)	*hecto*liter (hl)	*hecto*gram (hg)
× 1000	*kilo*meter (km)	*kilo*liter (kl)	*kilo*gram (kg)
× 0.1	*deci*meter (dm)	*deci*liter (dl)	*deci*gram (dg)
× 0.01	*centi*meter (cm)	*centi*liter (cl)	*centi*gram (cg)
× 0.001	*milli*meter (mm)	*milli*liter (ml)	*milli*gram (mg)

Activity 2: Speaking Metrically

Examine the table of Metric Units of Measure. How many patterns do you see? That table, along with Target Practices 1 and 2, may get you started "speaking metrically."

Target Practice 1: The Value of Metric Prefixes

These prefixes alter the *value* of the root words meter, liter, and gram to the tune of the powers of 10. The measured value of one *milli*gram is *one-thousandth* the weight of a gram. A *kilo*meter is the length of *one thousand* meters. Use the table above to complete this table. Speak it as you read it and fill in its values.

Prefix	Symbol	Value	Operation Used on Base Unit
1 _____	k	means _____	multiply by 1,000
2 hecto	h	means one hundred	_____ by 100
3 deca (or deka)	dk	means _____	_____
4 _____	d	means _____	multiply by 0.1 (or divide by 10)
5 _____	c	means _____	_____ or _____
6 _____	m	means _____	_____ or _____

TEST TIP

Memorize the meanings of kilo-, deca-, centi-, and milli-. Memorize the way they change the value of gram, liter, and meter.

Target Practice 2: Apply Them Again

Power-of-ten prefixes appear in other words in our language as well.

1 A **deca**de is a period of _____ years. In a **deca**thlon, athletes compete in _____ events.

2 Per**cent** means *out of a* _____. A **cent** is _____ of a dollar.

3 Bytes measure computer memory or software program size. A **kilo**byte ≅ _____ bytes.

4 It takes from 1 to 1.5 **kilo**watts of electricity to operate a vacuum cleaner. A kilowatt = _____ watts. 1.5 kilowatts = _____ watts.

Time is measured in the same units all over the world:

1 minute = 60 seconds (sec)	1 year = 365 days
1 hour = 60 minutes (min)	1 year = 52 weeks (wk)
1 day = 24 hours (hr)	1 year = 12 months (mo)
1 week = 7 days	10 years = 1 decade
	100 years = 1 century

Activity 3: Consult and Convert

The operations used to convert large units of measurement to smaller ones, and vice versa, is the same in both systems.

STUDY TIP

Multiply to convert a large unit to smaller units.
Divide to convert small units to a larger unit.

Kilograms to grams? Multiply by _____. Days to years? Divide by _____.
Gallons to quarts? _____ by _____. Minutes to hours? _____ by _____.

Target Practice 1: Customary Equivalents

Consult the charts and the Study Tip above to answer these questions.

1 John steps on the scale and see that he has gained 7 pounds. How much weight has John gained in ounces? _____

2 Barbara and Rita were talking about retirement. They compared how much longer they each had to work before they could collect Social Security. Barbara figured she had to work 12 more years. Rita figured she had to work 14 more years.

A How many more months does Barbara have left to work? _____
B What about Rita? _____

3 Roberto has to schedule 15 interviews over the next workweek. He works five days a week, nine hours per day. Each interview will take approximately 1½ hours. He wants to complete the interviews in as few days as possible.

A With an hour out for lunch, how many interviews can Roberto schedule per day? _____
B How many days will it take him to do all 15 interviews? _____

4 Use the following chart to answer A through D:

Yardage Requirement—Wedding Dresses			
Sizes	8	10	12
Dress A:	5½	5⅞	6⅜
Dress B:	5⅛	5¼	6
Lace for A:	2	2¼	2⅝
Lace for B:	2¼	2½	2¾

Rosa is a dressmaker who has been asked to make two wedding gowns for two clients who are getting married a week apart. She is planning her materials needs.

A How much fabric will she need to buy to make both dresses (A and B) in size 12? _____
B How much lace will she need to make those two dresses? _____
C The client who ordered Dress A called. She said she had lost weight and now wore a size 10. How much *extra* fabric has Rosa purchased?

_____

D How much *less* lace will she need now? _____

Target Practice 2: Work with Metric Measures

1 Rich ran a 3-kilometer (km) road race on Saturday. How many meters is that? _____

2 Roberta is carpeting three rooms. They measure 9 meters (m) by 6 m, 4 m by 5 m, and 3.5 m by 4.5 m. How many square meters of carpet does she need? _____

3 Lucho is on the college swim team. The last five days he swam 4.2 km, 520 m, 3 km, 1,280 m, and 2.8 km. How many meters did he swim altogether? _____

4 The undercover agents discovered 1.5 kilograms of the drug X-pletive when they searched the trunk of the suspect's car. How many grams of X-pletive is that? _____

Activity 4: Compare and Convert

Conversion Table: Customary to Metric/Metric to Customary

Length		Weight	
1 inch	= 2.54 centimeters	1 ounce	= 28 grams
1 foot	= 0.3048 meter	1 pound	= 0.453 kilograms
1 mile	= 1.6 kilometers		
		1 gram	= 0.035 ounce
1 centimeter	= .3937 inches	1 kilogram	= 2.2 pounds
1 meter	= 39.37		
1 kilometer	= 0.62 miles		

Target Practice: In Other Words

1 In the delivery room, Peter and Kristin watched their newborn child being weighed by Eleanor, the pediatric nurse. "He's a healthy 4 kilograms," she announced. When she saw the parents look at her with questions in their eyes, she quickly converted the kilograms to pounds. "In other words, your son is a bouncing _____ pounds."

2 The speed limit on the Canadian Highway was posted at 100. It took awhile for the visitors from Texas to realize that the sign was not referring to miles per hour. Convert that speed limit (100 kilometers per hour) to miles per hour: _____

3 Hank won first place in the 10-km footrace. How many miles did he run? _____

TARGET Formulas: Recipes and Workouts

Remember the two systems for measuring temperature? The Celsius-Fahrenheit graphic on page 155 is easy to use for making general comparisons. But for people who work in jobs where temperature readings (and temperature conversions) must be very specific, *that graphic is not good enough.* They need to understand how to use a mathematical plan such as this one for converting between degrees Fahrenheit (F) and degrees Celsius (C). $F = 1.8\ C + 32$ This plan is called a formula. It may look intimidating, but it works the same way as the geometry formulas you used in Lesson 4.

Reconnect with Formulas

"This geometry formula page is like having a 'cheat sheet' for answering measurement questions." Lisa said to her study group. "I love it: As long as I pick the right formula for the shape I'm working on, the formula tells me what numbers I need to collect and what to do with them to get the answer. For me, it's just like choosing and using a good recipe—*I get the results I want every time.* And you know how I like to cook."

Activity 1: Follow the Recipe

Select a formula from Lesson 4 to assist you in answering the next question.

Target Practice: Measuring Containers

A packaging manufacturer makes shipping containers for businesses. This drum is one of their containers. It measures 4 feet high and has a radius of 1 foot. How many cubic feet of space does it contain? _____

    Check your answer before you move on to make sure you're on the same wavelength as Lisa.

Words to Know

Formula	An equation that shows the relationship between two or more quantities by using numbers, variables, and operational symbols.
Variable	A symbol (usually a letter) in a formula that stands for a number that changes as other numbers in the formula change.
Vary	To change

Can You Explain that Relationship to Me?

A formula is based on observations of *how two or more things relate mathematically.* It is a *model* to follow for answering questions about how that pattern of relationship works. In Lesson 4, you used formulas to calculate the measurements of shapes, objects, and space. Over time, people have figured out formulas that explain "how the numbers work" in many other situations as well—all to make their jobs easier. There are formulas to use in business, in construction, in sports, in medicine, and in cooking. There are formulas for finding the best buy when you are shopping. The list goes on and on.

STUDY TIP

Formulas are like recipes: The more you use them, the better your results.

As you gain experience using formulas to solve problems, you will gain understanding of *why* certain ingredients are important and *how* those ingredients interact. Like an expert chef, you will realize that a successful result depends on *technique* as well as ingredients.

The Main Ingredients of Formulas Are Variables

Our daily lives are filled with conditions that can change from one moment in time to another—the weather, our moods, and the price of gas, to name a few. Many times a change in one condition will cause a change in another.

Activity 2: Variables? Let's Get Going

Think about the last time you traveled somewhere. How far did you go? How long did it take you to get there? Why? Could you have traveled faster if conditions had been different? No matter what type of trip you are making, the trip *variables* (conditions that can change) are the same: distance, rate, and time. How does that relationship work? Distance, rate, and time are in a *three-way relationship* and are dependent on each other. Travel distance depends on, *and is equal to,* the rate of travel (usually measured in miles per hour) *times* the length of time spent traveling (measured in hours). The way this relationship works is explained with this equation: **d**istance = **r**ate × **t**ime.

FYI

Single letters usually represent variables in equations: $d = r \times t$

Target Practice: Go the Distance with $d = r \times t$

Read about Jack's commute, then see how the facts of the situation fit into the "Take Five" format (steps for solving formula questions) that follows.

Jack commutes to work on his motorcycle. He figures his average speed is 40 miles per hour. It takes him about ¾ of an hour to travel the distance each time. How many miles does he commute by motorcycle in one day? *Hint:* Jack's total commute is a round-trip

QUESTION: How many miles does Jack commute each day?

1 **Formula:** $d = r \times t$

2 **Facts** matched with variables: $r = \underline{40}$ mph

$t = \frac{3}{4}$ hr $\times \underline{2}$ (round-trip) $= 1\frac{1}{2}$ hr

3 **Substitute** facts in the formula $d = 40 \times 1\frac{1}{2}$

4 **Solve** $d = 60$

SOLUTION: Jack commutes 60 miles each day.

5 **Check by substitution:** $60 = 40 \times 1\frac{1}{2}$

$60 = 60$

Use the Take Five format above to solve Questions 1, 2, and 3. Write the steps and calculations in your math notebook. Record your results below.

1 Mel drives a big rig on cross-country runs. The mountains really slow him down. He figures that he averages about 35 miles per hour driving in the mountains. If he has 3½ hours left of daylight to drive through the mountains, how many miles can he expect to travel? _____

2 Connie's pace in the first two hours of the marathon averaged 6.5 mph. What distance did she run in those two hours? _____

3 Rich loves to ocean kayak. In a moderate sea, he paddles about 4.5 miles an hour. This summer he plans on taking 3 days to kayak up the coast. Rich figures he will paddle 5 hours a day. How far can he expect to paddle in moderate seas on this trip? _____

Activity 3: Take a Rest Stop: Learn the Side-By-Side Signal

In Lesson 3, you reviewed several ways to signal the operation of multiplication. Here are two more ways to signal multiplication when a letter is used to represent a number:

- A letter *next to* a number means multiply. For example, $4y$ means four multiplied by the value of y.
- A letter *next to* a letter means multiply. rt means the value of r multiplied by the value of t.

Target Practice: Translate

Translate these signals into <u>words</u> of *operation*.

1. $7y^2$ means 7 _____ y^2
2. xy/z means x _____ y _____ z
3. $\dfrac{8z + 5\,(13) - 15}{2}$ means $[(8 \underline{\quad} z) \underline{\quad} (5 \underline{\quad} 13) \underline{\quad} 15] \underline{\quad} 2$

The Mechanics and the Format Are the Same

All formulas work the same basic way as the $d = r \times t$ formula above. Use the "Take Five" outline-format shown below to write down all the steps *even if you think you can "do it in your head."* When situations get complicated, this practice will pay off. Refer to these mechanics—and the outline format—for the remainder of the formula problems in this lesson.

STUDY TIP: PROMOTE AND PREVENT

Remember the Problem Solving Template in Lesson 2, page 100? The idea is the same: Structure and neatness *promote* logical thinking and help *prevent* error.

Read to focus on the question and choose the correct formula.

Question _____?

1. **Formula** _____
_____

2. **Facts** _____
_____

3. **Substitute** _____
4. **Solve** _____
Solution _____
5. Check by **Substitution** _____

STUDY TIP: READING AND REFLECTING ARE MATH SKILLS

They are the first *and* final steps when you tackle word problems. *Read your way* to solutions. *Reflect* on the results.

Activity 4: Formula Workout

Getting familiar with formulas means trying them out in various situations. The next two Target Practices are a start.

Target Practice 1: Help Eva Investigate Options

The Situation: Eva's grandfather left her $3,000 in his will. She decided to start an education fund for her children. She wondered the best way to invest this money. She heard friends talking about the interest rates of various investments. She also heard about the interest rates some of them were paying to borrow money! *She wants to know what the $3,000 will earn in one year* if she deposits it in a savings account at her local bank. The annual interest rate is 1½%. Next, she wants to know what her returns will be if she has an opportunity to invest the $3,000 (her principal) at these rates for one year: 5% and 8%.

Formula: **i**nterest = **p**rincipal × **r**ate × **t**ime (time is measured in years).

Use the Take Five formula format. Do the work in your notebook and write your answers below.

Reminder: When you use a percent in calculation, change it to its decimal form (Lesson 5, page 149)

1 Option 1: Savings Account. Interest rate, 1½% (use: 0.015)   Result: _____

2 Option 2: Investment A. Interest rate, 5%   Result: _____

3 Option 3: Investment B. Interest rate, 8%   Result: _____

Target Practice 2: Celsius to Fahrenheit

The Situation: Doris arrived in the Emergency Room at 2 P.M. with a temperature of 40°C. She told the admitting nurse she started feeling ill that morning, and had checked her temperature at 11 A.M. At that time, it was 37°C.

Use the following formula: $F = 1.8C + 32$ to convert Doris' temperature readings from °C to °F. (Reminder: °F = degrees Fahrenheit; °C = degrees Celsius)

1 What was Doris's temperature at 11 A.M. as measured in °F? _____

2 What was her temperature at 2 P.M. as measured in °F? _____

Activity 5: Your Choice

Practice Unlimited, Times Two:

1 *Formulas:* Choose a formula included in this lesson, in Lesson 4, or search for one that is used in a work field that interests you. Think of a question it will help solve. Write your question down and answer it using the formula format. If you work in a study group, exchange questions to make it more interesting.

2 *Measurement:* Refer to the tables of Equivalents and Conversions. Observe your world in measurement terms. Write down your observations.

Answer Key: Section 3, Lesson 6

TARGET Systems of Measurement:

Activity 1: How Cold Is That?

TARGET PRACTICE
1. 0 (zero)
2. 21 or 22 degrees
3. True

Activity 2: Speaking Metrically

TARGET PRACTICE 1: THE VALUE OF PREFIXES
1. kilo; one thousand
2. multiply
3. 10; multiply by 10
4. deci; one tenth
5. centi; one hundredth; multiply by 0.01 or divide by 100
6. milli; one thousandth; multiply by 0.001 or divide by 1,000

TARGET PRACTICE 2: APPLY THEM AGAIN
1. 10 years; 10 events
2. one hundred (100); one hundredth (0.01) (one out of the hundred parts)
3. 1,000 bytes
4. 1,000 watts; 1,500 watts

Activity 3: Consult and Convert

1,000; 365; *Multiply* by 4; Divide by 60

TARGET PRACTICE 1: CUSTOMARY EQUIVALENTS
1. 112 oz.
2. **A** 144 months
   B 168 months
3. **A** 5
   B 3
4. **A** 12⅜ yd.
   B 5 yd.
   C ½ yd. extra
   D ⅜ yd. less

TARGET PRACTICE 2: WORK WITH METRIC MEASURES
1. 3,000 meters
2. 89.75 square meters
3. 11,800 meters
4. $1.5 \times 1,000 = 1,500$ grams

Activity 4: Compare and Convert

TARGET PRACTICE: IN OTHER WORDS
1. 8.8 pounds (8 pounds, 12.8 ounces)
2. 62 mph (100×0.62)
3. 6.2 miles (10×0.62)

TARGET Formulas: Recipes and Workouts

Activity 1: Follow the Recipe

TARGET PRACTICE: MEASURING CONTAINERS
Did you choose the formula for Volume of a Cylinder?
V = pi × radius^2 × height = 12.56 cubic feet

Activity 2: Variables? Let's Get Going

TARGET PRACTICE: GO THE DISTANCE WITH $d = r \times t$
1. 122.5 miles
2. 13 miles
3. 67.5 miles (22.5 miles per day × 3 days)

Activity 3: Rest Stop

TARGET PRACTICE: TRANSLATE
1. *times* (or multiplied by)
2. x *times* y *divided by* z
3. [(8 *times* z), *plus* (5 *times* 13) *minus* 15] *divided by* 2

Activity 4: Formula Workout

TARGET PRACTICE 1: HELP EVA INVESTIGATE
1. $45.00
2. $150.00
3. $240.00

TARGET PRACTICE 2: CELSIUS TO FAHRENHEIT
1. 98.6°F
2. 104°F

LESSON 7 The Other Side of Zero

"I hear, and I forget. I see, and I remember. I do, and I understand."
An Old Chinese Proverb

Getting Started

Consider the following questions:

- How many yards were gained and lost in the first half of the football game?

- What was that company's profit record last year?
- How many degrees below normal was his temperature after his rescue from the frigid sea?

Numbers with + and − signs attached to them can be used to answer questions like these. Do you know how? Do you know why?

A Matter of Perspective

When numbers are used to answer questions about size or quantity, this number line is a useful picture of how the numbers work:

$$0 \quad 5 \quad 10 \quad 15 \quad 20 \quad 25 \quad 30 \longrightarrow$$

But when numbers are used to communicate information about *opposites* in size, direction, or quantity, this line with numbers on *both sides of zero* is needed to explain the whole story:

$$\longleftarrow -30 \quad -25 \quad -20 \quad -15 \quad -10 \quad -5 \quad 0 \quad +5 \quad +10 \quad +15 \quad +20 \quad +25 \quad +30 \longrightarrow$$

Information about opposite values is communicated with *signed* numbers. Signed numbers are also known as *integers*.

Words and Symbols to Know

Absolute value	The measure of a number's distance from zero. The absolute value of a number is *the number itself,* without a sign.
Integers:	Positive and negative numbers and zero; also called *signed numbers*
Negative numbers:	Numbers with values less than zero *always* carry a minus sign. For example, −5.
Positive numbers:	Numbers with values greater than zero *sometimes* carry a plus sign. A number *without* a + is *assumed* to be positive. For example, 6 = +6
Zero	The digit, 0, dividing positive from negative numbers on the number line. Zero has no value of its own. It represents a starting point or baseline.
| |	Symbol for absolute value. The value of a number placed within these parallel lines is equal to the number itself, *without* its sign. For example: | −34 | = 34 | +34 | = 34

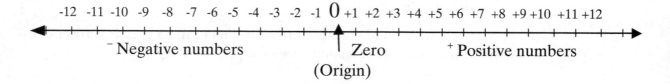

-12 -11 -10 -9 -8 -7 -6 -5 -4 -3 -2 -1 0 +1 +2 +3 +4 +5 +6 +7 +8 +9 +10 +11 +12

‾ Negative numbers   Zero   ⁺ Positive numbers
                            (Origin)

Signs: You are familiar with + and − standing for addition and subtraction. When *attached* to a number, they stand for the *value* of that number in relationship to zero. On a number line, + is a signal to *go above* zero or *to the right* of zero. Positive (+) numbers are greater in value than zero. On a number line, − signals *below* or *to the left of* zero. Negative (−) numbers are less in value than zero.

Words: Words that represent opposites are used to signal *shifts* in the value and direction of things in relationship to a zero point. For example: credit/debit, above/below, gain/loss.

Numbers: Numbers tell *how far* the value being measured is from the starting point, or zero. Zero itself is neutral; it has no value of its own.

Activity 1: Get Acquainted with Integers

Drawing a picture of a mathematical idea is a way to understand what that idea means. It is an active learning strategy. Keep graph paper and a ruler handy as you work through this lesson.

Target Practice 1: Draw the Line

Make an accurate copy of the integer line shown above. Draw it out on a piece of graph paper. Include all the signs and labels. "Talk your way through it" as you draw. Notice how the positive and negative numbers relate to each other and to zero.

STUDY TIP

- Symbols for *greater than* (>) and *less than* (<) always *point to* the smaller value: For example, 9 > 4, "9 is greater than 4", and 14 < 20, "14 is *less than* 20".
- The greater the negative number, the *smaller* its value: −53 < −23

Target Practice 2: Use the Line

Compare the value of the following integers. Use the symbols for *greater than* (>) and *less than* (<) to explain their relationship. Locate the integers on the line as you compare them.

1 −5 _____ −15

2 −1 _____ −2 _____ −3

3 +4 _____ +7 _____ +4

4 −5 _____ 0 _____ +5 _____ −6

5 +2.5 _____ +2.25

6 −2.5 _____ −3.50

Circle the expressions that are true in each line:

7 7 < −5   5 > −7   −5 < −7   −7 < −5

8 −11 > 12   −12 > −11   −11 > −12   −12 > 11

Put these integers in order by value, from smallest to greatest:

9 0   −3   −1   6   −7   2 _____

10 −2   −2.5   25   −5   1.25 _____

Activity 2: It is |Absolutely| True

A number's distance from zero on a number line is called its *absolute value.* Opposite numbers, such as +5 and −5, have the *same* absolute value: 5. The absolute value of a number is *the number itself,* without a sign. Here is the symbol for absolute value: ||. The statement | −2 | = 2 is read, "The absolute value of negative 2 is 2," or "The absolute value of minus 2 is 2."

Connect with the Idea of "Absolute"

<u>Think about sleep, lost and gained.</u> In Lesson 3, André told Ken he lost a lot of sleep when his dad was in the hospital. (p. 103) Let's say he *lost* three hours of his usual eight-hour sleep one night (−3). Let's say he was able to make it up the next day by going to bed 2 hours earlier and sleeping 1 hour later (+3). Losing 3 hours of sleep and gaining 3 hours of sleep are opposites, but the number of hours of sleep counted in each case are *absolutely the same:* 3. | −3 | = 3 | +3 | = 3

    <u>Now think about pounds, gained and lost.</u> Do you want them to be *absolutely* the same?

Target Practice: Evaluate These Absolutes

Follow this example:

- |30| + |−2| = 30 + 2   = 32

1 |−17| − |+7| = _____   = _____

2 |−2| + |−4| − |−5| = _____   = _____

3 |30| − |6| + |−4| = _____   = _____

4 |−29| − |−9| = _____   = _____

Activity 3: Integers and Life

Target Practice: Assign Signs

<u>Underline</u> words in these sentence that are clues for whether the numbers referred to are positive or negative. Write the correct integer and the name of what it is measuring.

For example: The temperature is 4 degrees <u>below</u> zero. <u>−4 degrees</u>

1 The football team lost 12 yards on the play. _____

2 They hit water at 125 feet below ground level. _____

3 The water in the reservoir was 7 feet above normal. _____

4 She lost $1,250 at the casino. _____

5 The child's fever rose 3.5 degrees. _____

6 When they flew from California to Singapore, they went back in time 11 hours. _____

Activity 4: Integers in the World of Work

Study the graphs on the following page. What has happened to this business operation? Do you see the connection between the things being measured in the three graphs? Look at the employees; they are right in the middle of it all.

Target Practice 1: The Big Story

1 The bar graphs display data for _____ years of business operations.

2 How many years does the line graph's data cover? _____

3 The topic of graph 1 is _____. It is measured in _____

4 The topic of graph 2 is _____. They are counted in _____

5 The topic of graph 3 is _____. It is measured in _____

Target Practice 2: Profit + and −

The x-axis of the first bar graph has a value of 0. It represents the baseline from which the company measured its gains and losses during each fiscal year. The bars measure the approximate amount of those gains and losses.

1 Company profit in 1983 was approximately
   A +$0.82 billion
   B +$8 billion
   C +$0.92 billion
   D +$9 billion

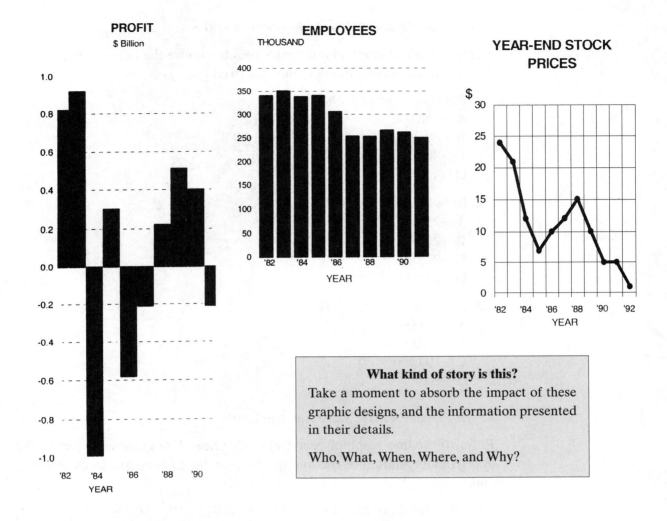

PROFIT
$ Billion

EMPLOYEES
THOUSAND

YEAR-END STOCK PRICES

What kind of story is this?

Take a moment to absorb the impact of these graphic designs, and the information presented in their details.

Who, What, When, Where, and Why?

2 Company profit in 1984 was approximately
   A +$0.9 billion
   B −$1 billion
   C −$0.80 billion
   D +$0.99 billion

3 The sum of company profit for the years '84, '86, '87, and '91 can be expressed this way:
   A −$2 billion
   B +$2 billion
   C −$1.3 billion
   D +$1.3 billion

4 The <u>absolute value</u> of profit gained *and* lost over the 10 year period was about
   A $3.25 billion
   B $52 billion
   C $5.2 billion
   D −$1.3 billion

Target Practice 3: Employee Numbers, + and –

Refer to the bar graph about Employees to choose the best estimate of the changes in employee numbers that occurred

1 Between 1985 and 1986:
- **A** –350,000
- **B** –40,000
- **C** –300,000
- **D** +40,000

2 Between 1988 and 1989:
- **A** +255,000
- **B** +20,000
- **C** +275,000
- **D** –20,000

3 Between 1982 and 1991:
- **A** –10,000
- **B** –250,000
- **C** –100,000
- **D** –100

Target Practice 4: The Story Is in the Line

Refer to the line graph of year-end stock prices. Use integers to record the approximate amount of rise and fall of the value of company stock at years' end:

- Price per share of stock in 1986 ≅ $\underline{\$10}$ In 1988 ≅ $\underline{\$15}$ Change ≅ $\underline{+5}$

1 Price per share of stock in 1982 ≅ _____   In 1985 ≅ _____   Change ≅ _____

2 Price per share of stock in 1985 ≅ _____   In 1988 ≅ _____   Change ≅ _____

3 Price per share of stock in 1988 ≅ _____   In 1992 ≅ _____   Change ≅ _____

TARGET Integer Operations: Think Money, Lines, and Rules

STUDY TIP

Use money, number lines, and common sense to guide your operations with integers. Rules are cool, but understanding is better.

Activity 1: Adding Integers

Use common sense: You start out the day with $10.00 in your wallet. You spend $6.00 on food and $20.00 on CDs. Luckily, your friend has money to lend you to make up the difference, but he will not forget. You *owe* your friend $_____. That transaction with money looks like this with signed numbers: +10 −26 = −16. Is that what you pictured when you figured out what you owed? Chances are, no. You probably *found the difference between* what you spent, and what you had in your wallet and thought of it this way: $26 − $10 = $16 *owed*. You probably did not think about what "signs" were on the dollars because you understood the transaction. The word *owe* took the place of a minus sign.

Speaking mathematically, you found the *difference* between the *absolute* values of +10 and −26. You understood that the answer, 16, was a *negative 16* when you used the word *owe*. What you did automatically (whether you knew it or not) was follow the rule for the following:

Adding Integers with Different Signs

Negative + Positive

Positive + Negative

Find the *difference* between the absolute values of the numbers.

The answer takes the sign of the larger absolute value.

- −$75 + $100 = +$25.   The *difference* carries a positive sign.
- $50 + −$75 = −$25   The *difference* carries a negative sign.

Adding Integers with the Same Signs
(This *really* is common sense.)

- Positive + Positive

- Negative + Negative

Add the *absolute values* of the numbers.

The answer takes the *common* sign.

$|+5| + |+5| = +10$

$|−5| + |−5| = −10$

Adding Several Signed Numbers
Simplify the expression by combining all the negative numbers and all the positive numbers. Find the difference between the absolute values of the sums. The answer takes the sign of the sum with the largest absolute value:

$(−5) + (7) + (3) + (−13)$

Positive total	Negative total
$7 + 3 = 10$	$5 + 13 = 18$

$$(+10) + (−18) = −8$$

Target Practice 1: Think About Money

These integers could represent deposits (+) and withdrawals (−) from your bank account.

Find the *difference* between the absolute values of the numbers. The answer gets the sign of the larger absolute.

1 $15 + (-5) =$

2 $(-9) + (+4) + (-2) =$

3 $(-\$12) + (\$15) + (-\$3) =$

4 $(75) + (-150) =$

Target Practice 2: Add Them on the Line

Another way to calculate the addition of signed numbers is to use a number line. Get out your own line or use the one above.

$-4 + (-4) = ?$ Start at the first signed number (-4). The sign on the second number $(-)$ tells you in which *direction* to move ($-$ means "go left"). The number itself tells you how many steps to take in that direction (4). Where do you land? Hopefully, at -8. Try it again: $-6 + (-2) + (5) = ?$. Did you land on -3? Now try these:

1 $4 + (-10) =$

2 $(-7) + (-5) =$

3 $-11 + 15 =$

4 $-15 + (-21) =$

Target Practice 3: Add Them on the Slopes

1 When the skiers woke up, the thermometer registered 12 degrees below zero. By the time they hit the slopes, it was 15 degrees warmer. At lunch time, it had risen another 15 degrees, and they sat in the sun on the deck to eat. An expression for the lunchtime temperature is:
A $(-12) + (15) - (15)$
B $(-12) - (15) + (15)$
C $-12 + 15 + 15$
D $2(15) - (-12)$

2 The base lodge was 2,000 feet above sea level. The gondola lift took them up 2,750 feet. From there they skied a run that ended at the mid-station, which was 3,300 feet above sea level. How many feet did they descend on that run? (Read that again. Don't grab numbers and run.)
A 2,750 feet
B 4,150 feet
C 1,450 feet
D 5,300 feet

Activity 2: Subtracting Integers

The rule for subtracting signed numbers is as follows:

1 Change the sign of the number being subtracted. $7 - (+3) \rightarrow +3$ becomes -3

2 Change the subtraction sign to addition $7 - (-3)$ becomes $7 + (-3)$

3 Follow the rules for adding signed numbers. $7 + (-3) = 4$

Subtract a Negative Number? That's a Double Negative – (–)

"I do *not* want to *not* go to the party." Think about the meaning of that sentence. The second "not" cancels the meaning of the first "not." What that person really means is, "I *do* want to go to the party." *Two negatives make a positive:* $-(-25) = +25$. Two minus signs next to each other can be as confusing as the two words "not" together in one sentence. The result is the same: What appears to be a negative statement is communicating a positive thought.

Think Money: You borrow $75 from a friend: –$75. You want to *subtract* (–) as much of that *debt* (–) as you can. When you subtract debt, you *pay back* what is owed and *reverse* the flow of money. Subtracting debt is the same as adding money to the balance. Subtraction of debt is a *positive* occurrence. You know you are moving in a positive direction (both literally and figuratively). The result of subtracting –(–$25) *is the same as adding* or "applying" $25 toward your debt to your friend. This is written mathematically –$75 – (–$25) = –$50.

Again, two negatives make a positive: $-75 - (-25) = -75 + 25 = -50$.

Target Practice: Tackle Double Negatives Positively

$(-8) - (-10) = -8 + 10 = +2$

$-8 - (-5) = -8 + 5 = -3$

1 $14 - (-20) =$

2 $48 - (-38) =$

3 $6 - (-2) =$

4 $-6 - (-2) =$

STUDY TIP

Two negatives make a positive

Understand, then memorize, this rule.

Target Practice 2: A Review

1 $(-7) + 6 =$

2 $3 + (-8) =$

3 $|-7 + 6| = |-1| =$

4 $|3 - 8| = |$ _____ $| =$

5 $-2 + (-4) + (-15) + |-5| =$

Activity 3: Multiply and Divide Integers—Take Multiple Leaps on the Line

What pattern do you see in these rules?

RULES	
Multiply Integers	1. with the same sign . . . the answer is always positive
	2. with different signs . . . the answer is always negative
Divide Integers	1. with the same sign . . . the answer is always positive
	2. with different signs . . . the answer is always negative

Do you see that the same rules are true for both multiplication and division? Here is the short and sweet of it: Same signs? Positive. Different signs? Negative.

Here are the explanations for those rules, with examples. Take time to work through them before trying problems on your own.

RULE 1: Same Sign? Answer Is Positive

- Two positive numbers? This one is self-explanatory. Remember, numbers without signs are assumed to be positive ones. For example, $+5(+3) = 5(3) = 15$; $+64 / +4 = 64/4 = 16$.
- Two negative numbers? The rule *two negatives make a positive* that you worked through on page 175 holds true. For example, $-5 (-3) = 15$; $-64/-4 = 16$.

RULE 2: Different Signs? Answer Is Negative

- $5 (-3) = -15$. Try it on the line: The minus sign carried by the 3 means *leap to the left of zero*. Do it five times: $5 (-3) = -15$.
- $-12/4 = -3$. Try it on the line: Start at -12. Leap over 4 of those 12 negative steps at a time, moving to the right (since 4 is positive). You end up with 3 groups of negative numbers; the answer is -3.

Target Practice: Multiplying and Dividing Integers

Follow the rules above, as well as the order of operations.

1 Sheila had $536.00 in savings. She bought lottery tickets with her savings for 7 weeks, $25 each week. Choose the expression that will result in the dollars she spent: -175

    A $-7(-25)$

    B $7(-25)$

    C $7(25)$

2 Sheila did not win the jackpot during those 7 weeks. Choose the expression with integers that represents the dollars she has left in her savings account: +361

   A 7(–25) –536

   B 7(536 – 25)

   C 7(–25) + 536

3 –15 × –4 =

   A –60

   B –19

   C 60

   D 19

4 –22 × 2 =

   A 44

   B –44

   C –20

   D 20

5 –3(+3)(–3) =

   A +27

   B –27

   C +9

   D –9

6 $\dfrac{-800 \div 50}{4} =$

   A –4

   B –16

   C 16

   D +4

7 6(–36) =

   A 216

   B –6

   C –216

   D –42

STUDY TIP: WHEN THE RULE FOR THE ANSWER'S SIGN IS SHORT AND SWEET, WHY LEAP?

Memorize this rule for multiplying and dividing integers:

   Same signs? +Answer   Different signs? –Answer

TARGET Patterns and Trends: Detective Work

Patterns are sequences of events or of design. They are found in nature, in human behavior, and in the numbers that track changes in society over time. Numbers give people a way of identifying, talking about, and understanding life's patterns in a structured and logical way. The language and science of mathematics grow from patterns.

Words to Know

Pattern   An organized arrangement or sequence that follows a rule

Sequence   In a row, one after the other

Activity 1: Warm Up to Patterns

Knowing how *identify* and *understand* number patterns is a valuable skill that will help you solve math problems and analyze data. You will learn and practice this skill here. You will use it in the next lesson as you work with the tools of algebra to find solutions to word problems and solve for unknowns in equations.

Make Your Own Patterns—From Scratch

The best way to understand how number patterns are formed is to create some of your own. The routine that follows may remind you of the repeated multiplication you do when evaluating powers of numbers.

1 Begin with a number: 3

2 Decide on a rule of operation: Multiply by 2

3 Apply the rule repeatedly: $3 \times 2 = \mathbf{6} \rightarrow 6 \times 2 = \mathbf{12} \rightarrow 12 \times 2 = \mathbf{24} \rightarrow 24 \times 2 = \mathbf{48} \rightarrow 48 \times 2 = \mathbf{96} \rightarrow 96 \times 2 = \mathbf{192} \rightarrow 192 \times 2 = \mathbf{384}$

4 Record the results in sequence: 3, 6, 12, 24, 48, 96, 192, 384

5 Look at the sequence. Can you *see* what went on "behind the scenes" to create it?

Target Practice: Apply These Rules Repeatedly

Apply each rule below six times to create a six-number pattern. Write your calculations in your math notebook. Record the results in sequence below:

	Start With	Rule of Operation	Number Pattern: 6 in a row
A	2	**Add 7** each time	**2**, 9, _____, 23, _____, _____
B	96	**Subtract 12** each time	**96**, _____, _____, _____, 48, _____
C	100,000	**Divide by 5** each time	**100,000**, _____, _____, _____, _____, _____
D	25	**Subtract 1**, then **2**, then **1** . . .	**25**, _____, 22, _____, _____, _____
E	6	**Multiply by 2 and add 2**, repeat	**6**, 14, _____, _____, 126, _____

Activity 2: What Is Going On and Why?

Detectives *collect and analyze evidence* to answer questions. They examine the pieces of evidence they collect and look for *how the pieces are related.* Is there a pattern? If so, what does that pattern say about the way events happened and the *way* the people involved *operated?* Think like a detective when you search for the rule for numbers in sequences.

Step 1: Look for a General Trend. Read the number sequence from left to right. Is there a general trend occurring? Do the numbers get larger or smaller? Does the change happen slowly or quickly? Does that trend continue all the way across the row?

Step 2: Record the Evidence of Change. Confirm your observation by recording the details. *Find the difference* between the first and second number. Write it down. *Find the difference* between the second and third number, the third and fourth number, and so on. Note the change with integers.

Step 3: Look for a Pattern in the Changes. Which operation is the cause? Larger: addition or multiplication? Smaller: subtraction, or division? Is *more* than one operation at work?

Step 4: Formulate a Rule of Operation. *Apply that rule to each number* in the sequence. Does the rule work each time? Then you have it solved.

Step 5: Try out the Rule. Predict what comes next.

Target Practice 1: Follow and Predict

Follow these examples. Steps 1, 2, and 3 from above have been done for you. Examine how each rule was discovered. Predict the next three numbers in each sequence.

A   3, 7, 11, 15, 19   . . . . next ____ ____ ____
    Difference: +4 +4 +4 +4   Rule: Add 4 to each number

B   1, 2, 4, 8, 16, 32   . . . . next ____ ____ ____
    Difference: +1, +2, +4, +8, +16 Rule: Multiply each number by 2

C   28, 21, 15, 10, 6   . . . . next ____ ____ ____
    Difference: −7, −6, −5, −4,   Rule: Subtract 1 less from each number
                                          than the number before it

Target Practice 2: Detective Work

Detect the rule for each sequence. Write it down. Apply it three times. Use signed numbers to record the direction (as well as the size) of the change.

A   72, 63, 54, 45, 36 . . . . next _____ _____ _____
    Difference: _____
    Rule:_____

B   0, 1, 3, 6, 10 . . . . next _____ _____ _____

Differences: _____

Rule: _____

C   1, 4, 10, 22, 46 . . . . next _____ _____ _____

Differences: _____

Rule: _____

Target Practice 3: Review

Detect the pattern of change.

A 11, 18, 25, _____, 39, _____, 53

B 3, _____, 15, 31, 63, 127, 255 _____

C 100, 99, 97, 94, _____, 85, 79, _____, 64, 55

Activity 3: Patterns in Nature

The natural world is filled with rhythms and patterns of change. In your part of the world, what pattern of change have you noticed in the times of sunrise and sunset throughout the year? Can you predict the approximate time the sun will rise in mid-December? About how late in the day does the sun set in mid-July?

Examine the statistics in the chart below showing sunrise-sunset times for Cincinnati, Ohio. Notice *how* the numbers change, month to month, across the rows.

Sunrise, Sunset Cincinnati, Ohio 2002

Months	Jan	Feb	Mar	April	May	June	July	Aug	Sept	Oct	Nov	Dec
Sunrise a.m.	7:53	7:22	6:40	5:53	5:20	5:12	5:29	5:57	6:25	6:54	7:28	7:54
Sunset p.m.	5:46	6:22	6:51	7:21	7:50	8:07	8:00	7:25	6:37	5:51	5:20	5:19

Times recorded on the 20th day of each month

Source: http://mach.usno.navy.mil/cgi-bin/aa_rstablew.pl

Target Practice 1: Sunrise, Sunset—Trends

1 Look for a trend in the Sunrise row. Sunrise time is
  A Earlier, month to month, January to December
  B Later, month to month, January to December
  C Earlier, month to month, January to June, then later month to month, July to December
  D Later, month to month, January to June, then earlier, July to December, for the second half

2 Sunset time, January to December, is _____ month to month, _____ to _____, then _____ month to month, _____ to _____

Target Practice 2: Sunrise, Sunset—Details

Calculate the number of minutes by which sunrise and sunset times changed, month to month, from January to December in Cincinnati, Ohio. Record the results of your calculations in the two tables below. Show whether those minutes represent changes to earlier or later times. **Record details in changes with integers.** Record changes to *later* times *as positive;* record changes to *earlier* times *as negative:*

- January to February sunrise times changed by <u>31</u> minutes. Sunrise happened *earlier.* −31
- January to February sunset times *change by* <u>36</u> minutes. Sunset happened *later.* +36

1 Changes in Time of Sunrise, Cincinnati, Ohio, USA, 2002

Jan	Feb	Mar	Apr	May	June	July	Aug	Sep	Oct	Nov	Dec
	−31										

2 Changes in Time of Sunset, Cincinnati, Ohio, USA, 2002

Jan	Feb	Mar	Apr	May	June	July	Aug	Sep	Oct	Nov	Dec
	+36										

When you have filled in all the data, check your answers before moving on to the last activity.

Activity 4: Picture the Pattern

After all the pattern puzzling you have been doing, take a moment to relax and reflect as you connect the dots of the data points in the line graph below.

Target Practice: Draw the Line

Do you recognize this data in picture form? The data points that mark the value of sunrise and sunset times come from the chart in Activity 3.

1 Connect the data points with line segments. How well do the trend lines match the trends you observed in Activity 3?

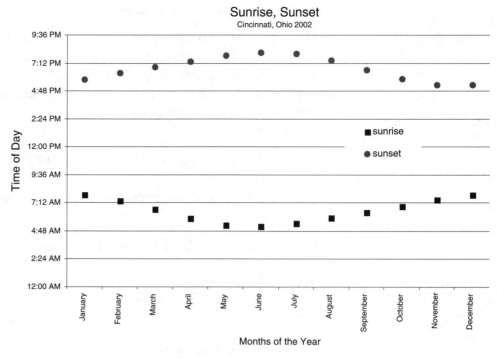

Sunrise, Sunset
Cincinnati, Ohio 2002

Source: Sunrise, Sunset (Cincinnati, Ohio 2002)
http://mach.usno.navy.mil/cgi-bin/aa_rstablew.pl

Use the data as displayed in the table and the line graph to answer these final questions.

2 The longest days of the year 2002 in Cincinnati, Ohio (the time between sunrise and sunset) had approximately this many hours of daylight:
A 10
B 12
C 15
D 17

3 The shortest days had approximately this many hours of daylight:
A 7
B 9
C 11
D 12

4 Days were about the same length in the months of
A June and August
B March and April
C September and October
D May and July

Add to your luck. People who are good at solving problems—all kinds of problems, not just in math class—are good at looking for and analyzing patterns. When questions are asked about a situation, and you see a pattern developing, you can make a plan to figure out *what is going on.* Luck at solving problems is wonderful when it happens. Add to your luck by strengthening your pattern-discovery skills.

Answer Key: Section 3, Lesson 7

TARGET Signed Numbers: Integers Speak of Opposites

Activity 1: Get Acquainted with Integers

TARGET PRACTICE 1: DRAW THE LINE
Check the signs and labels on your line for accuracy.

TARGET PRACTICE 2: USE THE LINE
1. >
2. >>
3. < >
4. << >
5. >
6. >
7. $5 > -7$ and $-7 < -5$ are true
8. $-11 > -12$ is true
9. $-7, -3, -1, 0, 2, 6$
10. $-5, -2.5, -2, 1.25, 25$

Activity 2: It Is |Absolutely| True

TARGET PRACTICE: EVALUATE THESE ABSOLUTES
1. $17 - 7 = 10$
2. $2 + 4 - 5 = 1$
3. $30 - 6 + 4 = 28$
4. $29 - 9 = 20$

Activity 3: Integers and Life

TARGET PRACTICE: ASSIGN SIGNS
1. lost; -12 yards
2. below; -125 feet
3. above; $+7$ feet
4. lost; $-1,250$ dollars
5. rose; $+3.5$ degrees
6. back; -11 hours

Activity 4: Integers in the World of Work

TARGET PRACTICE 1: THE BIG STORY
1. 10 years
2. 11 years
3. Profit; billions of dollars

4. Employees; thousands of people

5. Year-End Stock Price; dollars

1. C; +$0.92 billion

2. B; −$1 billion

3. A; −$2 billion

4. C; $5.2 billion

1. B; −40,000 employees

2. B; +20,000 employees

3. C; −100,000 employees

Note: Your estimate may vary by 1 or 2 dollars from these estimates, but the *sign* of the change should be the same

1. $25, $8   Change: −$17

2. $8, $15   Change: +$7

3. $15, $1   Change: −$14

TARGET Integer Operations: Think Money, Lines, and Rules

Activity 1: Adding Integers

You owe your friend $16

1. 10

2. −7

3. 0

4. −75

1. −6

2. −12

3. +4

4. −36

1. C

2. C

Activity 2: Subtracting Integers

1. 34

2. 86

3. 8

4. −4

TARGET PRACTICE 2: A REVIEW

1. −1
2. −5
3. 1
4. |−5| = 5
5. −16 (This one was difficult; how did you do?)

Activity 3: Multiple Leaps on the Line

TARGET PRACTICE: MULTIPLYING AND DIVIDING INTEGERS

1. B
2. C
3. C
4. B
5. A
6. A
7. C

TARGET Patterns and Trends: Detective Work

Activity 1: Warm Up to Patterns

TARGET PRACTICE: APPLY THESE RULES REPEATEDLY

A. 2, 9, <u>16</u>, 23, <u>30</u>, <u>37</u>
B. 96, <u>84</u>, <u>72</u>, <u>60</u>, 48, <u>36</u>
C. 100,000; <u>20,000</u>, <u>4,000</u>, <u>800</u>, <u>160</u>, <u>32</u>
D. 25, <u>24</u>, 22, <u>21</u>, <u>19</u>, <u>18</u>
E. 6, 14, <u>30</u>, <u>62</u>, 126, <u>254</u>

Activity 2: What Is Going On and Why?

TARGET PRACTICE 1: FOLLOW AND PREDICT

A. 23, 27, 31
B. 64, 128, 256
C. 3, 1, 0

TARGET PRACTICE 2: DETECTIVE WORK

A. Differences: −9, −9, −9, −9
   Rule: Subtract 9 each time
   Next: 27, 18, 9
B. Differences: +1, +2, +3, +4
   Rule: Add 1 more to each number than the number before it
   Next: 15, 21, 28
C. Differences: +3, +6, +12, +24
   Rule: Double the amount that is added, each time
   Next: 94, 190, 382

TARGET PRACTICE 3: REVIEW
  A. 11, 18, 25, <u>32</u>, 39, <u>46</u>, 53
  B. 3, <u>7</u>, 15, 31, 63, 127, 255, 511
  C. 100, 99, 97, 94, <u>90</u>, 85, 79, <u>72</u>, 64, 55

Activity 3: Patterns in Nature

TARGET PRACTICE 1: SUNRISE, SUNSET—TRENDS
  1. C
  2. later, month to month, January to June; then earlier, month to month, July to December

TARGET PRACTICE 2: SUNRISE, SUNSET—DETAILS
  1. −31, −42, −47, −33, −8, +17, +28, +28, +29, +34, +26
  2. +36, +29, +30, +29, +17, −7, −35, −48, −46, −31, −1

Activity 4: Picture the Pattern

TARGET PRACTICE: TREND LINES
  1. Answers will vary. Did you enjoy this activity?
  2. C
  3. B
  4. D

LESSON 8 The Value of Logic

> "If A equals success, then the formula is:
> A equals X plus Y plus Z . . . with X being work, Y play,
> and Z keeping your mouth shut."
> *Albert Einstein*

> "Try not to become a man of success, but rather
> try to become a man of value."
> *Albert Einstein*

Getting Started

André's high school friend, Dave, moved out-of-state after graduation. Now, five years later, he is back for a visit. André invited Dave to help him set up a new computer system at the Academic Success Center. They arrived just as the math study group was getting underway. Lisa, Ken, and three others were discussing the use of formulas to find solutions. As usual, formulas reminded Lisa of cooking.

"Remind me to bring in a sample of my latest recipe for cheesecake," Lisa said to the group. "It's a winner."

"You're on, Lisa," Ken replied with a grin. "I can always use more energy for math work. Seriously, I'm having trouble with these formulas you think are so great. They work fine for straightforward questions that ask me to solve for area, interest, distance, or volume. But how do I use them when I need to solve for a part of the formula on the other side of the equal sign? How can I move the variables around and be confident the formula will work?"

"Sometimes, I can picture what is going on and figure it out. Other times, I don't know where to begin. It seems upside down and backwards to me."

Learner Update:

Ken is getting closer to his goal of scoring high enough on the Math Admissions Test to qualify for college credit coursework. The study group has played a positive part in his progress. Ken finds that working with others on math has some of the same benefits as working with others at the construction site: the work goes faster, they learn from each other, and even have fun in the process.

 FYI

It is possible to answer a problem and not understand how you did it. As Ken said, sometimes he can just picture it. Some people have a mind that seems *to see* how math situations work, but they may not know how to explain it. Are you one of those people?

Back to the group "Maybe I can help Ken," Dave said to André. "Do you think he would mind if I make a suggestion?" "You've got to be kidding, Dave," André said. "You're an athlete, not a formula-type guy." "I surprised myself," Dave admitted. "Believe it or not, after I moved out west, I learned to use formulas to help me meet my training goals—even some of my social goals. Matter of fact, a new friend and I used formulas just last week. We met to compare notes on the distance, rate, and time of our favorite bike trips." "What makes me think your new friend might be a she?" observed André.

TARGET Logic at Work: The Tale of the Scale

Words to Know

Logic   Reason, judgment, and common sense

Activity 1: Planning for R_1 and R_2 . . . When R_1 = Recreation, and R_2 = Relaxation

Dave is thinking about biking to Crystal Lake for a day of swimming and fishing. He wonders if traveling by bike will leave him enough time to swim, fish, relax, and get back home before dark.

The plans: Get up early. Bike to Eric's house to pick up a fishing rod. Return by the same route, pass home, and continue to Crystal Lake. Eat, fish, swim, sleep in the sun. Bike back to Eric's, return the fishing rod, then bike home. Get there before dark.

The question: How much time will the biking part of the day take?

The facts: Eric's house is 17 miles south of home. Crystal Lake is 52 miles north of home. Dave averages 20 miles per hour on distance bike trips. Sunrise: About 5:30 A.M. Sunset: About 8 P.M.

Can You Answer Dave's Question?

After he figures out how long to allow for biking, Dave will decide whether that *travel time* will leave him as much *relaxation time* as he wants. There is more than one way to figure out the answer to Dave's question. If you have an idea of how to do it, bookmark this page and try it now. Remember to jot down the facts that are known about the bike route before you close the book.

Which way? Here are three different ways to figure out the answer (there may be others as well)

Target Practice: Travel Along. Fill In the Facts.

Travel along with this script. Fill in the facts that are stated above as you go. As you travel these three different ways, ask yourself which way is the most comfortable way for you to figure out the answer to Dave's question.

Way 1: Draw a diagram. Use number facts, symbols, lines, and labels.

Eric's apartment   Dave's apartment   Crystal Lake

	←	_____ miles				
	→	_____ miles				
	= _____ miles		+ _____ miles		= _____ miles
Miles	20	_____		_____	_____	+ 6 miles
Hours	1	2		3	4	+ 6 miles at _____ mph =

4 hours will get Dave to _____ miles, plus _____ of an hour more for the 6 miles.

<u>The Result:</u> Travel time by bike one way _____ hours. Round trip, _____ hours. Practically speaking, better round that up to 9 hours for travel time.

Way 2: Visualize the action. Write down the numbers below as you replay the action and talk it through to yourself.

Picture this: Biking to Eric's place is _____ miles. Back again is another _____. That adds up to _____ + _____ = _____ miles for that part of the trip. Then it's another _____ miles to the lake = _____ miles altogether. Biking _____ miles each hour for 4 hours looks like _____ + _____ + _____ + _____, which will get him to _____ miles in 4 whole hours. Then he has _____ more miles to go @ _____ mph which will take _____/_____ or _____ of an hour. <u>The Result:</u> Travel time by bike one way—_____ and _____ hours. Double that for a round-trip, the total is _____ and _____ hours. Rounded up to the nearest hour, that's about _____ hours travel time.

Way 3: Use the formula distance = rate × time. Solve it for time.

Formula:	**d**istance = **r**ate × **t**ime	$d = rt$
Formula **re**arranged:	**t**ime = **d**istance/**r**ate	$t = d/r$
Facts:	$d =$ _____ miles	
	$r =$ _____ mph	
	$t =$ _____ hours	
Substitute:	$t = 86/20$	
Solve for t:	$t = 4.3$	
Solution:	$t = \mathbf{4.3}$ hours	

Check by Substitution:

$$\mathbf{t}ime = \mathbf{d}istance/\mathbf{r}ate$$

$$4.3 = 86/20$$

$$4.3 = 4.3$$

<u>The Result:</u> Travel time by bike one way will be _____ hours. Round-trip, _____ hours. Practically speaking—allow at least _____ hours for travel time.

Any way you look at it, it figures. Based on the numbers, Dave makes the decision to go ahead with his plans. If he leaves his apartment at 7 A.M., he can get to the lake by about _____ A.M. That gives him about _____ hours to eat, swim, fish, and sun before heading back home. He should probably start biking at _____ P.M. in order to arrive before sundown at _____ P.M.

Which way was the best way for you to work through this situation? _____

All three methods of problem solving should have resulted in the same approximate answer. Can you guess which method Dave used? Right. For Dave, Way 3 was "best." For him, it was the quickest way *and* he trusted the results. He knew a tried-and-true formula to use to guide him to the answer.

How did Dave change the formula $d = r \times t$ to $t = d/r$? He knows formulas are equations, and he has learned how to make equations and other tools of algebra work for him.

Words to Know

Equation	A number sentence that says two quantities, or expressions, have the same value. An equation is balanced around an equal sign.

Formula	An equation that states a general rule or fact about the relationship between two or more quantities. Relationships are expressed using numbers, variables, and signs.
Variable	A symbol (usually a letter) in a formula that stands for a number that changes as other numbers in the formula change.
Inverse	Opposite
Inverse operations	Operations that have the *opposite effect on* number values. Addition and subtraction are inverse operations, as are multiplication and division.

Activity 2: Relationships Can Be Rearranged (Not Changed) and Still Remain True

How do equations work? You've been working with them for years! You have a good idea already of the basics. You know that the quantities on each side of the equal sign have the same value. You can easily solve for this *unknown value:* 2 + _____ = 4 You do not need to rearrange anything. Actually, to answer the question you probably did the rearranging without knowing it. Keep that in mind as you learn how to rearrange equations with variables.

Equations work like old-fashioned balance scales. Values represented by numbers, letters, and signs are balanced around an equal sign. These values can be *manipulated,* just like the weights on a scale. As long as the balance of value is maintained, the truth of the equation is maintained. The value of a formula to lead to a solution is kept intact when its parts are moved around with logic.

Target Practice: Visualize "The Tale of the Scale"

Your job in this Target Practice is to read and *understand* this tale. Put this "active reading" strategy to work: Make a "mind-movie" version of the tale. Use your imagination to visualize the motion described.

A quantity of something that is <u>un</u>measured (its value in weight is <u>un</u>known) is placed on one side of the balance scale (see Figure 1). *Measured* weights (their numbers are *known*) are placed on the other side of the scale until the scale is balanced (see Figure 2).

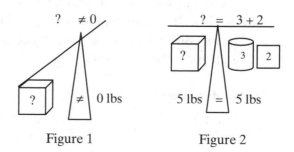

Figure 1   Figure 2

Now the quantities on both sides of the scale are known to have the same weight. Their *values* are in balance and equal. Since you already *know* the measure of the weights on the right side, the question of how much the quantity on the left weighs is now answered. Both sides weigh 5 pounds. Because the scale is in perfect balance, you can be sure that the value measured is *correct.*

But what if . . . ? Let's look at how Ken's question applies here. What do you do if the *unknown* part of a formula is on the *other* side of the equal sign along with some parts that are *known?* Look how it works with a scale:

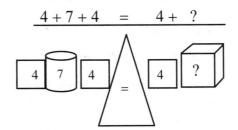

$$4 + 7 + 4 \quad = \quad 4 + \; ?$$

The problem here is *not* which side of the scale the unknown part is on.

The problem is this: The unknown part is *not alone.* How can you get the *unknown* weight (the box) alone and still keep the scale in balance? "That's easy as 1, 2, 3," you are probably saying. "All you need to do is take away the 4-pound weight from the right side *at the same time* you take away a 4-pound weight from the left side."

$$
\begin{array}{r}
4 + 7 + 4 = \; 4 + \square \\
-4 \qquad\qquad -4 \\
\hline
7 + 4 = \qquad \square
\end{array}
$$

"The scale is still in balance. It is obvious that the box must weigh 11 pounds." Does it bother you that the box is on the right side of the scale? When you work with equations, you can always "turn the scale around." It will not change the values. No matter which way you read or write it, $7 + 4 = 11$ is the same fact as $11 = 7 + 4$. These equations are equivalent.

Two Actions to Do, Tried-and-True, Balance Scales and Solve Unknowns Too

1. Isolate the unknown (weight of the box) on one side. Take action to move *known* weights away.
2. Manipulate weight with an even hand on both sides: Keep the scale in balance.

- *Question:* What will happen if you forget to keep the scale balanced?
- *Answer:* The scale will tip *and* worse yet: The true weight of the box will remain unknown.

   The news is good. It's common sense. The two steps you followed to discover the weight of the mystery box are steps of common sense. If you use a balance scale regularly, these actions become automatic. Can rearranging parts of formulas be this simple? Yes.

When we say something *is logical,* we are saying it *makes sense*—common sense. Algebra is a tool of logic. It provides us with an orderly way of tackling and finding answers to how things work. Understanding *how* and *why* to use these two common-sense procedures is *the key* to solving equations with unknowns. The more you practice using them . . . (you know the rest).

Activity 3: Take Opposite Action: Operate Inversely

Words to Know

Inverse   Opposite

Addition and subtraction are *inverse* operations. They have opposite effects on values.

- A gain of 4 lb (+4, addition) can be reversed by a loss of 4 lb (−4, subtraction)

Multiplication and division are *inverse* operations. They have opposite effects on values.

- Doubling your money in the stock market (×2, multiplication) will be reversed if your stock loses half its worth (÷2, division).

> Note: Remember how it worked with those boxes on the scale? You used an inverse operation when you *subtracted* the 4-pound weight that had been *added.*
>
> Apply the common sense of the balance scale to rearranging variables in formulas.
>
> > **Isolate** an unknown variable to discover its value.
> >
> > **Use inverse operations** to move values.
> >
> > **Keep the balance.** Whatever you do to one side of a formula, you must do to the other to keep it in balance.
>
> Note: A balanced scale weighs values accurately. A balanced equation results in a solution.

 STUDY TIP: MEMORIZE THIS ADVICE
Follow it as you solve for unknowns in equations: "Isolate the Unknown. Use Inverse Operations. Keep Your Balance."

Target Practice 1: Practice Isolation

Follow this routine, step by step, as you answer the three questions below. Follow the two examples.

Step 1 **Mark** the part of the formula you must isolate. Use a check mark ✔.

Step 2 **Identify** the operation that *relates* that checked part to variables or numbers on *its* side of the equation.

Step 3 **Choose** the opposite (*inverse*) operation to use as you move to a solution

Step 4 **Do it** on both sides (keep your balance)

Example One:

- Solve for <u>C</u>:　　　　$A = B + \overset{✔}{C}$

　　　Think:　　　　　　　B and C *are related by* <u>addition</u>.
　　　　　　　　　　　　To isolate C, I must use <u>subtraction</u>.

　　　Do it:　　　　　　$A = B + C$
　　　　　　　　　　　$\underline{-B = -B}$
　　　　　　　　　　　$A - B = C$

Example Two:

- Solve for Width:　　$Area = Length \times \overset{✔}{Width}$

　　　Think:　　　　　　　Length and Width *are related by* multiplication.
　　　　　　　　　　　　To isolate Width, I must use division.

　　　Do it:　　　　　$\dfrac{Area = Length \times Width}{Length = Length}$

　　　　　　　　　　　$Area/Length = Width$

1 Solve for Y:　　　$Y - X = Z$

　　　Think:　　　　　　Y and X *are related by* _____
　　　　　　　　　　　To isolate the Y, I must use _____

　　　Do it:　　　　　$Y - X = Z$

　　　　　　　　　_____

　　　　　　　　　$Y =$ _____

2 Solve for diameter:　$Circumference = \pi \times diameter$

　　　Think:　　　　　π and diameter *are related by* _____
　　　　　　　　　　　To isolate the diameter, I must use _____

　　　Do it:　　　　　_____

　　　　　　　　　_____

　　　　　　　　　$diameter =$ _____

3 Solve for C:　　　$F = 1.8\,C + 32$

　　　Think:　　　　　　C is related to 32 by _____
　　　　　　　　　　　To isolate C, I must use _____

Do it: _____

_____

_____

Think Again: C is related to 1.8 by _____

To isolate C, I must use _____

Do it: _____

_____

C = _____

Target Practice 2: Move It on Your Own

Continue the thinking process you've practiced above. This time do the figuring in your math notebook and write the rearranged formula below:

1 $A = b - c$ Solve for b $b =$ _____

2 $Q = R + S$ Solve for S $S =$ _____

3 $x = y/7$ Solve for y $y =$ _____

4 Which of these equations is equivalent to $i = p \times r \times t$?
   A $p = i/rt$
   B $p = i - r - t$
   C $p = i(r \times t)$
   D $t = pr/i$

5 Which of these equations is equivalent to $R = a\,t$?
   A $R = t/a$
   B $a = t/R$
   C $a = R/t$
   D $t = a \times R$

6 Alan built a rectangular frame for a raised vegetable garden in his back yard. The raised garden bed was 2 feet high and 3 feet wide. Four cubic yards (or 108 cubic feet) of a compost-loam mixture filled the frame to the brim. What is the length of the frame? _____

Hint: Use the formula for a rectangular solid, $V = lwh$, and solve for l.

Activity 4: $c = n \times r$

If $c = n \times r$, then $r = ?$

$c =$ total cost of purchase; $n =$ number of units purchased; $r =$ rate per unit

Words to Know

Per   For each

When you comparison-shop to find the best buy among competing brands (or different-sized packages of the same brand) you need to figure out the value of *r*. Rate in the shopping formula stands for *price* per unit. This unit could be per ounce, per foot, per day, and so on.

Target Practice: Which Is the Best Buy?

Inverse operations rearrange the formula to solve for *r*.
Round your answers up to the nearest cent.

Pre-Paid Telephone Cards

| **A** ☏ 30 minutes $17.99 | **B** ☏ 60 minutes $24.99 | **C** ☏ 150 minutes $49.99 |

1 What is the cost per minute of Card A? _____

2 What is the cost per minute of Card B _____

3 What is the cost per minute of Card C? _____

TARGET Algebraic Equations: Where There's a System, There's a Way

Algebra is a branch of mathematics that is based on, and enhances, the familiar language, tools, and operating rules of arithmetic. It is a problem-solving tool used to find the value of quantities that are *unknown* or *that can change or vary* under certain conditions. Letters called *variables* stand for numbers you want to find. Letters are used along with numbers to solve problems that cannot be solved in other ways.

Algebraic equations are equations that contain the *known* facts of a situation together with the *unknown* facts, and explain the relationship between them.

Does all this sound familiar? You bet. The formulas you have been working with for several lessons are algebraic equations. You have been using the language, tools, and operating rules of algebra all along.

Time for a change. Let's step away from using formulas to answer questions we can picture. Put aside thoughts of phone cards, building materials, and bikes. Focus now on the mechanics of manipulating terms in algebraic equations. It's another way to sharpen the logical side of your mind.

Words to Know

Enhance	To make better or more useful.
Evaluate	To find the value or amount of something.
Solve	To determine the value of an unknown (often by the use of inverse operations).
Solution	The result when the unknown becomes known; the answer.
Terms	Numbers or letters that represent values.

Unknown   A number fact that is not known. A *fixed unknown* has only one correct answer. A *variable unknown* can have various correct answers; it's solution is based on the value of other variables in the equation.

Tools and Rules to Use

Tools: (1) Variables are letters that represent *unknown values* (the ones you *want* to know).

(2) Equations state *the relationship of* the facts you know to the facts you want to know.

Rules: (1) Use *inverse operations* to isolate the unknown on one side of the equation.

(2) Keep the equation in balance by operating the same way on both sides of the equal (=) sign.

Activity 1: One-step Solutions

Use the tools and rules of algebra to solve these equations.

Target Practice: Go Directly to Solve

Use this template to organize calculations in your math notebook. For this target practice, all the facts are given in the starting equation. Write down the equation (Step 1 in the template). Next, go directly to Solve (Step 4).

For example:

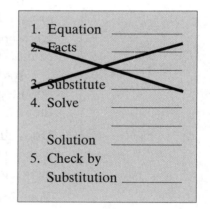

1. Equation _____
2. Facts _____
   _____
3. Substitute _____
4. Solve _____
   _____
   Solution _____
5. Check by Substitution _____

- Equation $m + 8 = 48$
  Solve $m + 8 = 48$
  $$\underline{-8 \quad -8}$$
  Solution $m \quad = 40$

Check by Substitution $40 + 8 = 48$
$$48 \ = 48$$

1 $n/15 = 6$ $n = $ _____

2 $1000 = 25 + j$ $j = $ _____

3 $y - 12 = -10$ $y = $ _____

4 $15p = 45$ $p = $ _____

5 $\frac{1}{2}n = 10$ $n = $ _____ Hint: Flip the fraction for the inverse operation

Activity 2: Make It Simple

When sorting fruit into cartons to get an accurate count of each kind, you would not mix apples and oranges. Likewise, do not combine different terms representing unknowns: Similar ≠ same.

Like terms: $15x^2y + 2x^2y = 17\,x^2y$ **Unlike terms:** $15x^2y + 15\,xy$
                                                                                cannot be combined,

$3xy + xy = 4xy$ $3xy + y = 3xy + y$

$7x^2 + 5x^2 = 12x^2$ $7x + 5x^2 = 7x + 5x^2$

<u>Follow the Order of Operations:</u> $3y + 3 + 7(y + 2)$ multiply first

<u>Combine "like" terms:</u> $3y + 3 + 7y + 14$, then combine

$10y + 17 =$ the y terms and the *numerical* terms.

Target Practice 1: Simplify by Combining Like Terms

1 $9xy + 6x - 4xy + x$ $=$ _____

2 $2(3z + 5) + 6z$ $=$ _____

3 $8(x - 2) - 3(2x + 1)$ $=$ _____

4 $15 + 2c + 7d - c + 4$ $=$ _____

Target Practice 2: Simplify, then Solve

Use inverse operations to isolate the unknown on one side of each equation, then calculate (solve) to arrive at the solution.

   Note: For problems 3 and 4, use inverse operations to move all R's and y's to one side in order to combine them.

1 $6x + 1 + 3x = 19$ $x =$ _____

2 $3c + 2 - c = 12$ $c =$ _____

3 $R + 4 = 13 - 2R$ $R =$ _____

4 $15 - 3y = 3 + 9y$ $y =$ _____

Activity 3: Where There Is a System, There Is a Way

STUDY TIP: ACCURATE COPYING IS AN ACTIVE LEARNING STRATEGY
Make an accurate copy of a procedure you want to understand and remember. Examine the details of the model. As you copy it, you are activating your senses of *sight, touch,* and *kinesthesia* (movement). *Speak,* and therefore *hear,* the details at the same time you *see* and *do* them. **Multi-sensory experiences strengthen memory and understanding**

Target Practice 1: Be a Copy Cat

Activate your senses. Use the strategies explained in the Study Tip above. Make an accurate copy of this solution-model in your math notebook.

MODEL FOR SOLUTION: AN EQUATION WITH TWO VARIABLES

Question: What is the value of w in the following equation if $h = 1.5$?

1 Equation: $\dfrac{w}{h^2} = 20$

2 Information: $h = 1.5$

$h^2 = 1.5 \times 1.5 = 2.25$

3 Substitute: $\dfrac{w}{2.25} = 20$

4 Solve: $\dfrac{w}{2.25} \times 2.25 = 20 \times 2.25$

Solution: $w = 45$

5 Check by Substitution: $\dfrac{45}{2.25} = 20$

$20 = 20$

Target Practice 2: Your Turn to Model

Question: What is the value of w if $h = 2$ in this equation?

Equation: $\dfrac{w}{h^2} = 27$

Work this one out in your notebook. Set up your calculations using this format:

Solution: $w = $ _____

> 1 Equation _____
> 2 Information _____
> _____
> 3 Substitute _____
> 4 Solve _____
> _____
> 5 Solution _____
> Check by Substitution _____

TARGET Writing Equations: How to Speak of the Unknown

Question: If A = success, or A = value, how do you write the formula?

Answer: Use the language, tools, and rules of algebra.

The Mystery of the UNKNOWN

When you are asked to calculate the answer to a problem in which all the number information (except the answer) is *known,* the tools of arithmetic are all you need. But when a question is asked and some of the number information you need is missing (*unknown*), you can use the tools of algebra to figure out the solution. The steps are as follows:

1 Read the problem statement.

2 Translate that statement into an equation, using letters for number information that is missing.

3 Solve the equation for the unknown—using the mechanics of inverse operations.

Activity 1: Read and Translate—Words to Equations

Target Practice 1: What's My Number?

Use the letter n for the word *number*. Use the equal sign in place of *is*, *get*, or *give*.

Statement:	A number is **twice as large as** 14.
Translation/Equation:	n = 2×14
Solution:	n = 28

Translate these word statements to equations with unknowns. Solve for the solution.

1 My number, increased by 52, is 86.
   Equation: _____

   What's my number?
   Solution _____

2 Three times my number plus 1 is 10.
   Equation: _____

   What's my number?
   Solution _____

3 My number squared plus 5 is 30.
   Equation: _____

   What's my number?
   Solution _____

4 If you multiply my number by 10, you will get –30.
   Equation: _____

   What's my number?

   Solution _____

Names of Unknowns: Who Gets to Choose the Letters?
Y*ou* do when you are the "translator."

Target Practice 2: Translate Words to Algebraic Expressions

Follow this procedure for statements A and B in the 4 exercises that follow:

   A Underline the <u>words</u> that stand for an *unknown* value. Give the unknown a letter name (variable).
   B Use the variable *in combination with information in this statement* to write an algebraic expression.

1
   A The <u>number of kittens</u> born to Joey's cat _____
   B The number of kittens *left after Joey gave away 3* _____

2

    A The weight of Jack's truck _____

    B The truck's weight after being loaded with 550 pounds of lumber _____

3

    A Sal's hourly wage _____

    B Sal's wages for a 48 hour week _____

4

    A Skip's bowling average_____

    B A bowling average 15 points higher than Skip's_____

Template for Solutions:
A New Variation
Use this version of the template as you translate and solve word problems that require algebraic equations.

Note: **A new line has been added to the top for naming the variables involved.**

1. Variables _____
2. Equation _____
3. Information _____
_____
4. Substitute _____
5. Solve _____
_____
_____
6. Solution _____
✔ by Substitution _____

Activity 2: Put It All Together—Translations to Solutions

Read the statements below. Assign a symbol to each variable. <u>Underline</u> the words that describe the *relationship* of the variables to each other. These words inform you how to write the equation. Use *additional information* that you find in the question statement. Substitute it in the equation and find the solution to the question. Follow this model:

Statement: Your cat <u>is 2.5 pounds heavier</u> than my cat:

    A Variables: y = your cat; m = my cat

    B Equation: $y = 2.5 + m$ (the relationship between *unknown* and *known* information)

Question: If *my cat weighs 5 pounds,* what does your cat weigh?

Equation:	$y = 2.5 + m$
Information (found in the question statement):	$m = 5$
Substitute:	$y = 2.5 + 5$
Solve/Solution:	$y = 7.5$
Check by Substitution:	$7.5 = 2.5 + 5$
	$7.5 = 7.5$

Target Practice 1: Follow the Model

1 Statement: Cindy *is* 3 years *younger than* Daisy.
   A Variables: Cindy = _____ Daisy = _____
   B Translation/Equation: _____ (What is the age relationship?)

2 Question: When *Cindy is 91,* how old will Daisy be?
   Use the information in this question statement. Substitute it for one of the variables.
   A Substitution: _____
   B Solution: _____ Does it check out?

3 Statement: Josh is 7 inches taller than Fran.
   A Variables: _____ _____
   B Translation/Equation: _____ (What is the height relationship?)

4 Question: If Fran just makes the height requirement of 42 inches to go on that roller coaster, how tall is Josh?
   A Substitution _____
   B Solution _____ Does it check out?

Target Practice 2: Solutions on Your Own

1 Eighty adults and children attended the Company Picnic. There were 4 times as many children as adults. How many adults attended the picnic?

   _____

2 Deanna and Carol decided to go into business together. They needed start-up money. Deanna was able to contribute 3 times as much money as Carol. In the first year, their business made a profit of $500,000 dollars (it was a hit.) If they split that profit between them according to the proportion of start-up money each contributed,
   A How much will Carol's share be? _____
   B Deanna's share? _____
   C Do you think they will decide to split the profit that way?

TARGET Graphing Relationships: Chart and Plot

Activity 1: Making Plans—How Fast and How Far?

Jen wants to join Dave on the bike ride to Crystal Lake, but she doesn't think she'll be able to keep up with him for the whole ride. She bikes a lot and knows her average speed is slower the longer she bikes. Jen does not want to be left behind, so she gets out her biking notebook. In the notebook, Jen has kept records of her average biking speeds after different length bike trips. She looks through it and starts to record the facts she knows in a chart.

Hours I spend biking	0	1	2	3	4	5	6
My average rate of speed	24						

Jen knows that she starts out biking at 24 mph, but after one hour her average speed usually falls to 22.5 mph. At 3 hours, her average speed is 19.5 mph. By 6 hours, her average speed is only 15 mph. How does she know this for sure? She has an odometer on her bike that measures average speeds.

Target Practice 1: Fill in Jen's Chart with Her Speed Data

Check your answers before you move on. Jen wants to know how far she can go in 4.3 hours, *and* how far behind Dave she might be at that time. She uses the same equation as Dave: $d = s \times t$ (distance = speed × time).

She knows $t = 4.3$ hours, but what value should she use for s? *For Jen, this variable is more variable over time.* How can she know what to put for her average speed if she knows it continues to slow down the longer she bikes? If Jen cannot figure out her correct average speed, then she cannot really be sure how far she can bike in 4.3 hours—*and* she will not know how far behind Dave she might end up. Can Jen figure this out, or should she just be prepared to be left in the dust?

What is the critical factor at work here?

Here is the key: The critical factor is *the amount of time spent biking.* Jen needs to figure out a separate equation for her speed. She needs to do something else to "see" what is going on with her speed as time passes. "I know!" she exclaims. "I'll graph it."

Activity 2: Plot to See (the Relationship of) Variables *s* and *t*

Jen will use her chart of data (above) as she plots her records of speed and time. She hopes the graph will *show* her the *true relationship* between these two variables.

Step 1: Jen sets up the structure for a line graph. She draws a horizontal line (the x-axis) near the bottom of a piece of graph paper. She meets it with a vertical line on its left side (the y-axis).

Step 2: Jen labels the horizontal line "Hours I have been biking" and spaces the numbers 1 through 6 evenly along it. Next, she labels the vertical line "My speed in mph" and spaces out the numbers 15 through 25.

Question: Why doesn't she start with 0 on the vertical line?

Answer: Because her biking speed records do not fall below 15.

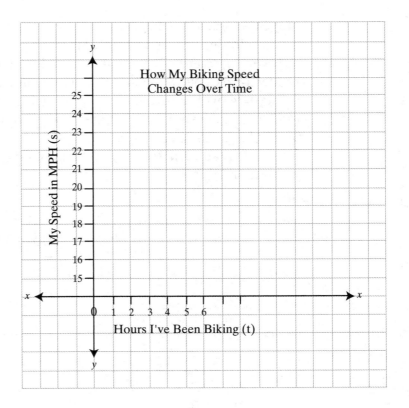

Target Practice 1: Make the Line Graph along with Jen

Use the grid below, or get out your own graph paper, and create the same graph Jen is drawing. Follow her example in Steps 1 and 2. Then go on to Step 3.

Step 3: Jen records her personal biking rate as points on the graph. This is called "plotting the data points." Here is how to do it: Refer to the number data you wrote in Jen's chart above. Find the line labeled 0 hour on the horizontal x-axis. Follow the line up until you are at 24 on the y-axis. Mark that point (0, 24) with a big dot. Next, find the line labeled 1 hour and follow it up to 22.5 (1, 22.5) Mark it. Continue, looking for the next two points indicated by the data in the chart.

Do you see what Jen sees as she looks at the way the points fall? There seems to be a trend.

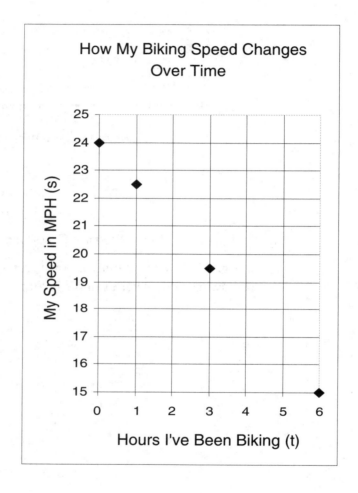

Jen sees that the data points *seem to fall in a straight line.* Do your points do the same? If your points do *not* seem to fall in a straight line, double-check the way you plotted them.

Question: What do you call it when plotted points fall in a straight line?

—————

Answer: You call them <u>line</u>ar. The <u>line</u> is on the graph and the <u>line</u> is in the word as well.

What a line. Just make sure that the line is a straight one. Curved lines don't count.

FYI

When the relationship between two variables forms a *straight* line on a graph, that relationship can be expressed by a simple equation. The term for an equation expressing this kind of relationship is *linear equation* (in other words, an equation that can be graphed as a straight line).

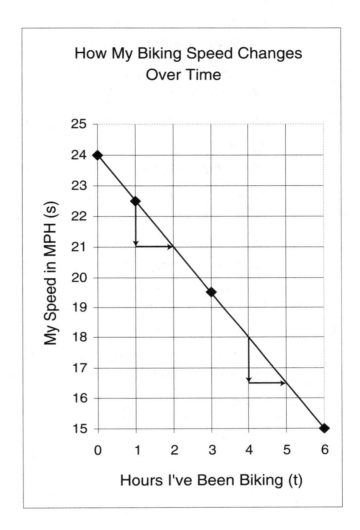

How My Biking Speed Changes Over Time

My Speed in MPH (s)

Hours I've Been Biking (t)

Finish up your line graph by connecting the points. Jen can see on the graph that her average speed (*s*) falls 1.5 mph for every hour (*t*) biked. She believes her average speed at any time can be expressed by this equation:

$$speed = 24 - 1.5\,t$$
or
$$s = 24 - 1.5\,t$$

See it. Measure it:

The arrow lines, which form right triangles under the trend line, help you measure what the trend line shows.

↓ The vertical line measures 1.5: the amount Jen's speed falls in mph.

→ The horizontal line measures 1: the time over which the slow-down in speed occurs.

Target Practice 2: True or False?

Make sure this equation holds true. To do so:

1 Substitute the following times for t in the equation: $s = 24 - 1.5\,t$.

2 Solve for s. Write your solution on the blank.

3 Third: Check your solution against the line in the graph above. Your solution should be a point on that trend line.

For example: At the zero hour, what is Jen's biking speed? Substitute 0 for t in the equation: $s = 24 - 1.5\,t$

- If $t = 0$ hour, what is her average speed?
  $\underline{\quad s = 24 - 1.5\,(0) \quad s = 24 - 0 \quad s = 0 \text{ mph} \quad}$ Check the graph. (T) or F?

1. If $t = 0$ hour, what is her average speed?
  $\underline{\quad s = 24 - 1.5\,(.5) \quad s = \quad\quad\quad\quad\quad\quad\quad}$ Check the graph. T or F?

2. If $t = 2$ hours, what is her average speed?
  $\underline{\quad s = 24 - 1.5\,(.2) \quad s = \quad\quad\quad\quad\quad\quad\quad}$ Check the graph. T or F?

3. If $t = 4$ hours, what is her average speed?
  $\underline{\quad\quad\quad\quad\quad\quad\quad\quad\quad\quad\quad\quad\quad\quad\quad\quad}$ Check the graph. T or F?

4. If $t = 5$ hours, what is her average speed?
  $\underline{\quad\quad\quad\quad\quad\quad\quad\quad\quad\quad\quad\quad\quad\quad\quad\quad}$ Check the graph. T or F?

Now Jen can solve for d using the formula $d = s \times t$ because she has figured out how to represent her *true* speed over time.

Formula:	$d =$	$s \times t$
Facts:		$t = 4.3$ hours
		$s = 24 - 1.5\,t$ mph
		$= 24 - (1.5 \times 4.3)$ mph
		$= 24 - (6.45)$ mph
		$= 17.55$ mph
Substitute:	$d =$	17.55 mph $\times 4.3$ hours
Solution:	$d =$	75.465 miles

Jen sees that she will be able to bike 75.465 miles in 4.3 hours. Rounding those miles to the nearest half mile, she figures she will probably be at mile 75.5 after 4.3 hours. That means she will be a little more than 10 miles behind Dave who will have finished 86 miles by then.

If Dave is smart, he will slow down a little.

Answer Key: Section 3, Lesson 8

TARGET Logic at Work: The Tale of the Scale

ACTIVITY 1: Planning for R_1 and R_2

TARGET PRACTICE: TRAVEL ALONG, FILL IN THE FACTS

Way 1:

Eric's apartment		Dave's apartment		Crystal Lake

__17__ miles

__17__ miles

= __34__ miles   + __52__ miles   = __86__ miles

Miles	20	40	60	80	+6 miles
Hours	1	2	3	4	+6 miles at __20__ mph =

4 hours will get Dave to __80__ miles, plus __3/10*__ of an hour more for the 6 miles   *(or 0.3)__

<u>The Result:</u> Travel time by bike one way __4.3__ hours. Round trip, __8.6__ hours. Practically speaking, better round that up to 9 hours for travel time.

Way 2:

Picture this: Biking to Eric's place is __17__ miles. Back again is another __17__. That adds up to __17__ + __17__ = __34__ miles for that part of the trip. Then it's another __52__ miles to the lake = __86__ miles altogether. Biking __20__ miles each hour for 4 hours looks like __20__ + __20__ + __20__ + __20__, which will get him to __80__ miles in 4 whole hours. Then he has __6__ more miles to go @ __20__ mph which will take __6__ / __20__ or __3/10__ of an hour. <u>The Result:</u> Travel time by bike one way— __4__ and __3/10__ hours. Double that for a round-trip, the total is __8__ and __3/5__ hours. Rounded up to the nearest hour, that's about __9__ hours travel time.

Way 3:

Facts: $d =$ __86__ miles

                          $r =$ __20__ mph

                          $t =$ __?__ hours

Substitute: $t = 86/20$

Solve for t: $t = 4.3$

Solution: $t =$ **4.3** hours

Check by Substitution:

$$time = distance/rate$$

$$4.3 = 86/20$$

$$4.3 = 4.3$$

The Result: Travel time by bike one way will be __4.3__ hours. Round-trip, __8.6__ hours. Practically speaking—allow at least __9__ hours for travel time.

Any way you look at it, it figures. Based on the numbers, Dave makes the decision to go ahead with his plans. If he leaves his apartment at 7 A.M., he can get to the lake by about __11:30__ A.M. That gives him about __4__ hours to eat, swim, fish, and sun before heading back home. He should probably start biking at __3:30__ P.M. __8__ P.M.

Which way was the best way for you to work through this situation? __Answers will vary.__ ~~in order to arrive~~ before sundown at

Activity 2: Relationships Can Be Rearranged . . .

TARGET PRACTICE: VISUALIZE "THE TALE OF THE SCALE"
Did you use the active reading strategy? Would your "mind-movie" film be nominated for an Oscar?

Activity 3: Take Opposite Action; Operate Inversely

TARGET PRACTICE 1: PRACTICE ISOLATION
1. subtraction;
   addition;

$$Y - X = Z$$
$$\underline{+ X = Z + X}$$
$$Y \quad = Z + X \qquad \text{or, } Z + X = Y$$

2. Think: multiplication; division;
   Do It: $C = \pi \times diameter$
   $C/\pi = \pi/\pi \times diameter$
   $C/\pi = diameter \qquad \text{or, } diameter = C/\pi$

3. Think: addition; subtraction;
   Do it: $F = 1.8\,C + 32$
   $$\underline{-32 = -32}$$
   $$F - 32 = 1.8C$$

Think Again: multiplication; division

Do it:
$$\frac{F - 32}{1.8} = \frac{1.8C}{1.8}$$

$$\frac{F - 32}{1.8} = C \qquad \text{or, } C = \frac{F - 32}{1.8}$$

TARGET PRACTICE 2: MOVE IT ON YOUR OWN
1. $b = A + c$
2. $S = Q - R$
3. $y = 7x$
4. A
5. C
6. 18 feet

Activity 4: $c = n \times r$

TARGET PRACTICE: WHICH IS THE BEST BUY?
1. $0.60
2. $0.42
3. $0.34

TARGET Algebraic Equations: Where There's a System, There's a Way

Activity 1: One-step Solutions

TARGET PRACTICE: GO DIRECTLY TO SOLVE
1. $n = 6 \times 15 = 90$
2. $j = 1{,}000 - 25 = 975$
3. $y = -10 + 12 = +2$ (or just 2)
4. $p = 45/15 = 3$
5. $n = 10 \times 2/1 = 20$

Activity 2: Make It Simple If You Can

TARGET PRACTICE 1: SIMPLIFY BY COMBINING LIKE TERMS
1. $5xy + 7x$
2. $6z + 10 + 6z = 12z + 10$
3. $8x - 16 - 6x - 3 = 2x - 19$
4. $19 + c + 7d$

TARGET PRACTICE 2: SIMPLIFY, THEN SOLVE
1. $x = 2$
2. $c = 5$
3. $R = 3$
4. $y = 1$

Activity 3: Follow This System

TARGET PRACTICE 1: BE A COPY CAT
Note to student: You can use this "copy-to-learn" method for other subjects, too. Just make sure that the model you choose to use is a good one.

TARGET PRACTICE 2: YOUR TURN—TRY IT WITH A DIFFERENT VALUE
$w = 108$

Activity 1: Read and Translate: Words to Equations

TARGET PRACTICE 1: WHAT'S MY NUMBER?

1. $n + 52 = 86$ $n = 34$
2. $3n + 1 = 10$ $n = 3$
3. $n^2 + 5 = 30$ $n = 5$
4. $10n = -30$ $n = -3$

TARGET PRACTICE 2: TRANSLATE WORDS TO EQUATIONS

A = Your letter   B = Your letter in relationship

Note: The letters used in these answers are samples. Your answers are correct as long as your letter has the same relationship to the number as the sample letters do below.

1.
    A <u>number of kittens</u> k
    B $k - 3$ (left after Joey gave away three)

2.
    A <u>weight of Jack's truck</u> t
    B $t + 550$ (loaded with 550 pounds)

3.
    A <u>hourly wage</u> w
    B $48w$ (for a 48 hour week)

4.
    A b <u>Skip's bowling average</u>
    B $b + 15$ (15 points higher than)

Activity 2: Put It All Together—Translations to Solutions

TARGET PRACTICE 1: FOLLOW THE MODEL

Note: The names of your variables may be different, but the translation and solutions will be the same

1. Cindy <u>is 3 years *younger than*</u> Daisy.
    A Cindy = C   Daisy = D
    B $C = D - 3$

2. When <u>Cindy is 91</u>, how old will Daisy be?
    A $91 = D - 3$
    B $D = 94$

3. Josh is <u>7 inches taller than</u> Fran.
    A Josh = J   Fran = F
    B $J = F + 7$

4. If Fran <u>just makes the height requirement of 42 inches</u> to go on that roller coaster, how tall is Josh?
    A $J = 42 + 7$
    B $J = 49$

1. 16 adults a = adults; c = children

$$a + c = 80$$
$$c = 4a$$
$$a + 4a = 80$$
$$5a = 80$$
$$a = 16$$

2.

A Carol's share: $125,000   C = Carol's contribution to start-up money

D = Deanna's contribution to start-up money

B Deanna's share: $375,000

$$C + D = \$500,000$$
$$D = 3C$$
$$C + 3C = \$500,000$$
$$4C = \$500,000$$
$$C = \$125,000$$
$$D = 3C$$
$$D = 3\,(\$125,000) = \$375,000$$

C Not a chance! Actually, how Deanna and Carol decide to split the profits will depend on many other variables, such as the number of hours each worked in the business that year, the value of their contributions toward its success in terms of creativity, problem-solving, customer relations, and so on. Imagine the possible variables.

TARGET Graphing Relationships: Chart and Plot

Activity 1: How Fast and How Far?

TARGET PRACTICE: FILL IN JEN'S CHART

0	1	2	3	4	5	6
24	22.5		19.5			15

Activity 2: Plot it to See . . . Variables s and *t*

TARGET PRACTICE 1: MAKE THE LINE GRAPH ALONG WITH JEN
How is your graph turning out?

TARGET PRACTICE 2: TRUE OR FALSE?

1. $24 - 0.75 = 23.25$ T
2. $24 - 3.0 = 21$ T
3. $24 - 6 = 18$ T
4. $24 - 7.5 = 16.5$ T

Language

LESSON 1: Surprises

When Mike Rinaldi first interviewed for a job at Ace Computer Chip Company, he wondered why the Human Resources Manager, Sue Mendez, asked him about school subjects. You recall that Mike liked and excelled in math and computer courses. He did not like his English courses, especially writing. He thought that he was finished with English composition when he started working at Ace Computer. He was wrong.

The first surprise occurred when he enrolled at Brightwater Community College.

Words to Know

Matriculating	Enrolling at a college
Inflammatory	Able to arouse strong emotion
Employee evaluation	A written or oral statement of the employee's work

New Information

Sue had prepared Mike by giving him information about the college. He recalled that Ace Computer had an alliance with Brightwater. Mike was still surprised by the fact that he was required to take the TABE, which, of course, included a test of his English language skills. He even asked Sue if he could skip that test. After all, he was just going to be working on the computer. Sue answered, "Mike, as I told you, our agreement with Brightwater Community College allows you to take any course that Ace does not offer in its training program. However, the college still requires that all *matriculating* students take the TABE for placement in courses."

Mike was almost afraid to ask the next logical question, but he did. He asked, "What kind of writing will I have to do for the company?" Mike's next surprise was to learn that he would have to write weekly summaries and monthly reports of his work. He would write even more if he wanted to advance in the company. In fact, his skill in handling those reports would be reflected in his *employee evaluations*. He had no idea how the reports were done. Ms. Mendez, suspecting that this was a surprise to Mike, told him that either she or Alicia Buchanan would work with him on the first few reports that he submitted.

At Brightwater Community College, Mike saw Michelle frequently. They talked about her progress in pursuing her goal to become a registered nurse. She, too, was concerned about the writing that she would be doing at the job she hoped to get some day. At the moment she was concentrating on writing a résumé. She needed to find a new part-time job that would accommodate her school schedule. Eventually, Michelle and Mike found themselves—and each other—in a business/career writing course. At its second meeting, the entire class took a language pretest not unlike the one you are about to experience. But first, students took a few minutes to think about writing in their lives. You should start by filling out the form that follows.

Reflection: Writing in My Daily Life

I estimate that I write _____ hours a week, including reminder notes or lists for myself and notes or letters to communicate with others.

I estimate that I write _____ hours a week for work-related tasks.

I enjoy writing _____.

I want to improve my ability to write _____ for my personal satisfaction.

I want to improve my ability to write _____ for job or career advancement.

Composition

I am able to organize my thoughts and express myself clearly when I need to write

Instructions:	___Yes	___No	___Need practice	___I don't know
Business letters:	___Yes	___No	___Need practice	___I don't know
Reports:	___Yes	___No	___Need practice	___I don't know

I understand the meaning of "Standard English" and can recognize it when I read it

___Yes ___No ___Need practice ___I don't know

Editing

I am able to correct ___Yes ___No ___Need practice ___I don't know
my own writing:

	Yes	No	Need practice	I don't know
I know how to check it for				
Plan, purpose, and tone	___	___	___	___

	Yes	No	Need practice	I don't know
Correct use of words	___	___	___	___
Complete sentences	___	___	___	___
Organized paragraphs	___	___	___	___
Spelling	___	___	___	___
Punctuation	___	___	___	___
Capitalization	___	___	___	___

Spelling

I am able to identify the correct spelling of a word when I am given more than one choice.   ___Yes ___No ___Need practice ___I don't know

I can identify the correct spelling of a word by the way it "looks."   ___Yes ___No

I can identify the correct spelling of a word by knowing the rules.   ___Yes ___No ___Need to review the rules

I know how to use a Spell-Checker   ___Yes ___No ___Need practice

Language Skills Assessment

Read the following memo. Use it to answer Questions 1 to 3.

> **MEMO**
>
> Date: December 11 2002
>
> From: Steve Forrest, Sales Manager
>
> To: Staff
>
> Subject: Holiday party
>
> The Christmas holiday will be here very soon. Brown Auto Maintenance's management invites all employees to dinner on December 13th. Betsy Murphy our favorite party planner has reserved The Willows at 7 P.M. To help the company plan please sign up for the dinner by the 5th of the month. Let me know if you have any questions.

1 Choose the phrase that needs a comma.

   A sign up for the dinner,

   B December 11, 2002

   C Let me know

   D Subject: Holiday party,

2 A comma should appear in which line?

   A To staff

   B In the third line of the message, after *Murphy* and after *planner*.

   C After *questions* in the last line.

   D After *MEMO*.

3 A comma should be inserted following the words

   A To help the company plan

   B The Christmas holiday

   C Let

   D None of the above

Read these paragraphs from a company manual. Each is a segment taken from a longer discussion. For Questions 4 through 13, look at the numbered underlined parts and choose a word or phrase that best fills those spaces.

> **Company Manual**
> Preparing for Meetings
>
> (4) <u>Meetings is</u> an essential part of every business environment. We want every meeting (5) <u>you</u> attend to be productive and <u>taking place</u> in a positive environment. One of the best ways you can assure a productive meeting is to prepare an agenda. All attendees should know, in advance, the purpose and direction of the meeting.

4

    A   Some meetings is

    B   Meetings is scheduled

    C   Every busyness environment schedule meetings

    D   Meetings are

5

    A   to take place

    B   to taking place

    C   in place

    D   None of the above

Managing Conflict

(6) How do we manage conflict among staff at Davenport Health Care <u>Center.</u> First, we take the emphasis off people and concentrate on gathering ideas. We discourage (7) statements <u>such as "Bill,</u> why did you ever decide to close the recreation room between 7 P.M. and 9 P.M.? You know very well that that is (8) <u>our residents'</u> favorite hour to use the facility. How could you do that?"

6

    A   Center?

    B   Center!

    C   , Center.

    D   Center;

7

    A   such, as "Bill

    B   such as, "Bill

    C   such as Bill

    D   Correct as is

8

    A   our resident's

    B   hour residents'

    C   our residents

    D   Correct as is

(9) What does it mean to take the emphasis off people and <u>then concentrating</u> on gathering ideas? To begin, it means that the leader of the group diffuses personal statements by redirecting attention to gathering facts. For example, in the situation (10) detailed above, what could the leader or a participant say <u>and that would</u> get to the (11) facts yet not be *inflammatory?* Think about how this would work<u>; Let's</u> look at our daily schedule. When can we free the recreation room for residents' use?

9

    A   go on to

    B   in order to concentrate on

    C   and what if we concentrate on

    D   concentrate with

10

    A   that would

    B   and do you think that would

    C   and that wouldn't

    D   and that would likely

11

  A , "Let's

  B , Let's"

  C ? "Let's

  D : "Let's

For Questions 12 and 13, read the paragraphs from a progress report. In each case, choose the sentence that best fills the blank in the paragraph.

12 _____. As the committee predicted, we will have the new procedure in place by January 1. Our first task was to choose several new suppliers. Now, three months before our start date, we have lined up all the suppliers we need.

  A Our plan to revamp the stock ordering system is progressing according to schedule.

  B We have just begun to plan our approach to choosing new suppliers.

  C Yesterday, I met with the committee for the first time.

  D There are no suppliers who want to do business with us.

13 The companies we chose have excellent records for on-time, on-budget deliveries. In addition, they will guarantee to deliver stock to us two to three days faster than our former supplier did. _____.

  A We can't say that these new companies ever deliver on schedule.

  B Since speed of delivery is not important to us, we chose companies based on different *criteria*.

  C Better service to us will result in our giving our customers the faster service they demand.

  D Fortunately for our company, service to our customers is no longer important.

Read the following sentences. For Questions 14 through 19, choose the sentence that is written correctly *and* shows the correct capitalization and punctuation.

14

  A The employees, and the owner, and some of the management.

  B One of those employees is giving a talk on benefits she offers very important information.

  C They'll all meet at dinnertime to talk about the seminars.

  D Know that the main speaker is the vice president of the United States.

15

  A Will and me gave our shopping list to someone else that was not complete.

  B After walking for a very long time, Will and me gave up.

  C Me and Elezondo was fixing the tire lying in the dirt.

  D Looking intently at the computer system on display, we both had the same question.

16

A Ann asked the manager about the team's performance reviews and she had very little to say.

B I told the operator that John's phone was not working.

C Let your customers know that they're looking for feedback.

D New manuals should not be given to Teams until they have been checked into the company library.

17

A On the northeast corner of Simpson Avenue, you will see a new office building.

B She wrote a book called, "Adventures of a house Cat."

C He said, "don't forget to meet me in the cafeteria at 12 sharp!"

D She replied, "If I can't be there on time, i'll call you?"

18

A The Officer thanked them for their loyalty, dedication and because they never left their stations during the blackout.

B This computer is fast, user-friendly, and able to handle all of the applications.

C Let's give more emphasis to education, training, and then we can throw in some travel experiences.

D Why don't you choose your courses, sign up for them, and then you'll meet us for dinner.

19

A Pick up the following supplies; 2 dozen pencils, 6 legal pads, and cartridge for my printer.

B Mr. Sadwin; from Illinois, is a member of the house of representatives.

C I dislike one of my office mates; however, I don't allow that to effect how well I do my job.

D I never did expect my boss to be my best friend; just to be fair.

For Questions 20 through 22, choose the answer that best completes the sentence.

20 An estimate of costs for new bathrooms, office furniture, and window treatments _____ beyond the scope of this report.

A are

B is

C are going

D are spiraling

21 We think this fabric is _____ than the one we originally chose.

A more appropriate

B most appropriate

C more appropriater

D more better

22 Many of our best ideas _____ left out of the final version of the report.

    A was

    B is

    C has been

    D were

In Questions 23 and 24, read the underlined sentences. Then choose the answer that best combines those sentences into one.

23 <u>We could not locate the file.</u>
<u>The file was missing.</u>

    A We could not locate the file, it was missing.

    B We could not locate the file and it was missing.

    C We could not locate the file ever since it was missing.

    D We could not locate the file because it was missing.

24 <u>Finally, one of the associates recalled what had happened.</u>
<u>It was that her secretary had taken it home to retype.</u>

    A Finally, one of the associates recalled that her secretary had taken it home to retype.

    B Finally, one of the associates recalled that she had asked her secretary to take it home to retype. And she did that.

    C Finally, one of the associates recalled a secretary she volunteered to take it home to retype.

    D Finally, one of the associates recalled what had happened. It was that her secretary had refused to take it home to retype.

For Question 25 choose the word or phrase that best completes the sentence.

25 Whoever calls the _____ has the advantage of an early appointment.

    A sooner

    B more sooner

    C most soonest

    D soonest

To the Student: As you check your answers, record the results in this chart. Use the three columns next to the Answer Key to mark your answers as *Correct, Error,* or *Skipped.* Use the other columns to record additional information you want to remember about the individual questions. Total the number of your responses in each column at the bottom of the chart. Then read the recommendations that follow.

Language Skills Assessment: Answers and Skills Analysis

Item Answers	Correct T	Error X	Skipped O	I have this question.	I need instruction.	Refer to these lessons.	Reading Skill Categories*
1 B						1	32
2 B						5	26
3 A						5	26
4 D						2	4
5 A						6	13
6 A						5	25
7 B						5	29
8 D						5	30
9 B						6	13
10 A						6	13
11 D						5	29
12 A						6	15
13 C						6	16
14 C						2	12
15 D						2	1
16 B						2	2
17 A						5	20
18 B						5	26
19 C						5	27
20 B						2	4
21 A						4	6
22 D						5	29
23 D						6	12
24 A						6	12
25 D						4	6
TOTALS	correct	errors	skipped	Questions	Instruction	Lessons	Skills

*Key to Language Skill Categories
1 Usage
2 Antecedent Agreement

3 Tense
4 Subject/Verb Agreement
5 Easily Confused Verbs
6 Adjective
7 Adverb
8 Choose Between Adjective/Adverb
9 Use Negatives
10 Sentence Formation
11 Sentence Recognition
12 Sentence Combining
13 Sentence Clarity
14 Paragraph Development
15 Topic Sentence
16 Supporting Sentences
17 Sequence
18 Unrelated Sentence
19 Connective/Transition
20 Capitalization
21 Proper Noun
22 Name
23 Title of Work
24 Punctuation
25 End Mark
26 Comma
27 Semicolon
28 Writing Conventions
29 Quotation Marks
30 Apostrophe
31 City/State
32 Letter Part

Note: These broad categories of reading skills are broken down into subskill categories. Question numbers are aligned with the subskill titles as well as the lesson to which you can return for a review.

Language Skills Analysis

USAGE

PRONOUN

Subjective   15   (See Lesson 2)

Objective

Possessive

NAME	
Geographic Name	
TITLE OF WORK	
PUNCTUATION	(See Lesson 5)
END MARK	
Question Mark	6
COMMA	
Series	
Appositive	2
Introductory Element	3
Parenthetical Expression	
SEMICOLON	19
WRITING CONVENTIONS	(See Lesson 5)
QUOTATION MARKS	11, 22
Comma with Quotation	7
End Marks with Quotation	
APOSTROPHE	
Possessive	8
CITY/STATE	
LETTER PART	
Date	1
Address	
Salutation	
Closing	

To discover your areas of skills improvement in the Language Section, do three things:

1. Total your number of correct answers out of the 25 possible answers. You should have 90 to 95 percent correct (or 23 correct answers).
2. Total the number of correct answers in each subset of skills. For example, in the subset *Comma,* there are three correct answers. To score a passing grade, you should have 95 percent correct (or at least 2 correct answers).
3. Wherever your score is below 95 percent, go back to that lesson (indicated in parentheses) and review the skill.

Mike and Michelle met for coffee to compare notes about their first writing assignment. The assignment had just been returned, and neither of them looked too happy. As a matter of fact, they decided that they both had a lot of work to do to bring their work up to a higher standard.

Mike was puzzled about some of the errors and the teacher's markings. "What's wrong with this part?" Mike asked Michelle. Michelle read the following from Mike's assignment, a personal statement on a résumé:

"I really enjoy learning new business software. Me and my friends keep up with all the new developments."

Michelle thought she knew what was wrong with the second sentence. Do you? Read on for answers to your questions.

Words to Know

Perceived	Noticed in a special way
Image	Picture
Résumé	A summary of work and education

The Bottom Line

Whenever we speak or write, we put ourselves on display. We want to be perceived in a positive way. Errors in writing and speaking, however, project a negative image. Can we allow a résumé to go out with errors in usage or spelling? At work, should we send memos that have punctuation or grammatical errors? We need to ask ourselves what we can do about it. In this section we will answer that question for you as you read about the most common errors made by writers and speakers of English.

Years ago, your English teachers probably tried to convince you that it was important for you to understand English grammar. You may have hated the subject then. If you did, you probably feel the same way now. The bad news is that you will still need to learn some basics of English grammar. The good news is that you already know much more than you think you do. We'll help you put that knowledge to work.

The first thing you need to do is look at your results on the language pretest. Find the areas of obvious weakness. The chart on page 221 will help you to sort out your strengths and weaknesses. Although we suggest that you review all of the language areas covered in this section, remember to pay special attention to the items that you found difficult.

Let's begin by observing that you *do* know a great deal about English; otherwise, how would you be constructing English sentences from the moment you get up in the morning until you go to sleep at night (and in your dreams as well). And therein lies the secret: You know a great deal about constructing English sentences; you started learning how to do this complicated task from the time you were born. However, what you may not know is that the words in those English language sentences can be explained in at least two ways—that is, by using their names and by knowing their jobs.

We have a *name* for each of the words in the sentence below, for example, *noun, pronoun, verb, adjective, article,* and so on.

1. Article Adjective Noun Verb Article Noun Preposition Article Noun

   The talented ballplayer hits the ball over the wall.

2. Each of those above-named words has a *job* to do in the sentences we construct. For example, nouns either function as performers or receivers (known in grammatical terms as the subject or the object), verbs are *action* or *being* words, pronouns are words that *take the place of other words,* adjectives *describe other words,* and so forth.

 FYI

FYI One very important kind of adjective is called an "article". We use articles, *the, an,* and *a,* all the time, including in the example sentence above.

Apply this to the above sentence.

Describes Subject Action Describes Object IntroPrep Describes Object
Phrase

The ballplayer hits the ball over the wall

You've probably forgotten—or never really learned—the names, definitions, and uses of grammatical terms. That's OK. We can help you become very competent users of English, written and spoken, with a limited emphasis on grammatical terms and rules. The grammatical terms and rules that you *do* learn will help you to write and speak correctly.

Starting with Sentences

Although you don't stop to name them, you know that you use different types of sentences when you write or speak. The following are all sentences and complete thoughts.

- The statement: You wrote that letter.
- The question: Did you write that letter?
- The exclamation: You wrote that letter!
- The command: Write that letter.

What do these sentences have in common? That is the subject of this lesson: performers (also known as subjects) and actions (also known as verbs) and how they work in sentences.

In the sentences above, which word tells you the *action* that is taking place? Everyone would probably agree that the action word is *write/wrote.*

Now, can we agree on who performs/performed the action? In the first three sentences, the *performer* is quite obvious: The word *You* is the performer. What about the fourth sentence? Because it is a command, it starts with the action word, *Write,* but where is the performer (subject)? The simple answer is that we understand that the performer is there, implied—the same *you* as in the other three sentences. When someone shouts a command at you,

Arrive on time tomorrow!

Hand in your papers.

Turn off the lights before you leave.

do you have any doubt about the performer in the command? Certainly not; it's *you.*

Subjects and Verbs: Singular and Plural

What else do you have to know about performers and actions? Essentially, you have to know that one affects the other, especially in time and number. What does this mean? It means, first of all, that actions agree with performers in number: singular or plural.

Mike drives to the college library.

What action do you see in this sentence? Of course, it is *drives.* Who performs the action? Mike does; he is the performer. What changes take place in the following sentence?

Mike and Michelle drive to the college library.

What is the action word? You are right again; it is *drive.* Who are the performers? Mike and Michelle are the two performers. That is why the action word takes a slightly different form: *drive* instead of *drives.*

This may not seem logical to you because an "s" at the end of a word in English often signals more than one, or plural. For example, look at these words that might function as performers:

Employee

Computer

Car

Textbook

How do you change these words to their plural forms? Add an "s" to each:

Employees

Computers

Cars

Textbooks

But what does an "s" at the end of an action word mean? It means just the opposite. You add an "s" to an action word in order to agree with the *singular* performer. You remove the "s" to agree with the plural performer. Most of the time, we seem to do this correctly and without even thinking. Sometimes we are fooled by an extra word or two in the sentence. For example:

An important characteristic of computers make them easy to use.

What is wrong with this sentence? Use the same technique as you did above, to decide whether or not the verb agrees with the subject in number. The sentence talks about the subject, *characteristic*. The subject is singular. What is the action word or verb? It is *make*. Put those two words together without extra words between them and how would you write them?

An important characteristic make them easy to use.

or

A characteristic makes them easy to use.

You probably know that the second sentence is the correct one just by the way it sounds. You also know that it is correct because you have just learned that an *s* at the end of the verb shows that it is singular. *Characteristic* is singular and *makes* is singular; they agree.

Practice 1

Read each sentence. Decide whether the subject and verb agree in number. Correct any errors. Only one sentence is correct. *Hint:* Don't be fooled by extra words found between the subject and the verb.

1 The flower, in addition to other greens, sit in water.

_____

2 This book, with hundreds of pages, needs your attention.

_____

3 A bank account in any of those branches pay a higher dividend.

_____

4 The magazine, *Consumer Guides,* sell all over the world.

_____

5 The customers on Terry's list needs a new car or truck.

_____

In the sentences above, all the subjects or performers, are expressed in one word: flower, book, account, magazine, and customers. At times, you want to write about more than one person or thing (a compound subject) in a sentence. That makes the subject plural, and the action word/verb follows suit. For example:

Clarissa and Mario open the office every day.

The action word/verb in the sentence is *open.* If the subject were *Clarissa,* how would the action word (verb) change? Remember what you read above. You add an *s* to the action word (verb) if the subject is singular.

Clarissa open*s* the office every day.

Now try these sentences. Circle the correct action word (verb).

Practice 2

1 Ceil (try/tries) to be on time.

2 Raoul and his brother never (misses/miss) an episode of Star Trek.

3 Marie and John (plan/plans) the company's picnic each summer.

4 Tomas (rewrites/rewrite) his résumé every six months.

5 Paper and paint (provides/provide) the children with activity.

More Challenges

What other subject-verb agreement challenges do you need to know about? A few word combinations cause many common writing and speaking errors.

- The subject contains an *either/or* combination. Think of the subject as *either* one *or* the other, which makes the subject singular. Choose a singular verb.

  Either Marie *or* John plans the company's picnic each summer.

                                    BUT

- The subject is compound and contains an either/or combination. The verb is singular or plural depending on the number of the second subject word.

  Either my brother or his children plan the reunion.

  Brother and *children* are the two subject words. *Children* is the second subject word and it is plural; therefore, the plural verb form, *plan,* is correct.

- The subject of the sentence is *any.* Any is singular and used when the choice involves three or more.

  Any of your classmates takes that responsibility.

  You will learn more about subject-verb errors in later lessons. For now, let's face the challenges in the following practice exercise.

Practice 3

Choose the correct verb in each sentence. If you are in doubt, look back to the instruction above.

1 Either this course or that one (fill/fills) the requirement.

2 Any one of those dresses (look/looks) suitable for a job interview.

3 Hattie and her daughter (eat/eats) lunch together every Saturday.

4 Either this book or the videos (make/makes) a wonderful gift.

5 Children and a dog (make/makes) me smile.

Practice 4—Review

Correct each sentence. Look for errors in subject-verb agreement in number, use of pronouns as subjects, and use of special constructions.

1 Me and Amy share recipes all the time.

_____

2 Amy and me share CDs, too.

_____

3 Amy and I walks in the park every day.

_____

4 Amy's dog need to walk in the park twice a day.

_____

5 Either Amy or a family member walk the dog.

_____

Practice 5

In this practice, look for statements that are not complete thoughts. Rewrite them. Some of the statements are complete thoughts and won't require rewriting.

1 Concerning my request for a raise.

_____

2 I'll defer my request until next year.

_____

3 Return the cart to the store!

_____

4 A full explanation at the end.

_____

5 In community colleges where certificate programs are available.

_____

Practice 6

Read the following paragraph taken from a memo. Nick Bucci wrote the memo on January 4, 2003. Find any errors. Rewrite the paragraph to correct those errors.

About the recycling program. We needs to discuss what our community is doing now. What do the community recycle? We should compare what we do to the national model we read about. Us and members of the town council should sit down to talk and plan. When do you think we can get together?

Something Else About Verbs

Verbs also indicate time, or what grammarians call *tense*. We can use any of the sentences from the exercises in this lesson to demonstrate the time or tense of verbs.

1. **Present:** Marie plans the company picnic each year.
   Past: Marie planned the company picnic each year.
   Future: Marie will plan the company picnic each year.
   Past with helping word, has, have, or had: Marie has planned the company picnic each year.

2. **Present:** Mike walks to the library.
   Past: Mike walked to the library.
   Future: Mike will walk to the library.
   Past with helping word, has, have, or had: Mike has walked to the library.

3. **Present:** Jack listens to the radio.
   Past: Jack listened to the radio.
   Future: Jack will listen to the radio.
   Past with helping word, has, have, or had: Jack has listened to the radio.

So far, this is probably very easy for you; you change verb forms—drive, drove, will drive—without even thinking about it. We say that these verbs change time in an organized, *regular* way. Think of yourself as doing any one of these actions. Place a pronoun in front of the verb to start. For example, *I plan* or *they plan*. Then continue from there.

Present	Past	Future	Past + Helping word, has, have, had
I plan	planned	will plan	has, have, had planned
You walk	walked	will walk	has, have, had, walked
listen	listened	will listen	has, have, had walked
count	counted	will count	has, have, had counted
use	used	will use	has, have, had used

You have probably used all of these verb forms for some time. You never think about the changes because they come naturally to you after all this time. If you look at them very carefully, however, a pattern emerges.

Present	Past	Future	Past + Helping word, has, have, had
They walk	They walk + ed	They walk + will	They walked (past form) + helping word (have walked)
count	count + ed	count + will	counted (past form) + helping word (has counted)

What changes occur in these action words in the past tense and with helping words? The answer, of course, is that you add an -*ed* to form the past tense. You add a forward-looking word, such as *will,* to the present tense, in order to form the future tense. You add a helping word to the past tense form to express the past tense that continues into the present. *(They have walked to work for three years.)* And you do all this without even thinking about it!

Why do we even bring this up if we handle this automatically and correctly? The answer is that we don't always. English takes some strange turns. And that is why you need to beware of the common verb use errors. We'll explore the topic further in the section entitled "There's More?"

Practice 7

Place these action words on the chart. The first word, *call,* is done for you.

Present	Past	Future	Past + Helping word, has, have, had
Call	called	will call	have called
Change			
check			
include			
use			
clean			

Practice 8

Fill each space with one of these action words. The sentences will give you clues to the time of the verb. Change the verb endings when necessary.

load   guide   trip   enter   arrive

1 Yesterday I _____ over that wire.

2 According to the chart, you will _____ the dishwasher every night this week.

3 As I _____ the room, I can see my favorite chair.

4 My newspaper has _____ on time every Sunday.

5 Your map _____ me to the campsite.

There's More?

It would be comforting to think that you now know everything you need to know about action words/verbs. Unfortunately, that is not the case. You recall that you worked with verbs that changed tense in a regular pattern—adding *-ed* to the past, and so forth. Now you need to learn about *irregular* action words/verbs. These are verbs whose spellings change to a greater degree in order to indicate tense. They are called *irregular* verbs—for a reason.

Many errors in writing and speaking occur because of these irregular verb changes. Study the list that follows to see if you use the correct forms. As you study the list, what one characteristic do you see that remains the same with every verb? Hint: Look at the future tense.

Present	Past	Future	Past + helping word, has, have, had
begin	began	will begin	have begun
bend	bent	will bend	have bent
bet	bet	will bet	have bet
bite	bit	will bite	have bitten
bring	brought	will bring	have brought
burst	burst	will burst	have burst
buy	bought	will buy	have bought
chose	chose	will chose	have chosen
cost	cost	will cost	have cost
dig	dug	will dig	have dug
dive	dived or dove	will dive	have dived
drink	drank	will drink	have drunk
drive	drove	will drive	have driven
fling	flung	will fling	have flung
fly	flew	will fly	have flown
forbid	forbade	will forbid	have forbidden
forget	forgot	will forget	have forgotten
freeze	froze	will freeze	have frozen
get	got	will get	have gotten
grind	ground	will grind	have ground
hang	hung	will hang	have hung
have	had	will have	have had
know	knew	will know	have known
lay (place)	laid	will lay	have laid
lend	lent	will lay	have lent
lie (recline)	lay	will lie	have lain
mistake	mistook	will mistake	have mistaken
ride	rode	will ride	have ridden
ring	rang	will ring	have rung
run	ran	will run	have run

Present	Past	Future	Past + helping word, has, have, had
see	saw	will see	have seen
seek	sought	will seek	have sought
send	sent	will send	have sent
shake	shook	will shake	have shaken
shine	shone	will shine	have shone
shrink	shrank	will shrink	have shrunk
sing	sang	will shrink	have shrunk
sink	sang	will sing	have shrunk
slide	slid	will slide	have slid
speak	spoke	will speak	have spoken
spin	spun	will spin	have spun
spring	sprang	will spin	have spun
steal	stole	will steal	have stolen
sting	stung	will sting	have stung
strike	struck	will strike	have struck
swear	swore	will swear	have sworn
swim	swam	will swim	have swum
swing	swung	will swing	have swung
take	took	will take	have taken
tear	tore	will tear	have taken
think	thought	will think	have thought
throw	threw	will throw	have thrown
wake	woke	will wake	have waken
weep	wept	will weep	have wept
wind	wound	will wind	have wound
wring	wrung	will wring	have wrung

Practice 9

Choose the correct form of the verb in each sentence. Look back at the list whenever you are in doubt about the correct form to use.

1 I (did/done) my homework very carefully.

2 Mac has (sing/sung) in the choir for years.

3 Lydia and Tomas have (teared/torn) up their credit cards.

4 Last summer, I (swimed/swam) a half mile every day.

5 I went home again because I had (forgot/forgotten) my license.

6 Our dog (shaked/shook) his wet fur furiously.

7 The recipe said that I should have (grinded/ground) the meat.

8 Betsy and David (drived/drove) over an hour a day to work.

9 The student (laid/lain) his paper on the teacher's desk.

10 For vacation, their family (flew/flown) to Disney World.

Practice 10—Review

Practice everything you have learned in Lesson 2. Correct the error in each sentence.

1 Me and my dog start every day with a long walk.

2 Either you or me will have to lend Barney lunch money.

3 Ted, Dan, and Jose (play/plays) on the company's softball team.

4 This office, plus people from the other building (share/shares) a parking lot.

5 Any of your choices (work/works).

Practice 11

Read the following paragraph. All of the sentences, except two, contain errors. Rewrite them to correct the problems.

> I have learnt that the English language has a history of changing. What's wrong usage today may be accepted years from now. Just takes a long time. Me and my friends struggle to learn the rules. For example, Mike and me always say, "We swimmed the mile race last summer." That might be right some day. Don't know if we can wait that long!

_____

_____

_____

_____

Answer Key: Section 4, Lesson 2

Practice 1
1. flower–sits
2. book–needs (Correct as it is.)
3. account–pays
4. magazine–sells
5. customers–need

Practice 2
1. tries
2. miss
3. plan
4. rewrites
5. provide

Practice 3
1. fills
2. looks

3. eat
4. make
5. make

Practice 4
1. Amy and I
2. Amy and I
3. walk
4. needs
5. walks

Practice 5
1. I am writing this memo concerning my request for a raise.
2. Correct
3. Correct
4. I have provided a full explanation at the end.
5. Adults attend community colleges where certificate programs are available.

Practice 6
From: Nick Bucci

Date: January 4, 2003

Subject: The recycling program (Avoid the incomplete sentence in the paragraph. Use this as the subject line of the memo.)

We need to discuss what our community is doing now. What does the community recycle? We should compare what we do to the national model we read about. Members of the town council and we should sit down to talk and plan. When do you think we can get together?

Practice 7

Call	called	will call	have called
Change	changed	will change	have changed
Check	checked	will check	have checked
Include	included	will include	have included
Use	used	will use	have used
Clean	cleaned	will clean	have cleaned

Practice 8
1. tripped
2. load
3. enter
4. arrived
5. guided

Practice 9

1. did
2. sung
3. torn
4. swam
5. forgotten
6. shook
7. ground
8. drove
9. laid
10. flew

Practice 10—Review

1. My dog and I start every day with a walk.
2. Either you or I will have to lend Barney lunch money.
3. play
4. shares
5. works

Practice 11

1. I have learned that the English language has a history of changing.
2. Change (or It) just takes a long time.
3. My friends and I struggle to learn the rules.
4. For example, Mike and I always say, "We swam the mile race last summer."
5. I don't know if we can wait that long!

LESSON 3: The Good News and the Bad News

Mike had been going to his computer class for several weeks. Not only did he thoroughly enjoy all the new information he was learning, but he was also happy to meet people with whom he had a lot in common.

Leaving computer class one day, a new friend, Tim McNeil, talked to Mike.

"I love this class. I enjoy it because I understand it. Now, English is completely different for me. I been speaking English my whole life and I ain't got a decent grade on my work yet!"

Mike answered, "I know what you mean, Tim. My friends and I are having the same problem, but I think that if we stick with it, we'll get the idea."

The good news is that Mike has learned to say, "My friends and I . . . ," but Tim still has some work to do in agreement of subjects and verbs. Did you find Tim's errors? Read on for an explanation.

Words to Know

| DVD | A compact disc that stores a large amount of information |
| Construction | The way in which something has been built |

Contraction	A shortened form of a word or words
Infamous	Having a bad reputation

Another Kind of Verb

Up to now, we have discussed only one kind of verb: an *action* word such as *write, return, plan, arrive, make, look,* and so forth. The subjects of the sentences did something. For example:

The batter hit the ball over the wall.

The action in this sentence is very clear: *hit.* Who did it? The *subject,* or *batter,* did it.

Now we will explore another type of verb that does not tell what the subject was doing. This verb tells what the subject was *being.* Some people call these *being verbs,* while others refer to them as *non-action* or *linking verbs.* For example:

The other team *was* angry.

You can see that there is no action in the sentence, but there is a description of how the team members *felt*—how they *were.* The verb, *was,* links *team* to the describing word, *angry.* (We go into more detail about words that describe in Lesson 4.)

The being verb, *was,* is a good place to start the discussion because we use it so much. It is, in fact, one of the forms of the very common linking verb, *to be.* There are a number of others that you will see listed later in this lesson. For now, we will start by listing all the forms of *be,* using the same chart that you worked with in Lesson 2. The chart combines tense (present, past, and so forth) with number (we use singular or plural pronouns as subjects). Again, it is a convenient way to show how the number of the subject changes the spelling of the linking verb. With pronouns as subjects, the authors can show subject-verb agreement in number. In your writing or speaking, you use whatever subject is appropriate.

Linking Verbs

Present	Past	Future	Past with helping words have, has, had
I *am*	*was*	*will be*	*have been*
You *are*	*were*	*will be*	*have been*
He, she, it, *is*	*was*	*will be*	*has been*
We *are*	*were*	*will be*	*have been*
They *are*	*were*	*will be*	*have been*

Consider yourself very fortunate if you have heard and spoken English since birth. Most of what you have seen above simply comes naturally to you. Imagine what it must be like to learn this as a second language—so many changes to memorize!

But don't become too comfortable. Common errors occur when people use non-action or linking verbs. How many times have you heard this doubleheader?

Me and Jim was on our way to work.

The first error, of course, is the infamous pronoun error. You can easily correct it by *mentioning Jim first* and *choosing a subject pronoun for yourself, I.* Now decide whether the subject—*Jim and I*—is a singular or plural subject. Yes, it is plural (there are two people in the subject), and it requires a plural non-action verb. Look back at the chart. If you substituted a pronoun for *Jim and I,* which one would it be? Of course, *we* would be the correct pronoun.

We were on our way to work.

We is a plural subject and *were* is the plural linking verb.

Practice 1

Choose a linking verb in each sentence. If you need help, look at the chart above.

1 Angelo (is/are) the biggest eater in our crowd.

2 We (was/were) not even close to his ability.

3 Only one of us (were/was) a big enough eater to compete. (*Hint:* Don't be fooled by words between the subject and linking verb.)

4 Bill and Ann (is/are) always late.

5 This new computer program (is/are) much easier to install than the last one was.

When you read the instruction above, you learned that non-action verbs are also called *linking* verbs. You will see how appropriate this name is when you consider what follows linking verbs. For example:

Don is handsome.

Les is president.

I was really angry at her.

They were sick for a week.

Tomorrow is Thanksgiving.

What is linked in each sentence? In each one, the subject is linked to one of two things: a describing word (handsome, angry, sick) or a word that means the same as the subject (president, Thanksgiving). Because of the linking verb, you can turn any of these sentences around and still make sense of the meaning.

Now take a look at a longer list of linking verbs.

Linking Verbs

are	am	appear	become
is	feel	seem	smell
was	were	grow	taste
be	sound	remain	

Practice 2

Fill each blank with a linking word from the list above. There may be more than one correct choice for some sentences.

1 My children _____ tired of that TV show.

2 Do you _____ as groggy as I do today?

3 I'll _____ president of the PTA for this year at least.

4 The first apples of Fall _____ tart and crispy.

5 Marge _____ sick.

Practice 3

Underline the linking verb in each sentence above. What does the linking verb link? Draw an arrow from the subject to the describing word or the word that means the same as the subject. The first one is done for you.

My children <u>are</u> tired of that TV show.

1

2

3

4

5

Practice 4

Read the sentences and decide if they are correct. Change any words that are used incorrectly.

1 These pies tastes so good.

2 We was here on time; where was you?

3 A DVD sound so much better than a video cassette.

4 Ron, Fred, and Barney feels left out.

5 Either a guitarist or a pianist are needed.

6 Ellen and Lacy is co-chairs of the event.

7 The dog is a terrier.

8 The scouts growed weary from climbing the mountain.

9 The Santos' and their dog is home after their vacation.

10 The appliances appears broken.

Linking Verbs and Pronouns

Pronouns create a usage problem for many people. Many of these problems have to do with linking verbs. Is the correct form, "It is I"? Or is it, "It is me"? Should you say, "It's between you and he"? Or is this correct? "It's between you and him." Is there an easy way to make these decisions? Actually, there is. Just by dividing pronouns into three groups, you will avoid, not all, but many pronoun problems.

In Lesson 2, you learned that words have names (noun, verb, and so forth) and they have jobs (subject, action or linking word, and so forth). You can explain pronouns in the same way. You know that pronouns (that is their name) take the place of nouns (that is their job). In addition, pronouns can be placed in three groups according to what they do.

Pronouns that Act	Pronouns that Are Acted Upon	Pronouns that Own or Follow the Linking Verb (Receive Action)
I	me	my, mine
you	you	your, yours
he, she, it	him, her	his, her, hers, its
we	us	our. ours
they	them	their, theirs
who	whom	whose

Look at these sentences. Some contain linking verbs and others have action verbs.

The new council president is *she*.   (*She* follows the linking verb and equals the *council president*.)

Our greatest resource is he.   (*he* follows the linking verb and equals *resource*)

I gave the appointment to *him*.   (*I* acts; *him* receives the action)

The lunch bag is *yours*.   (*yours* shows ownership)

Betty and *I* gave *you* an extra   (*I* acts; *you* receives the action)
day off this week.

 FYI

As you work with the sentences below, remember this: The pronoun that follows a linking verb either (1) describes the subject or (2) equals the subject.

Describes the subject: The new office is *ours. Ours* is an ownership pronoun. *Ours* describes office.

Equals the subject: The fastest runner is *she. She* equals the subject. The best test of the subject and the pronoun being equal is this: You can turn the sentence around and achieve the same meaning.

> *She* is the fastest runner.
> She is the new council president
> He is our greatest resource.

The authors know that most people do not answer the phone by saying, "Yes, this is he/she." In many cases, that would be too formal and not natural. You need to make a choice based on the situation. At those time when being casual is not appropriate, you need to know the correct pronoun form.

Practice 5

Choose the correct pronoun in each sentence.

1 It was (they, them) who stole the money!

2 The winner is (him, he).

3 Tina and (I, me) called you.

4 The Smiths are (them, they).

5 The winner is (who, whom)?

Practice 6—Review

Use all that you have learned to choose the correct pronoun in each sentence.

1 The child had a new dog; the child loved (her, she) immediately.

2 Shirley and (me, I) leave for lunch at exactly 1 PM.

3 A new lunch hour was set for Shirley and (me, I).

4 Mike and (him, he) plan to share an apartment.

5 It is (she, her) who committed the crime!

Another Group of Pronouns

Just as you thought you had met every pronoun, here is another group. *Indefinite* pronouns are used often, but they are different in an important way. They don't replace a specific noun. That is why they are called *indefinite*. For example:

Each has the right to choose one person.

Someone chose Lynn.

Just as subjects and verbs have to agree in number, so do pronouns and verbs:

Each has a new uniform. (*Each* is singular, *has* is singular)

Both have new uniforms. (*Both* is plural, *have* is plural)

The following list will help you to match indefinite pronouns with the correct verbs.

Indefinite Pronouns

Singular	Plural	Singular or Plural
any	many	some
anybody	few	all
each	plenty	most
everything	more	none
nothing	several	
either, neither	both	
much		
one		
someone		
more		
plenty		
less		

Practice 7

Choose a verb to agree with the indefinite pronoun in each sentence. The pronoun is italicized.

1 *Both* of the recipes (is, are) delicious.

2 *Anybody* (are, is) welcome to come.

3 *Few* (was, were) able to attend.

4 *One* of us (has, have) to take responsibility.

5 *Several* of us (is, are) leaving at the same time.

6 *None* of us (is, are) responsible for the damage. (Meaning none of us as individuals.)

7 *None* (was, were) sad about the results. (Meaning none of a group of people.)

Another Pronoun Problem

Another problem occurs when a pronoun comes later in the sentence but refers to something before it. The word the pronoun refers to is called the *antecedent.* You learned that subjects and verbs must agree in number. The same rule applies to a pronoun and its *antecedent.* For example:

A new employee will pick up their own uniform.

What is the subject of the sentence and is it singular or plural? *Employee* is the subject, and it is singular. *Their* is a plural pronoun that refers to *employee,* the *antecedent.* But that can't be correct, can it? Either both words must be plural or both must be singular.

A new *employee* will pick up *his* or *her* own uniform.

or

All new *employees* will pick up *their* own uniforms.

Sometimes plural words come between the subject and the referring pronoun:

Each one of the women hired *their* own babysitter.

What is the subject? *Each* is the singular subject. No matter how many plural words (women) follow the subject, the next pronoun must be singular:

Each one of the women hired *her* own babysitter.

In addition to the singular/plural decision, you have one more decision to make. That is, is the pronoun reference clear? For example:

The employee told the repairman that his computer was down.

Whose computer is down? Does it belong to the employee? Or does it belong to the repairman? Rewrite the sentence:

The employee told the repairman that his, the employee's, computer was down.

Here's another example:

Larry and Juan moved the equipment to the new office, but he could not stay past 6 P.M.

Who could not stay? Larry? Juan? Rewrite the sentence:

Larry and Juan moved the equipment to the new office, but Juan could not stay past 6 P.M.

Practice 8

Choose the correct pronoun in each sentence. If necessary, rewrite the sentence for clarity. One sentence is correct.

1 Don't give new employees materials until they have been date stamped.

2 Laura told the receptionist her phone was not working. [*Hint:* Whose phone was not working?]

3 Each of our sons wants a car for themselves.

4 Many of their friends get their cars before they are eighteen years old!

5 Anybody in this group who thinks they are done are sadly mistaken.

Special Forms of Linking Verbs

We often take shortcuts when we write or speak. We can take a shortcut using linking words. A linking word can be combined with another word to construct a new word, a *contraction*. In each case, one letter is left out of the combination.

Contraction	Example	Letter Left Out
I'm = I am	I'm here to help.	a
He's = He is	He's always right!	i
She's = She is	She's my best friend.	i
It's = It is	It's your turn.	i
You're = You are	You're wrong as usual.	a
We're = We are	We're a great team.	a
They're = They are	They're following us.	a

Note: Without the apostrophe, *its* is used to indicate possession. For example: The cat took the kitten to *its* new home.

Once again, if you have been speaking and writing English all of your life, the information above is not a great challenge. However, the same problem—agreement in number—does remain a challenge. Sometimes we use a contraction when we should not. For example:

There's many problems with your plan. = There is many problems with your plan.

What is wrong with this sentence? *Problems* is the subject, and it is plural. A plural subject agrees with a plural linking verb. Change *is* to *are*. The construction should be

There are many problems with your plan.

Following is another example:

Here's the magazines you asked for. = Here is the magazines you asked for.

What is wrong with this sentence? *Magazines* is the subject and it is plural. Once again, you need to use a plural linking verb. Change *is* to *are*. The construction should be

Here are the magazines you asked for.

A New Wrinkle

What happens when the contraction is negative? Add *not* to the following:

is + not = isn't

are + not = aren't

will + not = won't

were + not = weren't

was + not = wasn't

Very Wrinkly

Never use the contraction *ain't*. Think about what it takes the place of and use the correct form instead.

I ain't (am not) finished yet.	I'm not finished yet.
You ain't (are not) finished yet.	You aren't finished yet.
She ain't (is not) finished yet.	She isn't finished yet.
They ain't (are not) finished yet.	They aren't finished yet.
We ain't (are not) finished yet.	We aren't finished yet.

Even though you will find *ain't* in some dictionaries, it is not correct usage, ever.

Practice 9

Find the errors in the following sentences. One is correct as written.

1 My problems isn't the worst in the world!

2 Wasn't you and Miguel expected at 8 A.M.?

3 Ain't I ever going to get any credit?

4 I can't sign up at the community college until September.

5 There's plenty of apples on that tree.

Practice 10—Review

Read the paragraphs. Decide if any underlined word is incorrect. Choose the letter of the incorrect word. Correct the error.

1 Employees, if <u>they're</u> smart, <u>prepares</u> for every performance evaluation. Preparations should <u>begin</u> immediately following the last evaluation session. Rewrite any notes that you took so that <u>they're</u> very clear to you. Look at the goals that you and the manager <u>decided</u> were appropriate for the next six months. <u>Plan</u> how you will implement the goals.
   A they're
   B prepares
   C they're
   D decided
   E plan

2 <u>Are</u> you interested in obtaining your education on-line? <u>There's</u> pluses and minuses that both students and teachers are concerned about. Being able to keep your own schedule as you learn <u>is</u> a very big consideration for some people. The computer <u>doesn't</u> know if you are learning at 5 P.M. or A.M. <u>Neither</u> does your instructor.
   A Are
   B There's
   C is
   D doesn't
   E Neither

3 On the other hand, <u>are</u> you independent and reliable enough to assume the responsibilities? There <u>ain't</u> going to be an instructor to face in person, therefore no face-to-face reminders about assignments. Although <u>you'll</u> have an online instructor, you <u>won't</u> have someone at your side to help you with homework and research.
   A are
   B ain't
   C you'll
   D won't

Another Kind of Agreement

Verbs also express time or tense.

I walk the dog each morning.

I walked the dog this morning.

I will walk the dog the tomorrow morning.

I have walked the dog every morning this week.

The action verb, *walk,* is in the present time; *walked* talks about the past; *will walk* talks about the future, *have walked* talks about the past and continues into the present.

Now let's look at the linking verb in time.

Present: I am angry.   I appear pale.

Past: I was angry.   I appeared pale.

Future: I will be angry.   I will appear pale.

Past with helping word: I have been angry. I have been pale.

The Challenge

In a sentence or a paragraph, the writer needs to keep the time of the verbs consistent. For example:

(1) The scene *is* set. (2) The atmosphere *is* hushed. (3) The curtain *rises* and the audience *applauds.*

Every verb in this paragraph—whether action or linking—is in the same tense.

1 is

2 is

3 rises, applauds

Obviously, the writer decided, in the first sentence, that all the verbs would be in the *present* time. You need to check your writing, as well as your speech, for inconsistencies in time. Start with the following practice:

Practice 11

Read the paragraphs. Look particularly for inconsistent verb tense. Choose the answer that shows the incorrect verb tense. Correct the error.

1 (A) We decided to leave for the airport three hours before our flight time. (B) Believe it or not, we didn't have any extra time. (C) It takes us a long time to park. (D) The airport parking lot was so crowded. (E) We ran to the departure gate.

    A decided

    B didn't

    C takes

    D was

    E ran

2 (A) We were last to board the plane. (B) None of us had window seats.
(C) This was a no-frills flight, which meant that no food was served.
(D) In the last minute rush, we also forget to buy some food for lunch.
(E) What a mistake that was!
A were
B had
C was, was
D forget
E was

3 (A) We settled in for a three-hour trip. (B) Unfortunately, we spent the first two hours waiting to take off. (C) Have you ever spent five hours on a plane with someone else's three year old? (D) By the time we took off, the child had visited every passenger. (E) Finally, the steward talks to the parents and they control the child.
A settled
B spent
C spent
D had visited
E talks, control

Answer Key: Section 4, Lesson 3

Practice 1
1. is
2. were
3. was
4. are
5. is

Practice 2
1. are, were, grew
2. feel
3. remain, be
4. tasted
5. was, is, became, felt, remained

Practice 3

1. My children <u>are</u> tired of that TV show.

2. Do you <u>feel</u> as groggy as I do today?

3. I'll <u>remain</u> president of the PTA for this year at least.

4. The apples <u>tasted</u> tart and crisp.

5. Marge <u>became</u> sick.

Practice 4
1. taste
2. were, were
3. sounds
4. feel
5. is
6. are
7. correct as written
8. grew
9. are
10. appear

Practice 5
1. they
2. he
3. I
4. they
5. who?

Practice 6
1. her
2. I
3. me
4. he
5. she

Practice 7
1. are
2. is
3. were
4. has
5. are
6. is
7. were

Practice 8
1. Don't give new employees materials until the materials have been date stamped.
2. Laura told the receptionist that Laura's phone was not working.
3. Each of our sons wants a car for himself.

4. Correct

5. Anybody in this group who thinks that he or she is done is sadly mistaken.

Practice 9

1. aren't

2. Weren't

3. Aren't

4. correct as written

5. There are

Practice 10

PARAGRAPH 1

1. B; prepare

PARAGRAPH 2

2. B; There are

PARAGRAPH 3

3. B; isn't

Practice 11

PARAGRAPH 1

1. C; took

PARAGRAPH 2

2. D; forgot

PARAGRAPH 3

3. talked, controlled

LESSON 4: SPEAK UP!

Mike met Ken on campus, after Ken's math class.

Mike asked, "How was class today?" Ken replied, "Same." "Coffee?" Mike asked. "Sure."

You may think that the authors are concerned about the non-sentences above. We are not. In casual conversation, incomplete thoughts are acceptable. You will see incomplete thoughts in written language as well as in conversation. What is noteworthy, however, is the lack of color in the sentences. Adding color to your speech and writing is the subject of this lesson.

Words to Know

Adjective	A word that describes a noun or pronoun
Adverb	A word that describes a verb, an adjective, or another adverb

Preposition	The first word in a group of words that describes another word in the sentence
Reluctant	Feeling no enthusiasm for something
Dilemma	A situation in which you must choose one of two unsatisfactory solutions

A More Colorful Approach

This bears repeating: A complete sentence must have a subject and a verb, and that makes it a complete thought. Does that make it an interesting thought? Not necessarily. You need to introduce more colorful additions to the basic thought. This is true whether the sentence is organized around an action verb or a linking verb. Look at a sentence with an action verb.

The child leads.

Subject = child   Action verb = leads

We don't usually write or speak such simple thoughts. We want to describe both the subject and the verb. We accomplish that by adding adjectives and adverbs to sentences.

The older child leads very effectively.

Older describes child. Effectively describes leads. Very describes effectively.

With these words, adjectives (*older*) and adverbs (*effectively* and *very*), the reader has more information. The question becomes, "If all of the words describe, why do they have different names?" The answer is simple. You recall that words have both *names* and *jobs*. In this case, the adjective's (that is its name) job is to describe or give more information about nouns, or names of people, places, or things. Following are a few examples:

Adjective	Noun
older	child
small	town
big	meal
tall	gentleman
large	crowd

As you learned in Lesson 3, adjectives also work with linking verbs. A linking verb links the subject of the sentence with a describing word (adjective). Retool the sentence above:

The older child is effective at work.

Child is still the noun/subject of the sentence. However, the verb is now a linking verb (is) instead of an action verb (*leads*). What two words does the linking verb bring together? The answer, of course, is *child* and *effective.* *Effective* describes *child.*

Here is another example:

My job is challenging.

Noun	Linking verb	Adjective
job (noun)	is (linking)	challenging (adjective describes job)

STUDY TIP

You have been studying adjectives that follow the linking verb. What about other adjectives in the sentence? For example, in the sentence above, what about the word *my? My* certainly describes job, telling whose job it is. *Job* is a noun; therefore, the describing word, *my,* is an adjective. If *my* looks as if it should be called a pronoun, you are right. Some pronouns act as if they were adjectives: The kind of job they do in the particular sentence affects what they are called! Remember, words have names and they have jobs, too.

Here's another example:

Your job seems impossible.

job (noun) seems (linking verb) impossible (adjective describes job)

After reading the study tip above, what job do you think the word *your* does in this sentence? If you said it describes, you were correct. What word does it describe? The correct answer is *job.* Again, you see a pronoun acting as an adjective.

Practice 1

Now try these sentences on your own. Underline the linking verb and find the subject. Draw an arrow from the adjective to the noun or pronoun it describes.

1 We grew tired of a very long argument.

2 That pie tastes so good.

3 You are swamped with work.

On the Other Hand . . .

The job of adverbs is to describe a verb, an adjective, or another adverb. For example:

The older child leads very effectively.

Effectively describes *leads.*

Very describes *effectively.*

Here's another example:

I gave the present reluctantly.

Reluctantly describes *gave.*

Practice 2

Now try these sentences on your own. Draw an arrow from the adverb to the verb it describes. In Sentence 3, there is also an adverb that describes another adverb.

1 In the neighboring room, the occupant played the radio loudly.

2 Our cousins arrived unexpectedly.

3 I'll ask very politely.

Practice 3

Read the five sentences in the "On the Other Hand" and Practice 2 sections above. List the adverbs that describe verbs

1

2

3

4

5

Note: What conclusion can you draw about the way adverbs that describe verbs are most often spelled? Yes, they very often end in -ly. That spelling will become a clue for you when you are trying to decide if a word is an adverb.

The Challenge

The challenge is to use adjectives and adverbs correctly. There are several very common errors that you will want to avoid.

Well vs. Good

Well can be used as an adjective when you talk about health. For example:

I feel well now. (*Well* describes *I.*)

At all other times, *well* is an adverb and, as such, describes the action word:

My boyfriend drives racecars well. (*Well* describes *drives.*)

Important: Good never describes an action. What kind of word does it describe in the next four sentences?

My boyfriend is a good driver. (Not, "My boyfriend drives good." *Good* cannot describe the action, *drives.*)

A good reader has an advantage on tests.

A good place to live is not always that easy to find.

Use good paper to print that report.

You read, *good driver, good reader, good place,* and *good paper.* The word *good* obviously describes people, places, and things. They are all nouns.

Practice 4

Choose the correct word to complete each sentence.

1 One of my office friends dresses (good/well).

2 Our manager has not felt (good/well) for weeks.

3 My brother-in-law is a (good/well) house painter.

4 The choir sings (good/well).

5 I rewrote my résumé, and it worked (good/well) for me.

Real vs. Really

Really describes another descriptive word. Did you notice the -ly? Yes, this is an adverb, and it describes other descriptive words. For example:

Clara's computer is really outdated. (*Really* describes the adjective, *outdated.*)

Aaron's excuse for being late was really lame. (*Really* describes the adjective, *lame.*)

Real describes a person, place, or thing—a noun. For example:

This is a real dilemma. (*Real* describes the noun, *dilemma.*)

The sofa is made of real leather. (*Real* describes the noun, *leather*)

Practice 5

Choose the correct word in each sentence.

1 The actress played a (real/really) lovable part.

2 The hat was (real/really) too small to protect me from the sun.

3 One problem is that our morning meetings are (real/really) early.

4 One (real/really) problem is that our meetings are in the morning.

5 Why don't you take a (real/really) break—an extra ten minutes.

Nice vs. Nicely

This is one of the most common errors in the use of descriptive words. Don't make this error!

The senator spoke nice at the town meeting.

Once again, you need to decide what job each word performs. *Nice* describes a person, place, or thing—a noun. *Nicely* describes an action. In the sentence above, what does *nice* try to describe? The answer, of course, is *spoke*. But *nice* cannot describe a verb; *nicely* does.

The senator spoke nicely at the town meeting.

If you wanted to describe the senator as nice, what would you say?

The nicely senator spoke at the town meeting.

or

The nice senator spoke at the town meeting.

Nice is an adjective and, as you know, adjectives do describe nouns or persons, place, or things.

Practice 6

Choose the correct word in each sentence.

1 Because it was a (nice/nicely) day, we walked to work.

2 "(Nice/Nicely) done!" yelled the enthusiastic fan.

3 The manager spoke (nice/nicely) at the district meeting.

4 The (nice/nicely) manager spoke at the district meeting.

5 He's really a (nice/nicely) person.

Practice 7

Read the paragraph below. Choose a correct adjective or adverb in each sentence.

Young people today have a (well/good) reason for learning to write a strong résumé. Research tells them that they will not have just one job in their lifetimes. It is (more/most) likely that they will have many jobs over time. For some, this is a (nice/nicely) opportunity to avoid boredom in their work lives. It is also a (real/really) good opportunity to become a lifelong learner. These young people—as well as older workers—must expect to change jobs. In addition, they will have to feel (good/well) about changing the kind of work they do. They have to be (real/really) ready, and trained for change.

An Important Change

There is another very important way that adjectives change in order to accommodate the meaning in a sentence. The change is called *comparison of descriptive words*. In the following examples, you can see just why that is an appropriate term.

The commuter train is *fast*.

The new Acela is *faster*.

The European train is the *fastest* one of all.

Obviously, each sentence talks about the degree of speed. The first sentence simply states a fact—a certain train is fast. Sentence 2 sets up the comparison between the first train and the Acela. The important fact here is that two things are compared and the English language adds an -er to indicate that of the *two,* one is faster. Proceed to the third sentence and you reach a new level of comparison. Now it is clear that of the three trains being compared, the European train is the fastest. The word ending, -est, is used to show that comparison of three or more.

This simple comparison exercise is probably not much of a challenge for you. You use the following words, and many others, without a problem.

Adjective	Comparison of Two	Comparison of More Than Two
fast	faster	fastest
green	greener	greenest
blue	bluer	bluest
pretty	prettier	prettiest

Trouble Ahead

We tend to run into trouble in comparisons in two ways:

1 Sometimes adjectives change spelling in ways other than the addition of -er or -est to the base word. Some describing words are too long and become awkward when we place an extra syllable on the end. Consider this:

That is the *advancedest* course in our program.

The writer or speaker compared all of the courses in a program. The person decided that one of many courses was the most advanced. Because *advanced* is a three syllable word and because it becomes a very awkward word, you must not add -er or -est to it. What is a good choice here? Add *more* or *most* and keep the base word, *advanced*.

That course is the most advanced in our program. (The sentence indicates a comparison among three or more courses. The word *most* is used instead of adding -est.)

or

That course is more advanced than the one I took last semester. (The sentence indicates a comparison between two courses. The word *more* is used instead of adding -er.)

We sometimes, mistakenly, use *more* or *most* plus the -er or -est ending, and that is too much of a good thing:

That TV show is *more funnier* now than it was in the past.

The sentence should read

That TV show is funnier now than it was in the past.

Here are some other words that need to use *more* and *most* in comparisons:

Adjective	Comparison of Two	Comparison of More than Two
enormous	more enormous	most enormous
difficult	more difficult	most difficult
beautiful	more beautiful	most beautiful
quickly	more quickly	most quickly
valuable	more valuable	most valuable
wonderful	more wonderful	most wonderful

2 Some adjectives are spelled entirely differently when they are used to compare two or more things. Look at the following chart:

Adjective	Comparison of Two	Comparison of More than Two
good	better	best
bad	worse	worst

What's wrong with this sentence?

That was the worse meal I've ever had.

I think we can assume that the writer has had more than two meals. How would you correct the sentence?

That was the worst meal I've ever had.

Try this:

That book is the better of the group.

This should read

That book is the best of the group.

Practice 8—Review

Find an error in all but one of these sentences. Write a correction in the space provided.

1 She has children who are enormouser than mine. _____

2 I run pretty quick for the bus. _____

3 Our garden looks good this year. _____

4 This is the worse training course I've had in my ten years with the company! _____

5 You'll never find a more wonderfuler friend. _____

6 Tod's known as the most tenaciousest trainer in our group of runners.

_____

7 I feel good today. _____

8 Jan lives nearest to me than Carl does. _____

9 That episode was more funnier than any of the others. _____

10 She's real unhappy. _____

Another Way to Describe

Occasionally, we need more than a single word to add meaning to a sentence. We add a phrase instead. For example:

The guitar screeched *on the high notes.*

The phrase *on the high notes* describes how the guitar screeched. The entire phrase acts as a descriptive word. If you had to decide whether the phrase was an adjective or adverb phrase, what would you say? You would first have to know what kind of word it describes. In this case, it is *screeched,* the verb. What kind of word describes a verb? If you said an adverb does, you are correct. You remember what you learned in the beginning of this lesson.

There is a practical reason for you to be able to recognize descriptive phrases. As you will see, they frequently come between or close to the subject or verb. For example:

A *summary* of all the chapters *is* in the last part of the book.

You needed to recognize that the word *chapters* is a part of the descriptive phrase. It is not the subject in the above sentence. The sentence below shows *chapters* as the subject. What happened to the verb? It became plural to agree with the plural subject.

The chapters are in the last part of the book.

STUDY TIP

Sometimes you need to identify the subject in order to decide if it is singular or plural. First, exclude the descriptive phrase. Then make your decision. Try it here:

The athletes at the stadium (park/parks) free.

What is the action verb? The answer is *park*. Who parks? The *athletes*. That is the subject. Is the subject singular or plural? The answer is plural. Which word should you choose? *Athletes park.* Try another sentence.

The recruits under the wire fence (was/were) stuck.

Remember, first remove the prepositional phrase, *under the wire fence*. What is left? *The recruits (was/were) stuck.* Now, choose the correct verb.

There is a group of words that typically start descriptive phrases. They are called *prepositions* and they are listed below.

Prepositions

after	at	along	alongside	among	around
before	beside	between	by	except	for
from	in	into	of	off	on
over	to	through	under	up	with

Practice 9

In the sentences below, you will find descriptive phrases. Each starts with one of the prepositions in the list. Find the phrases and decide which word the phrase describes. Then find the subject and the verb. Place an *S* over the subject and a *V* over the verb.

1 The change fell into his pocket.

2 They are among our best friends.

3 Our children do go through the woods to Grandmother's house.

4 The houses between the brook and the forest (are/is) green, white, or gray.

5 The houses of congress are divided in their thinking. (Hint: divided describes congress. What does *in their thinking* describe?)

STUDY TIP

Do you remember the three kinds of pronouns? You recall that they act as subjects, receivers of action, or show ownership. (If you need to, review Lesson 3, page 241.) Now you can follow this rule. Use a pronoun from the second column at the end of a prepositional phrase

Save the books *for them.*
John sent an invitation *to her.*
An argument raged between *George and him.*

Practice 10

Choose the correct word in each sentence.

   1 The discussion was between you and (I, me).

   2 We'll make that decision among (us, we).

   3 Any final decision must go through (me, I).

   4 Will anyone arrive before (me, I)?

   5 The winner is between Jorge and (he, him).

Warning!

A descriptive, or prepositional phrase should take its place next to the word it describes.

When prepositional phrases are misplaced, confusion results. For example:

The child yelled at her mother on the swing.

Who was on the swing, the child or her mother? You cannot say for sure after reading this sentence. Rewrite it like this:

The child on the swing yelled at her mother.

Or try this:

Tom ran down the newly polished hallway in slippery boots.

Who was wearing slippery boots, Tom or the hallway? Be more precise by placing the descriptive phrase closer to the word it describes. You can do this in more than one way:

In slippery boots, Tom ran down the newly polished hallway.

or

Tom, in slippery boots, ran down the newly polished hallway.

Practice 11

Find the incorrectly placed prepositional phrases in these sentences. Rewrite the sentences and place the phrases closer to the words they describe. If you have trouble recognizing the prepositions, look back to the list on page 260.

   1 The cow belongs to that farm with the black and white spots.

   2 The photographer relaxed after taking 100 outdoor pictures in his studio.

   3 I was finally able to hang on my wall my diploma.

   4 Show Lois in the collar the frisky dog.

   5 The drivers on the counter completed registration forms.

Answer Key: Section 4, Lesson 4

Practice 1

1. <u>grew</u> we (subject) tired

2. <u>tastes</u> pie (subject) good

3. are you (subject) swamped

Practice 2
1. played ← loudly
2. arrived ← unexpectedly
3. ask ← very → politely

Practice 3
1. effectively
2. reluctantly
3. loudly
4. unexpectedly
5. politely very

Practice 4
1. well
2. well
3. good
4. well
5. well

Practice 5
1. really
2. really
3. really
4. real
5. real

Practice 6
1. nice
2. Nicely
3. nicely
4. nice
5. nice

Practice 7
1. good
2. more

3. nice

4. really

5. good

6. really

Practice 8

1. more enormous

2. quickly

3. correct as is

4. worst

5. more wonderful

6. most tenacious

7. feel well

8. nearer

9. was funnier

10. really

Practice 9

1. change (subject) fell (verb) into his pocket (prepositional phrase describes *fell*)

2. They (subject) are (verb) among our best friends (prepositional phrase describes *they*)

3. Children (subject) go (verb) through the woods, to Grandmother's house (prepositional phrases describe the verb *go*)

4. houses (subject) are (verb) between the brook and the forest (prepositional phrase describes *houses*

5. houses (subject) are (verb) *of congress* and *in their thinking* are prepositional phrases. *Of congress* describes *houses. In their thinking* describes *divided.*

Practice 10

1. me

2. us

3. me

4. me

5. him

Practice 11

1. The cow with the black and white spots belongs to that farm.

2. The photographer relaxed in his studio after taking 100 outdoor pictures.

3. I was finally able to hang my diploma on the wall.

4. Show Lois the frisky dog in the collar.

5. The drivers completed registration forms on the counter.

LESSON 5: Punctuation

At the Brightwater Community College student café, Mike and some friends were having their usual after-class get-together. Ken had a great deal to say (complain) about his English class. "I'm doing good—I mean well on my tests now. But I don't think I'll ever understand the teacher completely." Mike and Michelle couldn't wait to hear why. Ken always had such good stories.

Ken continued, "Today Ms. Santos gave back our third paper. I worked real—really—hard on that paper. She gave me a C! And she said to me, 'I don't think you like me, Mr. Brinkley.' I had absolutely no idea what she was talking about, so I stayed after class and asked what I had done. She said, 'If you cared about your reader, and I am your reader in this class, you would use punctuation more carefully. Your thinking skills are excellent, but sometimes I have to read a sentence two or three times in order to sort out your idea'."

Ken asked, "What can I do about it?" She replied, "Come to see me during office hours and we'll go over your paper. I'll give you some extra materials to work through."

Here are the things Ken learned about punctuation and how it affects understanding. Ken was very surprised. Will you be?

Words to Know

Unenthusiastic	Not eager to do something
Interact	To have an effect on someone else
Diversity	Variety

Why Do We Need Punctuation?

Have you ever thought about the fact that we don't talk this way?

> today comma Iapostrophem going to the mall right after work period my coworker comma Jennie comma has promised to take me to the best discount clothing store in the state exclamation point

Of course, we don't have to supply the punctuation and capitalization as we talk. Our voices fill in all the necessary information. We pause for commas, and utter an end sound for a period. Our tone rises for a question. We show appropriate emotion for an exclamation point. Obviously, on paper, we can't express endings, beginnings, excitement, and so forth. We need punctuation marks. That is what Ken had not taken into consideration when he eliminated commas, occasionally ran two sentences together, and misused or forgot quotation marks.

For the most part, the use of punctuation is logical. We avoid run-on sentences, for example, by using a period or a semicolon. What is wrong with this sentence?

My friend is always hungry she'll want to eat before we shop.

My friend is always hungry, she'll want to eat before we shop.

This is a classic run on sentence. The sentence does exactly what its name implies; it runs on from thought to thought with no punctuation or with the incorrect use of a comma (called a comma fault). To correct the preceding sentences:

My friend is always hungry. She'll want to eat before we shop.

or

My friend is always hungry; she'll want to eat before we shop.

Either the period or semicolon is correct. You will learn more about making the choice between a period and a semicolon later in this lesson. For now, keep in mind that sentences have to end. Always choose one: **.** or **?** or **!**

End Marks

The period (.), question mark (?), and exclamation mark (!) are all end marks. They are the most common and the most easily used punctuation marks. Without them and capital letters, however, all would be chaos. For example:

> would you like to be able to learn something the minute you need to would you like to access information from a reliable source any time anywhere with new software and people friendly machines and knowledge of how people learn we will be able to create such a learning environment

The authors challenge you to quickly read and understand the above information. Probably, you did get some meaning on your first reading, but real comprehension came when you placed missing end marks and capital letters in the paragraph, like this:

> Would you like to be able to learn something the minute you need to? Would you like to access information from a reliable source any time anywhere? With new software and people friendly machines and knowledge of how people learn, we will be able to create such a learning environment

In this section, you will study end marks and capital letters simultaneously. One does, in fact, signal the other. There is a whole list of other uses of capital letters below. For the purposes of Practice 1, however, just remember that proper names of people and places are capitalized.

STUDY TIP

Here is a list of capitalization rules. Refer to this whenever you are unsure about using a capital letter.

Capitalize the following:

- *The first word in a sentence.*
- *The first word of a direct quotation.*

- The word *I*.
- Names of important historical events and ages (World War II, Declaration of Independence).
- The deity, place names, people's names, organization names, specific course names, languages.
- A title when it is a form of address: Lieutenant George Grant.
- The title of a book, play, magazine, or poem (just the first and important words in each, e.g., The Competent Writer: A Plan of Attack).
- Sections of the country, not directions. Example: I had lived in the East for many years.
- Days of the week, months, and holidays. Example: Christmas falls in the fourth week of December on Monday.
- The first word in every line of poetry.

Practice 1

In the following paragraphs, place end marks and capital letters where they are needed. Do not worry about commas or any other punctuation marks.

1. if you ask me, our leader bruce m wheeler needs to learn more about leading a group successful group work depends to a great extent on the skills of the leader our leader absolutely does not believe in imposing any standards would you rather have no rules or a few sensible rules of procedure and conduct anything less must lead to anarchy

2. in june, we'll move to our new two-room office our moving list will include paper and pencil supplies yours should concentrate on furniture and lighting dan will concentrate on the computers and other hardware the office can be moved quickly if we all cooperate do you think we can be ready by may 31

3. yesterday i told my boss that i would be happy to work on the new project he was very glad to get my message he's had trouble selling the idea to our team management really wants full cooperation what do you do when four of the five team members are unenthusiastic pray

When Should I Use a Comma?

For many people, the comma is the most challenging form of punctuation. If, however, you keep the idea of logical use in mind, the process will be easier. Commas are meant to clarify meaning. Read the paragraph below. Where would you insert commas?

When you use the English language some rules are very clear. For example there is no dispute about the word ain't. You should not use it—ever. Neither do you say "I don't never want to see that textbook again." However when it comes to commas we don't seem to be as confident sure or secure in making decisions. Now you will have the opportunity to study the important uses of commas and when you finish you will be very confident in your decisions.

Check your answers in the Answer Key. The following checklist will help you to understand the correct uses of commas and to correct any errors you may have missed in the sample paragraph.

Comma Use Checklist

1 Use a comma after a salutation in a friendly letter.

Dear Abby,

Use a comma after the closing in a business or friendly letter.

Sincerely,

Ruth

2 Separate items in a series with commas.

Feed the cat, walk the dog, and clean the bird's cage.

3 Use a comma to separate an introductory phrase from the complete thought.

When I am ready to leave for the airport, I go over my departure checklist one more time.

STUDY TIP

Take a careful look at this example. Writers sometimes make the error of thinking that the introductory words (When I am ready to leave for the airport) represent a sentence. They do not. When you finish reading it, you want to ask, "What happens?" That is simply because it is an incomplete thought, a sentence fragment. Don't fall into the sentence fragment trap!

4 Insert commas to separate words that interrupt the flow of the sentence.

An electronic organizer, although I don't own one, is an essential tool for business trips.

STUDY TIP

Use this tip to test the need for commas. Words that interrupt the flow of the sentence can be eliminated. Eliminating the words will not affect the sentence's meaning.

An electronic organizer is an essential tool for business trips.

5 Commas set off the words *however, nevertheless, inasmuch as, therefore,* when they interrupt a complete thought.

Our meeting, however, cannot take place in the usual meeting room.

6 A comma separates two complete thoughts that are joined by a connecting word such as *but, for, or, and.*

We will look at all the available rooms, and we will have to choose the largest one.

7 Use commas to separate more than one descriptive word describing the same word.

A Series B, handheld, electronic organizer is the newest version.

8 Insert a comma to separate the name of a city from the name of a state or country.

Juan Moniz

196 Union Street

San Francisco, CA 00000

9 Insert a comma to separate a direct quotation from the rest of the sentence. For example:

"I'll never get to work on time in this traffic," he complained.

He shouted in his empty car, "I'll never get to work on time in this traffic!"

"Margie, I know I won't make it on time," he said to his secretary, "so please start the meeting without me."

10 Insert a comma between the day and the year and between the year and the rest of the sentence.

Mike will graduate on June 14, 2004, from Brightwater Community College.

Practice 2

Insert commas where they are needed. If you are not sure of your answers, check the list of rules above.

Citizens can make a difference in their community and in the world. Without doubt, the first step is to identify problems. Look at community needs strengths and resources. As a result of their investigation people can form and express opinions. Of course all involved in community action must be willing to work with others. In this way, citizens can impact their communities and the world around them.

Practice 3

Insert or remove commas wherever necessary.

How, do things get done in a community? When citizens have a common purpose they interact with others to get things done. In order to do that people must respect others. They, need first to understand the power of diversity.

Practice 4

For questions 1 through 5, decide if the underlined parts need correction. Write the correction or *correct as is* on the line provided.

1 How many times have you heard people complain about others' failure to communicate<u>.</u>

_____

2 Believe it or <u>not people</u> benefit from poor <u>communication?</u>

_____

3 Poor communication allows people to hide their lack of <u>planning, others</u> can't see the whole picture. _____

4 <u>Or p</u>oor <u>communication, makes</u> it easier to deny what plan was made.

_____

5 If you don't say things clearly, who can say you were wrong?

_____

Use Commas Logically

Do not insert commas where they are not needed. Avoid the following common overuses of commas.

1 Do not use a comma to separate two actions if the sentence has one subject/performer.

Incorrect: <u>I bought</u> the car, and <u>went</u> for the registration immediately.

Correct: <u>I bought</u> the car and <u>went</u> for the registration immediately.

2 When a sentence starts with a complete thought, do not use a comma to separate it from the incomplete thought that follows.

Incorrect: You need to greet the guest, when he arrives.

Correct: You need to greet the guest when he arrives.

Reminder: You can see that the subject of commas frequently brings up the subject of sentence fragments. Keep this in mind as you do the review exercise.

Practice 5—Review

Find and correct errors in capitalization, end marks, and comma usage. For practice, look for three sentence fragments among these sentences.

1 I was ready to eat lunch, having finished the morning's work.

2 dear mom
please send money.
Love
Sam

3 I'll mow the lawn fertilize it and pull the weeds if you want me to

4 When I have finished and you are ready and the new equipment has arrived.

5 Because he was late six times this year John's pay was docked.

6 This long-standing committee will disband and a new team concept will be put in place.

7 If you think you can be available we'll meet on September 20 2004.

8 "I cannot attend" she responded.

9 Before the event and after my promotion.

10 After outrunning the children and entering the cool house.

Stronger Than a Comma

A semicolon is stronger than a comma; it is actually more like a period. It expresses the close relationship between two complete thoughts. You recall reading (page 265) that you can correctly put two thoughts together by using a semicolon. You read this example:

My friend is always hungry; she'll want to eat before we shop.

Remember that the two thoughts need to be closely related. Three rules apply.

1 Thoughts connected by a semicolon might <u>otherwise</u> be connected using a comma plus the words *so, for, but, and, or, nor.*

Use a period to end a declarative sentence, or use a question mark if it is a question.

or

Use a period to end a declarative sentence; use a question mark if it is a question.

2 What happens when you write two complete and related thoughts, one or both of which contain commas?

I was born on May 24, 1970, in Denver, Colorado; but my sister was born in Seattle.

According to Rule 1 above, two thoughts connected by *but* do not require a semicolon. In this sentence, however, there are three commas in the first thought. Using another one to separate the two thoughts might be very confusing. To avoid the confusion, use the stronger mark of punctuation, the semicolon.

3 When you use certain large connecting words to join two complete thoughts, use a semicolon. Use a semicolon, the connecting word, and a comma, in that order. The connecting words are *however, therefore, nevertheless,* and *inasmuch as.* For example:

I don't like my new schedule; however, I must stay on it for at least a year.

You haven't finished the report; therefore, I will not be able to present it.

We will continue our work; inasmuch as, we have a great number of facts to discuss.

Practice 6—Review

Insert commas, end marks, and semicolons wherever they are needed. Look for run-on sentences and correct them.

1 Rod is taking a computer course an introduction to health care and a writing course

2 I'll be very busy at work all week please don't call me.

3 Shelley said that we should meet in the parking lot

4 Shelley said "Meet me in the parking lot."

5 I've already made plans therefore I won't be there.

6 Rain hail and snow followed us all the way to our destination.

7 When you visit us you will travel on Route 95 for an hour.

8 The child needed to have a blood test he howled at the sight of the needle

9 His mother did all that she could to comfort him however nothing seemed to work.

10 I want a sleek red fast convertible for my birthday do you think I'll receive one

Quotation Marks

You have had some experience working with commas and quotation marks. You learned that quotation marks are used to set off the exact words said by a person.

Direct quotation: The President of the United States said, "We need to learn to work together to solve problems."

Indirect quotation: The President of the United States said that we need to learn to work together to solve problems.

What one word changes the direct quotation to an indirect one? The answer, of course, is the word *that.* The word *that* turns the statement into a *report* of what the President said.

In order to use quotation marks correctly, you need to know a number of rules.

Quotation Mark Checklist

1 As you saw above, use quotation marks to indicate the exact words of a speaker. *Important:* Note the period inside the quotation marks at the end of the sentence. Also note the comma between the speaker and the words spoken.

The policeman said, "Stay right and move along."

2 Some quotations are called "broken," because the name of the speaker interrupts the sentence. In the first example, note the small letter on the first word of the second part of the quotation. In the second example, the second part of the quotation is actually a new sentence and requires a capital letter. Also look at the exclamation points. Just like the period, they are placed inside the quotation marks.

"Sure," shouted Audrey, "now that I'm finished, you want to help me!"

"Now that you're finished, you don't need my help," said Audrey. "Why didn't you call me earlier!"

3 Place a semicolon after the closing quotation marks.

I heard, "Pull over to the right"; so I did.

4 Never use two forms of punctuation at the end of a quotation. Use logic to decide where question marks and exclamation marks should be placed. If the entire sentence is a question, but the quotation is not, place the question mark after the closing quotation marks. If the entire sentence is an exclamation, but the quotation is not, place the exclamation point after the closing quotation mark.

Question mark: Did Ms. Santos say, "Your final exam is next Thursday"?

Exclamation point: I was so furious when you said, "I never told you that the reconditioned equipment would work again"!

5 Use quotation marks to enclose titles of poems, chapters, articles, or any part of a book or magazine. When the quoted title is followed by a comma, the comma should be placed inside the quotation marks.

"To Brooklyn Bridge," by Hart Crane, was written in 1930.

6 Use single quotation marks for a quotation within a quotation.

The other day, Judy asked me, "Is it true that you said, 'I'm going on strike if I don't get more help at home' when you started spring cleaning?"

STUDY TIP

Here are some common mistakes in the use of quotation marks. You will see that the addition of other punctuation marks often causes the problem. Errors include the misuse of commas, periods, question marks, and capital letters.

STUDY TIP

Problem 1: "Take the newspaper with you" his father suggested.

Solution: Insert a comma between the quoted words and the person who said them. Remember to place the comma inside the quotation marks.

"Take the newspaper with you," his father suggested.

Problem 2: "Take the newspaper with you," his father suggested. "In case you want something to read in the car."

Solution: When you write a broken quotation, do not capitalize the first word of second part of the quotation unless it starts a new sentence.

"Take the newspaper with you," his father suggested, "in case you want something to read in the car."

or

"Take the newspaper with you," his father suggested. "You may want something to read in the car."

Problem 3: His mother warned, "We're not stopping to eat, so remember to take the food".

Solution: The period always goes inside the quotation marks at the end of a sentence.

His mother warned, "We're not stopping to eat, so remember to take the food."

Problem 4: My son asked, "Is this all there is to eat"?

Solution: The quoted portion is a question; the entire sentence is not. Place the question mark inside the quotation marks.

My son asked, "Is this all there is to eat?"

Problem 5: Did your son say, "There's only enough food for me?"

Solution: The quoted portion is not a question; the entire sentence is a question. Place the question mark outside the quotation marks.

Did your son say, "There's only enough food for me"?

Practice 7—Review

Punctuate these sentences. Add capital letters where necessary.

1 The announcer said the manager must get the field in shape for the season

2 The announcer said that the manager must get the field in shape for the season

3 Two other people said that the manager must get the field in shape for the season

4 The announcer asked when will the manager get the field in shape for the season

5 Why didn't the announcer ask when will the manager get the field in shape for the season

6 Imagine if the announcer had said that the manager should get the field in shape for the season

7 The announcer shouted into the microphone the manager should get the field in shape for the season

Practice 8

Punctuate these sentences. Add capital letters where necessary.

1 "We asked them to come for dinner, she said

2 She said, We asked you to come for dinner, too"

3 The salesman said that we would receive our order within two weeks

4 I believe him do you

5 "If you are planning to drive the car back home" I said "Please be sure to check the tires first

6 After finishing the fourth chapter entitled "Getting Your Puppy Trained" I thought I could do a good job

7 After you drive the car out of the garage take out all the gardening tools she instructed

8 Did you say "Meet me in one hour"

9 "Did you hear that" Alice inquired

10 "Get off the stands. They're collapsing" the announcer shouted.

More Punctuation: Colon, Hyphen, Apostrophe, Dash, Parentheses, Brackets

Although we use them less frequently, we need to know how to use these forms of punctuation. Study the checklist below, and then try the practice exercise.

1 The Colon

Use a colon to introduce a list. For example:
Don't forget to bring up the following: the attendance report, the new employee kitchen, and raises.

Use a colon after the salutation in a business letter. For example:
Dear Mr. White:

Use a colon between numbers that show time. For example:
Please be home for dinner by 7:30.

2 The Hyphen

Use a hyphen to divide a word at the end of a line. Always divide words between syllables. For example:
Some people are naturally-good spellers.

Use a hyphen to divide compound numbers from twenty-one to ninety-nine. For example:
forty-two, twenty-three, eighty-seven

Use a hyphen when you add some prefixes or when you add self- to another word. For example:

non-American   self-respect
ex-partner   self-reliant

3 The Apostrophe

Use an apostrophe to show that one or more letters have been left out of a word (a contraction). For example:
Mac isn't (is not) meeting us until 9 P.M.
I'll (I will) call you when we're (we are) ready to leave.
It's (It is) too hot in here.

Use an apostrophe to show possession. (a) Place the apostrophe before the *s* in singular words. (b) Place the apostrophe after the *s* in plural words. (c) Some words become plural by other spelling changes. For example:
the cat's meow (singular)
the cats' meow (plural)
the cow's pasture
the cows' pasture
the woman's office
the women's office
the baby's cries
the babies' cries
the child's school
the children's school

Names follow the same rules. For example:

Ms. Paulsen's coat   The Paulsens' property
Mr. Dawson's coat   The Dawsons' car
Ms. Jones's class   The Joneses' property

Use an apostrophe to show the plural of letters and numbers. For example:
Start the math game with the 1's in the top row.
Z's are the hardest letters to use in a word game.

STUDY TIP

Don't use an apostrophe in a possessive pronoun: theirs, its, hers, whose. For example:

The house is theirs.
The animal carried its weight in supplies.
The blue one is hers.
Whose is this?

4 The Dash

Use dashes to mark an important interruption in the sentence. For example:
Your voice—as beautiful as it is—should not be heard above everyone else's.

Use a dash to sum up previous words. For example:
Promptness, enthusiasm, and knowledge—these are the things we're looking for in our new candidate.

5 Parentheses

Words in parentheses are not directly related to the main thought of the sentence. They are an *aside* or an *addition* not absolutely necessary to the thought. For example:
We definitely saved that information (look in Doc. 1a).

Practice 9

Choose the correct word and punctuation in the parentheses.

1 (Its/It's) only 3 P.M.

2 Her thirteen-year-old is not as (self-reliant/self reliant) as she thinks she is.

3 That (restaurant's/restaurants) food is often stale.

4 In your backpack, carry the (following;/following:) water, a pen knife, and some crackers, cheese, and trail mix.

5 When I turned (thirty nine/thirty-nine), I stopped smoking.

6 Call me when (it's/its) time to go.

7 The mother cat carried (it's/its) kittens to safety.

8 Even though Evan knew the manager of the company, he started the letter, Dear Mr. (Murray,/Murray:).

9 The six, town (councilors/councilors') decided to table the issue.

10 We planned our get-away(—in an antique car—/in an antique, car) following the reception.

Answer Key: Section 4, Lesson 5

Practice 1

1. If you ask me, our leader, Bruce M. Wheeler, needs to learn more about leading a group. Successful group work depends to a great extent on the skills of the leader. Our leader absolutely does not believe in imposing any standards. Would you rather have no rules or a few sensible rules of procedure and conduct? Anything less must lead to anarchy.

2. In June, we'll move to our new two-room office. Our moving list will include paper and pencil supplies. Yours should concentrate on furniture and lighting. Dan will concentrate on the computers and other hardware. The office can be moved quickly if we all cooperate. Do you think we can be ready by May 31?

3. Yesterday, I told my boss that I would be happy to work on the new project. He was very glad to get my message. He's had trouble selling the idea to our team. Management really wants full cooperation. What do you do when four of the five team members are unenthusiastic? Pray!

WHEN SHOULD I USE A COMMA?

When you use the English language, some rules are very clear. For example, there is no dispute about the word *ain't*. You should not use it—ever. Neither do you say, "I don't never want to see that textbook again." However, when it comes to commas, we don't seem to be as confident, sure, or secure in making decisions. Now you will have the opportunity to study the important uses of commas, and when you finish, you will be very confident in your decisions.

Practice 2

Citizens can make a difference in their community and in the world. Without doubt, the first step is to identify problems. Look at community needs, strengths, and resources. As a result of their investigation, people can form and express opinions. Of course, all involved in community action must be willing to work with others. In this way, citizens can impact their communities and the world around them.

Practice 3

How do things get done in a community? When citizens have a common purpose, they interact with others to get things done. In order to do that, people must respect others. They need, first, to understand the power of diversity.

Practice 4
1. communicate?
2. not, people communication.
3. planning. Others
4. Or, communication makes
5. correct as is

Practice 5—Review
1. lunch having
2. Dear Mom,
   Please send money.
   Love,
   Sam
3. I'll mow the lawn, fertilize it, and pull the weeds if you want me to.
4. Fragment. Possible correction: When I have finished, and you are ready, and the new equipment has arrived, let's go home.
5. Because he was late six times this year,
6. will disband, and a new team
7. available, we'll meet September 20, 2004.
8. attend,"
9. Fragment. Possible correction: Before the event and after my promotion, we'll go out for dinner.
10. Fragment. Possible correction: After outrunning the children and entering the cool house, I showered.

Practice 6—Review
1. computer course, an introduction to health care, and a
2. week; please don't call me. OR week. Please
3. lot.
4. Shelley said, "Meet
5. plans; therefore, I
6. Rain, hail, and snow
7. visit us,
8. test. He
9. comfort him; however, nothing
10. sleek, red, fast convertible for my birthday. Do you think I'll receive one?

Practice 7—Review
1. The announcer said, "The manager must get the field in shape for the season."
2. The announcer said that the manager must get the field in shape for the season.
3. Two other people said that the manager must get the field in shape for the season.
4. The announcer asked, "When will the manager get the field in shape for the season?"

5. Why didn't the announcer ask, "When will the manager get the field in shape for the season"?
6. Imagine if the announcer had said that the manager should get the field in shape for the season!
7. The announcer shouted into the microphone, "The manager should get the field in shape for the season!"

Practice 8
1. dinner," she said.
2. She said, "We
3. weeks.
4. I believe him; do you?
5. back home, " I said, "please . . . first."
6. chapter, entitled, "Getting Your Puppy Trained," I . . . a good job.
7. "After you . . . garage, take out . . . tools," she instructed.
8. Did you say, "Meet me in one hour"?
9. "Did you hear that?" Alice inquired.
10. collapsing!" the announcer shouted.

Practice 9
1. It's
2. self-reliant
3. restaurant's
4. following:
5. thirty-nine
6. it's
7. its
8. Murray:
9. councilors
10. —in an antique car—

LESSON 6: Constructing Sentences and Paragraphs

Ms. Santos continued to press her students for perfect English usage. She also insisted that that they learn another skill. They must use their best English in well-constructed sentences and paragraphs. Ken, Mike, and Michelle all agreed about one thing: The earlier discussion of punctuation, especially commas and semicolons, helped them. Now they were thinking much more about using punctuation to combine ideas in sentences and in paragraphs.

Ms. Santos also wanted her students to think about the structure of paragraphs. After all, well-structured paragraphs would build their ideas. She would explain that each sentence must lead to the next. They would soon know more about writing topic sentences and supporting details. You will learn more about this toward the end of this lesson.

Words to Know

Subordination	Making one part less important than another
Data	Information, such as facts and figures
Succinct	With no wasted words
Sporadic	Occurring occasionally
Commonwealth	A nation in which the people govern

One of the first discussions took place after Ms. Santos asked the class to punctuate the sentences in Practice 1. She also advised them that the sentences exhibited another problem.

First, can you find any incorrect punctuation in these sentences? Then, can you explain what is structurally wrong with these sentences? *Hint:* Decide if the words and thoughts are parallel. That is, is each part of the sentence expressed in the same grammatical form? Before you try Practice 1, read this example:

Write your report honestly and record the facts in a succinct way.

In the first half of the sentence, the writer instructs you to report *honestly* (an adverb describes *write*). In the second half of the sentence, you are told to report the facts *in a succinct way.* How can you change that prepositional phrase (*in a succinct way*) to match the -ly adverb, *honestly?* The answer, of course, is to change the phrase to one word: *succinctly.* Now the sentence is parallel.

Write your report *honestly* and *succinctly.*

Practice 1

Correct any punctuation errors in these sentences. Rewrite the sentences so that they are parallel.

1 The long-time assistant was faithful; prompt, and with honesty.

2 Some doctors give patients very little nutritional advice; are saying little about exercise, and they're silent on lifestyle.

3 I like to sing in the shower and dancing in the kitchen.

4 My manager wrote the evaluation clearly; promptly, and fair.

5 This weekend I will buy fabric for the new drapes, choose a paint color, and then I'll be emptying the cabinets.

6 Mike is not only a good computer analyst but a gifted mathematician also.

You probably realized that these sentences have more than punctuation problems. They are not parallel. Sentence 1, for example, contains two descriptive words, *faithful* and *prompt,* followed by a prepositional phrase, *with honesty.*

As we have said, to be parallel, a sentence must repeat like structures. Change the prepositional phrase to a descriptive word. In addition, change the semicolon to a comma. (Look back to the comma-in-a-series rule.)

The long-time assistant was faithful, prompt, and honest.

Sentence 2 tries to inform us about where doctors are deficient in advice on three topics. How can you express those three topics in a parallel way? Start by changing the semicolon to a comma in a series.

Some doctors give patients very little nutritional, exercise, or

lifestyle advice.

Sentence 3 has no punctuation problem. However, the sentence is not parallel. The actions, or verbs, are not the same: *to sing* and *dancing.* One or the other needs to change.

I like to *sing* in the shower and *dance* in the kitchen.

or

I like *singing* in the shower and *dancing* in the kitchen.

Sentence 4 uses a semicolon instead of a comma in a series. In addition, only two of the three descriptive words (adverbs) are parallel: *clearly* and *promptly.* How would you change *fair* to give it a parallel form? Think about what you learned regarding adverb endings.

My manager wrote the evaluation *clearly, promptly,* and *fairly.*

Sentence 5 has two verbs that are parallel: *buy* and *choose.* The third verb, *emptying,* is in the -ing form. How can you change it to match the others? The answer, of course is, to remove the -ing. The correct form is *empty.*

This weekend I will *buy* fabric for the new drapes, *choose* a paint color and *empty* the cabinets.

Sentence 6 says that Mike is two things: a *good computer analyst* and a *gifted mathematician.* What two phrases relate computer analyst to mathematician? You probably realize that the answer is *not only* and *but also. Not only* comes directly before *computer analyst;* consequently, *but also* must be placed before *gifted mathematician.*

Mike is not only a good computer analyst but also a gifted mathematician.

You will read more about words that combine ideas later in this lesson.

Practice 2

Restructure these sentences. Correct errors to make each construction parallel.

1 Professor Egbert is fair and has intelligence.

_____

2 Yoga is both invigorating and makes me tired.

_____

3 Our mentoring program involves both managers and peers are involved too.

_____

4 I like to research the subject, write a first draft, and then I'm doing a final draft.

_____

5 I love gardening and to cook.

_____

Combining Ideas

Good writing is usually simple, correct, and natural-sounding. However, you need to learn to connect thoughts in order to make sentences more interesting and more meaningful. The punctuation you have studied, plus connecting words, will help you create better sentences and paragraphs. Read this paragraph from a personal evaluation:

> I had not had the opportunity to help my coworkers address their concerns. It was a test of my ability as team leader to succeed in a totally different task. I had to maintain a balance of leadership and acceptance. It was my job to provide a creative environment.

In this paragraph, there are no errors that we can point to. Still, there are ways to improve the flow of ideas by combining them. First, every time you start a sentence with "_It was, It is,_ or _This is,_" stop and ask yourself how you might join the sentence with the one before. You will need a combining word and punctuation. For example, how would you combine sentences one and two and delete "It was"? How could you combine sentences three and four and, again, delete "It was." Write your answers here.

_____

_____

_____

_____

You probably combined the sentences in this way:

> Before this, I had not had the opportunity to help my coworkers address their concerns, so it was a test of my ability as team leader to succeed in a totally different task. I had to maintain a balance of leadership and acceptance because it was my job to provide a creative environment.

or

Before this, I had not had the opportunity to help my coworkers address their concerns; consequently, it was a test of my ability as team leader to succeed in a totally different task.

or

Before this, I had not had an opportunity to help my coworkers address their concerns; therefore, it was a test of my ability as team leader to succeed in a totally different task.

STUDY TIP
The last words in a sentence get your reader's attention.

Combining sentences sometimes requires that you make one part less important than the other. Logically, this is called *subordination*. First, you decide on your emphasis. For example, look at the last sentence in the sample paragraph above. The complete thought that comes after the comma receives the greater emphasis. True of sentences in general, the final words do receive the emphasis. What if the writer decided that *a balance of leadership and acceptance* required emphasis? Then the sentence could be turned around. The introductory words would then begin with a subordinating word: *Because*. And this is where the punctuation you studied becomes very important. When you use a subordinating word to start a sentence, you need to punctuate before the complete thought. Note the comma before the complete thought:

Because it was my job to provide a creative environment, I had to maintain a balance of leadership and acceptance.

Subordinating words are important to know about. Here is a list of them.

Subordinating Words

although   after   if   though

as   because   unless

when   since   where   whereas

Practice 3

Subordinate one part of the sentence to the other. Choose a subordinating word from the list above. Insert the appropriate punctuation.

1 You shred the unusable paper. I'll put the report together.

2 We bought a new computer. We figured out which system would work better for us.

3 You need to get the report to me by July 2nd. The data won't be on time to be considered.

4 We requested the supplies three weeks ago. They have not arrived yet.

5 You didn't take my advice. I pleaded with you.

You have also learned about using commas or semicolons to connect sentences. Below is a list of words used with commas and semicolons. In the first list, you will find words that combine sentences of equal importance. The second group of words also joins ideas of equal importance. However, these are used in pairs.

Words that Link Equal Ideas

and	also	nor
or	however	but
yet	moreover	for
so	further, furthermore	then
therefore	thus	accordingly
also	besides	consequently

Practice 4

In these sentences, insert words that link equal ideas. Use the words in the list above. Remember that a semicolon follows longer connecting words.

1 I'll finish my work first. Then I'll leave.

2 I've put hours and hours into creating the new filing system. No one uses it.

3 You could take the bus. You could take the train.

4 Her boss wrote in the memo, "I like the work you've been doing. I'm going to recommend a promotion."

5 Our computers don't have enough memory. We will buy new computers for the support staff.

Words that Link One Sentence Element to Another

either—or

neither—nor

both—and

not only—but also

whether—or

Practice 5

Fill the spaces in the sentences below with words from the list above.

1 _____ you _____ I have a reason to complain.

2 I've decided that I'll carry _____ my computer _____ my gym bag.

3 The scientist couldn't explain _____ the cause _____ the effect.

4 Your employment agreement promises _____ _____ a week of vacation _____ _____ seven sick days.

5 We have to decide _____ we have enough staff _____ if we need to interview more people.

Practice 6

Michelle attended a training seminar to prepare for a job interview. The following paragraph is an incorrect version of the training manual. Use all that you have learned about commas and semicolons to make this paragraph flow smoothly. Look above at the two lists of words that link ideas. Use any of these that are appropriate.

> You will graduate from the college in June. You will go on interviews. Prepare for the interview. It is something like a final exam. The interview is the exam. Do your homework. Study the company for the interview. Think about the questions you will be asked. Think about the answers you will give. Pass the exam. It means more than answering a few questions. Be courteous. Be poised. Look good.

_____
_____
_____
_____
_____

Practice 7

The training manual continues. Continue to link ideas by using words that bring thoughts together.

> Few people think about the waiting room. The interview does not begin when you meet the interviewer. It begins earlier. It is in the waiting room where the interview begins. You know not to be late. Arrive about 10 minutes early. Introduce yourself to the receptionist. Choose a place to sit. It should not be in a chair where you know that you will slouch. Display good posture. Don't chew gum. Don't talk on your cell phone. Don't read a book. Remember that you are already on view.

Building Paragraphs

When you write anything—a report, a letter, or memo, for example—you are building paragraphs. Most of the time, you begin with a topic sentence. You want your reader to know as quickly as possible what to expect. Read the following paragraph. Start by asking yourself, "What is this paragraph about?" Where is the answer to that question? That is the *topic sentence*.

Note: The paragraphs below and in Practice 9 are all about Presidential Medal of Freedom winners, 1998 to 2001.

> Maya Angelou, an award-winning black writer, went through many changes in her life. She even started life with a different name. She was born Marguerite Johnson in 1928. As a child, she shuttled back and forth between St. Louis, a tiny town in Arkansas, and San Francisco. After she was assaulted, she stopped speaking for four years. Only her brother Bailey heard her voice in those years.

You would probably agree that you knew the topic of the paragraph as soon as you read the first sentence. You expected the sentences that followed to list the changes. They are the supporting details. Make a list of the changes below.

_____

_____

_____

Find the topic sentence in the following paragraph. Underline it. What details support the topic? List them on the lines that follow.

> The Medal of Freedom has been awarded for over 30 years. President John F. Kennedy wanted to honor American citizens. He wanted the award to be for great achievements in the arts and sciences. Many other fields have been recognized as well. President Lyndon B. Johnson gave the first Medal of Freedom award after Kennedy's death. President Kennedy's idea continues to this day.

_____

_____

_____

_____

Sometimes writers want to summarize the main idea in the last sentence. They can do that by placing the topic sentence at the end of the paragraph. Look at the following paragraph. Which sentence contains the topic? Explain your answer on the lines below.

> Maya Angelou went to high school in San Francisco until 1944. After she dropped out, she trained to become the first black cable car conductor in the city. Maya returned to high school and graduated in 1945. In the 1950s, she studied dance in New York and appeared as a singer in New York and San Francisco. Maya's education was sporadic and varied.

_____

_____

_____

Check your answer in the Answer Key.

Practice 8

Read these paragraphs. Find the topic sentence in each one and underline it. List at least two details that support the topic sentence.

A. Maya Angelou had a series of important jobs. She served as an assistant to the director of a school of music and drama in Ghana. She worked as an editor of *The Arab Observer*. She also worked as an editor for *The African Review*. In addition, Maya wrote "Black, Blues, Black" for educational television.

_____

_____

B. Maya Angelou's distinguished career continued. She became very well known in 1970 for her autobiography, *I Know Why the Caged Bird Sings*. She finished three more volumes of her autobiography by 1990. Many books followed into the year 2000 and beyond.

_____

_____

Now you have a topic sentence. How do you organize the paragraph? Ideas are organized logically. As you have seen, paragraphs can be organized by dates. You can tell where each idea should appear. Look at the next paragraph. Decide where this sentence should be inserted: She even acted on television in 1987.

C. Other creative activities followed as Ms. Angelou used all of her many talents. Angelou received an Emmy for her TV performance in *Roots*. On January 20, 1993, Angelou participated in the inauguration of President Bill Clinton. She recited her poem, "On the Pulse of Morning."

_____

_____

Practice 9

Follow the directions for each of the following exercises. Compare your answers to those in the Answer Key. Your answers may be different, yet still correct.

Insert this sentence where it logically belongs in time: She was reelected twice.

A. Wilma Mankiller: Campaigner for Civil Rights and Winner of the Medal of Freedom in 1998

Born in 1945, Wilma Mankiller rose out of poverty and great hardship. Mankiller was appointed principal chief of the Cherokee Nation of Oklahoma in 1985. In 1987, she became the first elected female leader of a major Indian tribe. Mankiller was known for being an effective leader. She worked to reduce Cherokee infant mortality. She also improved the health and educational systems. Ms. Mankiller was well known for promoting Cherokee business interests.

In the next paragraph, insert this sentence where it belongs: The name was given to the person charged with protecting the village.

B. Wilma Mankiller's family history goes back to 1907. Her great grand-father was given land in Oklahoma. She lives on that land today. Mankiller's name is a family name and a military title. She showed the same leadership. Wilma became the first female in modern history to lead a major Native American tribe.

In the next paragraph, do the same with this sentence: In 1974, she moved back to her homeland.

C. Wilma Mankiller's understanding of her people went back to her family's forced removal from Oklahoma. She was just a small girl when they were relocated to California. By 1969, though, her concerns for her people had grown immensely. She began teaching in preschool and in adult education programs. There, she worked to get grants for rural programs.

Move the Ideas Along

STUDY TIP

How else can you organize paragraphs? Instead of dates, you can use words to move the ideas along. These are called *transition* words. They move the reader from one idea to another. Here is a list of transition words. They fall into the categories named in the left column.

Category Transition Words

Time:	now, later, after, before, last, first, while, then, first, second, finally, meanwhile, formerly
Addition:	moreover, in addition, besides, too, also, furthermore
Similarity:	just as, similarly, in the same way, likewise
Contrast:	yet, but, however, although, nevertheless, on the contrary, on the other hand, whereas, nonetheless
Illustration:	for example, for instance, to illustrate, specifically, in this way
Emphasis:	indeed, clearly, in fact, certainly
Conclusion:	therefore, consequently, in conclusion, in other words

Use these words from the time category in the following paragraph: first, then, meanwhile, finally.

Making brownies includes these steps. Shop for all the ingredients in the recipe. Have all of them handy before you begin. Preheat the oven to 350°. Mix the dry ingredients and add the wet ones. Pour the mixture into a greased, 11 × 13 pan and bake for 25 minutes.

Your paragraph may look like this. Other answers are possible.

Making brownies includes these steps. *First,* shop for all the ingredients in the recipe. Have all of them handy before you begin. *Then,* preheat the oven to 350°. *Meanwhile,* mix the dry ingredients and add the wet ones. *Finally,* pour the mixture into a greased, 11 × 13 pan and bake for 25 minutes.

Practice 10

Use two of these connecting words (contrast words) to build your paragraph: *however, on the other hand,* or *nevertheless.* Check your answer in the Answer Key.

A. Luis Muñoz Marin, also a Medal of Freedom winner, was born in 1898. Puerto Ricans consider the year important for another reason: The United States gained Puerto Rico from Spain. It was Marin who showed Puerto Rican's how to use their freedom.

In paragraph B, you have two jobs. First, find the sentence that does not support the topic. Cross it out. Then use words that show addition of ideas. Choose one from this list: *in addition, besides, furthermore.* Insert the word in the paragraph.

B. As a senator, Luis Muñoz Marin was known for having started very important programs. He ran for the senate in Puerto Rico in the 1920s. While in the senate, he started Operation Bootstrap. This program encouraged Puerto Ricans to help themselves by improving health and education conditions. The program improved farming methods and created new industry.

In paragraph C, can you find two sentences that could easily be combined? Then, add the word *finally* to the beginning of a later sentence.

C. Marin was Puerto Rico's first elected governor. He was elected in 1949. He started Operation Commonwealth. The purpose of the program was to achieve more self-rule. In 1952, Puerto Rico became a commonwealth of the United States.

In the following paragraph, decide which sentence does not belong. Cross it out. Then, use these words to connect ideas: *for instance, in this way.*

D. Marin had one more phase to his plan. He put Operation Serenity into effect. Marin thought that Puerto Ricans could enjoy life more. Theater, dance, and literature could be a part of their lives. Marin encouraged development and enjoyment of the arts. In 1964, Marin decided not to run for a fifth term as governor.

Answer Key: Section 4, Lesson 6

Practice 1
1. The long-time assistant was faithful, prompt, and honest.
2. Some doctors give patients very little nutritional advice, say little about exercise, and are silent on lifestyle.
3. I like to sing in the shower and dance in the kitchen.
4. My manager wrote the evaluation clearly, promptly, and fairly.
5. This weekend I will buy fabric, choose a paint color, and empty the cabinets.
6. Mike is not only a good computer analyst but also a gifted mathematician.

Practice 2
1. Professor Egbert is fair and intelligent.
2. Yoga is both invigorating and tiring.
3. Our mentoring program involves both managers and peers.
4. I like to research the subject, write a first draft, and then do a final draft.
5. I love gardening and cooking.
   or
   I love to garden and to cook.

Practice 3
Your sentences may look something like this:
1. After you shred the unusable paper, I'll put the report together.
2. When we figured out which system would work better for us, we bought a new computer.
3. Unless you get the report to me by July 2nd, the data won't be on time to be considered.
4. Though we requested the supplies three weeks ago, they have not arrived yet.
5. Although I pleaded with you, you didn't take my advice.

Practice 4
Your choice of connecting words may be different, yet correct. In sentence 4, for example, you might have chosen *therefore, thus,* or *accordingly.*
1. I'll finish my work first and then I'll leave. Study Tip: When two short sentences are combined with *and,* you don't need to use a comma between them.
2. I've put hours and hours into creating the new filing system, but no one uses it.
3. You could take the bus or you could take the train. (See the Study Tip above.)
4. Her boss wrote in the memo, "I like the work you've been doing; consequently, I'm going to recommend a promotion."
5. Our computers don't have enough memory; therefore, we will buy new computers for the support staff.

Practice 5

1. Neither you nor I
2. both my computer and my gym bag
3. either the cause or the effect
4. not only a week . . . but also seven
5. whether we have enough staff or if we need

Practice 6

When you prepare for interviews, think of them as final exams. Do your homework not only by studying about the company but also by thinking about answers to the questions you will be asked. Passing the exam means more than just answering a few questions; courtesy, poise, and appearance all count.

Practice 7

Your paragraph may look something like this.

Your interview begins before you meet the interviewer; it begins earlier, in the waiting room. Of course, you know not to be late, but did you know that you should arrive about 10 minutes early? First, introduce yourself to the receptionist. Then choose a chair in which you won't slouch and you will display good posture. Don't chew gum, talk on your cell phone, or read a book, because you are already on view.

Building Paragraphs

Paragraph 1
Her name was changed.
She shuttled between Arkansas and California.
She stopped speaking for four years.

Paragraph 2
Topic sentence: The Medal of Freedom has been awarded for over 30 years.

Details:
JFK wanted to honor American citizens for achievements in the arts and sciences.
Many other fields have been recognized as well.
President Lyndon B. Johnson gave the first medal after JFK's death.
The idea continues to this day.

Paragraph 3
The main idea is summarized in the last sentence, "Maya's education was sporadic and varied." The other sentences support the main idea with details.

Practice 8

A. Topic sentence: Maya Angelou had a series of important jobs.
Supporting details:
1 Assistant to the director of a school
2 An editor of *The Arab Review*
3 An editor of *The African Review*
4 Wrote for educational television

B. Maya Angelou's distinguished career continued.

    1 had published *I Know Why the Caged Bird Sings*

    2 finished three more autobiographical volumes by 1990

    3 Many books followed into the year 2000.

C. Other creative activities followed as Ms. Angelou used all of her many talents.

    1 received an Emmy

    2 participated in Bill Clinton's inauguration

    3 recited her poem, "On the pulse of Morning," at the inauguration

Practice 9

A. Insert "She was re-elected twice" after sentence three.

B. Insert after sentence four.

C. Insert as the next-to-last sentence.

Practice 10

A. Luis Muñoz Marin, also a Medal of Freedom winner, was born in Puerto Rico in 1898. However, Puerto Ricans consider the year important for another reason: The United States gained Puerto Rico from Spain. On the other hand, it was Marin who showed Puerto Ricans how to use their freedom.

B. Delete this sentence: He ran for the senate in Puerto Rico in the 1920s. As a senator, Luis Muñoz Marin is known for having started very important programs. While in the senate, he started Operation Bootstrap. This program encouraged Puerto Ricans to help themselves by improving health and education conditions. Furthermore (or in addition), the program improved farming methods and created new industry.

C. Combine the first two sentences.

    In 1949, Marin became Puerto Rico's first elected governor. He started Operation Commonwealth. The purpose of the program was to achieve more self-rule. Finally, in 1952, Puerto Rico became a commonwealth of the United States.

D. Delete this sentence: In 1964, Marin decided not to run for a fifth term as governor.

    Marin had one more phase to his plan. He put Operation Serenity into effect. Marin thought that Puerto Ricans could enjoy life more. For instance, theater, dance, and literature could be a part of their lives. In this way, Marin encouraged development and enjoyment of the arts.

Spelling Pretest

1   A _____ wind blew the sailboat across the finish line.

   A   phenomenil

   B   phenominal

   C   phenomenal

   D   phenomenul

2   Was Tom _____ to you?

   A   referred

   B   refferred

   C   refered

   D   refurred

3   I am thinking of hiring him because of his reputation for great _____.

   A   stubility

   B   stabilaty

   C   stebility

   D   stability

4   We did three new _____ for that product.

   A   comercials

   B   commertials

   C   commercials

   D   commertiels

5   Some people require very close _____ at work; others don't.

   A   managment

   B   management

   C   manugement

   D   manigement

6   Is this a _____ time for you?

   A   convenient

   B   convienent

   C   convinient

   D   conveinient

7   That is a _____ in the problem that we had not thought of.

   A   vareable

   B   variable

   C   varible

   D   vareable

8   The new bookcase is so large that it will have to be _____.

   A   stationery

   B   stationury

   C   stationerery

   D   stationary

9 We didn't go to bed until _____.

    A midnite

    B midnihgt

    C midnight

    D midnieght

10 Your _____ whining will not get the job done any faster.

    A incessant

    B inseccent

    C insessant

    D incessunt

11 Can you imagine a _____ to *Titanic?*

    A seqel

    B sequal

    C sequel

    D sequil

12 We'll _____ at noon.

    A conveen

    B convene

    C conveine

    D conveene

13 Remember to show your _____ as you enter the conference.

    A credentials

    B credencials

    C credentails

    D credencails

14 That is one _____ step.

    A unneccasary

    B unneccesary

    C unnessary

    D unnecessary

15 This directive _____ all the others you have received.

    A superceedes

    B supersedes

    C superseeds

    D superceeds

16 That music has a _____ beat.

    A rhithmic

    B rhuthmic

    C rhythmic

    D rhithmyc

17 When this company decides to hire someone, they send a letter of _____.

    A acceptunce

    B acceptense

    C acceptance

    D acceptince

18 Our _____ is at least 30 hours per week.

    A requirement

    B requirment

    C requiremunt

    D requiremint

19 Some parking places are _____.

    A illegil

    B illegal

    C ilegal

    D illegall

20   Your children bear a remarkable
_____ to you.

A   resemblance

B   resemblence

C   resemblanse

D   resemblince

Answer Key: Spelling Pretest

1. C; phenomenal
2. A; referred
3. D; stability
4. C; commercials
5. B; management
6. A; convenient
7. B; variable
8. D; stationary
9. C; midnight
10. A; incessant
11. C; sequel
12. B; convene
13. A; credentials
14. D; unnecessary
15. B; supersedes
16. C; rhythmic
17. C; acceptance
18. A; requirement
19. B; illegal
20. A; resemblance

To the Student: As you check your answers, record the results in this chart. Use the three columns next to the Answer Key to mark your answers as *Correct, Error,* or *Skipped.* Use the other columns to record additional information you want to remember about the individual questions. Total the number of your responses in each column at the bottom of the chart. Then read the recommendations that follow.

Spelling Skills Assessment: Answers and Skills Analysis

Item Answers	Correct T	Error X	Skipped O	I have this question.	I need instruction.	Spelling Skill Categories*
1 C						1
2 A						2
3 D						1
4 C						2
5 B						3
6 A						1
7 B						1
8 D						3
9 C						2
10 A						3
11 C						1
12 B						1
13 A						2
14 D						3
15 B						1
16 C						1
17 C						3
18 A						3
19 B						2
20 A						1
TOTALS	correct	errors	skipped	Questions	Instruction	Skills

* Key to Spelling Skill Categories
1 Vowels
2 Consonants
3 Structural Units

Note: These categories of spelling skills are broken down into subskill categories as well. On the next page, question numbers are aligned with the subskill titles as well. Return to Section 5 to review the rules.

Spelling Skills Analysis

Vowel

Short	16
Long	6, 12, 15
Schwa	1, 3, 7, 11, 20

Consonant

Variant Spelling	4, 13
Silent Letter	9
Double Letter	2, 19

Structural Unit

Homonym	8
Similar Word Part	10, 14, 17
Root	5
Suffix	18

To discover your areas of skills improvement in the Spelling Section, do three things:

Total your number of correct answers out of the possible 20 answers. To score a passing grade you should have 95 percent correct (or 19 correct answers).

Total the number of correct answers in each subset of skills. For example, in the subset *Schwa,* there are five correct answers. To score a passing grade, you should have 95 percent correct (or 4 correct answers).

Keep a list of your spelling errors and follow the directions for improvement in the Study Tip on page 298.

How Do I Become a Better Speller?

 STUDY TIP
Some people seem to be "natural" spellers. For others, correct spelling is not an easy skill to acquire. If spelling is a problem for you, try a more organized approach to learning. First, understand that you cannot learn to spell every word you need in a short time. Instead, take your time and do a small amount of studying at any one time. Try the following plan.

- *Keep a small notebook handy to record words that you have spelled incorrectly or that are new to you.*
- *When you enter a word into the notebook, divide it into syllables. Make sure that you are spelling and pronouncing it correctly. Check with a dictionary or use the spelling/dictionary tool on your computer.*
- *Look at the word. Say it in syllables.*
- *Think about whether a common spelling rule applies.*
- *Close your eyes and picture the word.*
- *Write the word. Check it. Write it again if necessary.*
- *Review a word until you are sure you know how to spell it.*

 STUDY TIP
Do you remember the discussion of the different types of learners? You should think about how you prefer to learn when you study words. Do you prefer to move around as you study? Do it! Have your list handy and spell the words out loud as you walk.

If you learn better by listening, dictate the words into a recorder and then listen to the way the words are spelled. In any case, make writing one of the steps in the learning process. For some, the writing may not be the first step.

What You Have to Know

To improve your spelling, you need to know about four things:

1 Vowels, a, e, i, o, u, and sometimes y
   A Vowel sounds can be <u>short</u>, as the *a* in *apple* or the *e* in *test*
   B Vowel sounds can be <u>long</u>, as the *i* in *fine* or the *o* in *pole*
   C The vowel *y* provides different sounds depending on the word in which it is used: *scary* (long *e*), *rhythmic* (short *i*).
   D Vowel sounds are sometimes dropped, or not clearly long or short. Listen to the *o* in *conclude* or the first *e* in *absence*. They are dropped vowel sounds. A dropped vowel sound is called a *schwa*. In the dictionary, the schwa is printed this way: ə

2 Consonants, which are the rest of the alphabet
   A Single consonants such as *d* and *g* in *dog*
   B Combinations such as *sh* in *shut* and *ch* in *church*
   C Letters that have more than one sound, such as the *j* sound in *jaw* which becomes *dg* in *edge*

3 Combinations of consonants and vowels that sound the same but are spelled differently in different words: *partial*, *crucial*

4 Silent letters as in *night*

5 Homonyms, or words that sound the same but have different meanings, such as *stationary* (meaning *place*) and *stationery* (meaning *paper*)

6 Syllables, or how letters are put together in small units of sound. Any word that contains more than one syllable, has an accent on one of those syllables.

Example: bi-Ó-gra-phy. This word is made up of four syllables. Say it out loud. Can you hear the *accented* or *stressed* syllable? Yes, the second syllable is stressed; therefore, it has an accent mark over it.

Practice 1

Say each of these words. Put an accent mark over the syllable you hear stressed.

1 Eng-lish

2 Com-put-er

3 Ab-sent

4 Yes-ter-day

5 Sig-na-ture

6 Con-ta-gious

Rules

Don't try to learn too many rules at one time. Sometimes, however, a series of rules naturally go together. One such rule has to do with adding prefixes and suffixes to words. Prefixes are added to the beginning of a word; suffixes are added to the end.

Rule: In most cases, you can add a prefix to a word without changing the spelling of that word (add prefix *un-* to *necessary* and you have *unnecessary*).

Prefix	Meaning	Root Word	New Word
ir-	not	regular	irregular
un-	not	necessary	unnecessary
mal-	badly	nourished	malnourished

Practice 2

Use these negative prefixes to make new words. Choose prefixes from this list.

ir-   il-   im-   un-

1 possible

2 legal

3 reverent

4 complicated

5 available

Rule: When you add a suffix that begins with a consonant, the spelling does not change (with few exceptions).

Word	Suffix	New Word
quick	-ly	quickly
careful	-ly	carefully
careless	-ness	carelessness
economic	-al	economical

Exceptions

true   -ly   truly

due   -ly   duly

Rule: When you add a suffix that begins with a vowel to a word that ends in *e,* drop the *e* before you add the suffix.

Word	Suffix	New Word
continue	-ous	continuous
fame	-ous	famous

Exceptions: Words that end in *ge* or *ce* must keep the final *e* in order to retain the soft sound of *g* or *c.*

Word	Suffix	New Word
notice	able	noticeable

Another exception is the word *dye.*

Dye + -ing = dyeing

Rule: Suffixes change the spelling of words that end in *y*.

Word	Suffix	New Word
happy	-ness	happiness
necessary	-ily	necessarily
hearty	-ily	heartily

Practice 3

Circle an incorrectly spelled word in each sentence.

1 The movie was not fameous for its good story.

2 Happyness means different things to different people.

3 She was noticably thinner after her illness.

4 I am truely sorry.

5 Carlessness is not an option.

Rule: When a one-syllable action word ends in a consonant preceded by a vowel (*run*), double the final consonant before you change the form of the word.

run   runner

plan   planned

thin   thinner

Rule: When a two-syllable word ends in a consonant preceded by a vowel and is accented on the second syllable (*occur*), change its form by doubling the final consonant (*occurred*).

refer   referred

occur   occurrence

Rule: In a two- or three-syllable word, if the accent changes from the final syllable to a preceding one when a suffix is added (refer/reference), do not double the final consonant.

prefer   preference

confer   conference

Practice 4

Circle the letter of the incorrectly spelled word.

1 A unanimous **B** nominate **C** confer **D** suning

2 A occurred **B** painter **C** carelesness **D** satisfactory

3 A developped **B** prefer **C** funny **D** wonderful

4 A preferrence **B** reference **C** refined **D** conferred

5 A except **B** occurred **C** baddly **D** stun

Practice 5

Read each sentence. Correct any incorrectly spelled word. If there is no error, leave the space blank.

1 It ocured to me to check the weather report before I left. _____

2 John was refered to me as a possible candidate for the job. _____

3 Your bad attitude has never deterred me. _____

4 I consider myself a runer, not just a fast walker. _____

5 Suning yourself day after day is not a healthful thing to do. _____

Rule: *i* before *e* except after *c*.

believe

receive

Exceptions: *e* before *i* in words that have a long *a* sound (neighbor).

neighbor

weigh

More Exceptions: weird, leisure, neither, seize

Practice 6

Choose the correctly spelled word in each sentence.

1 I will feel great (relief/releif) once I have finished my report.

2 Does your (neice/niece) come to stay with you every summer?

3 "(Sieze/Seize) the day," is a famous saying.

4 Once she (deceived/decieved) me, I couldn't be her friend.

5 We'll have more (liesure/leisure) time next month.

Rule: Rules for forming plurals of words.

1 Add an *s* to most words.
rug   rugs
shoe   shoes

2 Add *es* to words ending in *o* preceded by a consonant.

hero   heroes

tomato   tomatoes

3 Add only an *s* to words ending in *o*, preceded by a consonant, but referring to music.

    alto   altos

    piano   pianos

4 Add *es* to words ending in *s, sh, ch,* and *x.*

    boss   bosses

    crush   crushes

    church   churches

    sex   sexes

5 Change *y* to *i* and add *es* in words that end in *y* preceded by a consonant.

    fly   flies

    story   stories

6 Words ending in *-ful* form their plurals by adding *s* to the end of the word.

    mouthfuls

    spoonfuls

7 A compound word forms its plural by adding *s* to the main word.

    mother-in-law   mothers-in-law

    babysitter   babysitters

8 Some words keep the same spelling for singular and plural forms.

    sheep

    deer

    Chinese

    trout

9 Some words form their plurals by irregular changes.

    child   children

    leaf   leaves

    tooth   teeth

    crisis   crises

    thief   thieves

    knife   knives

    woman   women

louse   lice

alumnus   alumni

appendix   appendices

Practice 7

In each line, circle the word that is spelled incorrectly.

  1 **A** holiday **B** bulletin **C** knifes **D** teeth

  2 **A** father-in-laws **B** chairs **C** bows **D** towels

  3 **A** lice **B** crises **C** childs **D** deer **E** bunches

  4 **A** gestures **B** occurrences **C** bulletin **D** radioes

  5 **A** trays **B** handsful **C** clients **D** women

    Rule: *sede, ceed,* and *cede.* Only three words are spelled with a *ceed* ending:

exceed   proceed   succeed

Only one word is spelled with an *sede* ending:

supersede

All other words of this type are spelled with a *cede* ending.

Practice 8

Choose the correct word in each sentence.

  1 This manual (superceeds/supercedes) the first one we received.

  2 (Procede/Proceed) to the corner and turn right.

  3 At the meeting, Manuel (preseeded/preceded) me on the program.

  4 Have you read about the states that wanted to (secede/seceed) from the union?

  5 Your praise (exceeds/excedes) what I expected.

Spelling Review

Part I Find the word in each line that is spelled incorrectly. Write the word correctly. If all the words are correct, write, *no error.*

  1 **A** deferred **B** hoping **C** differences **D** tomatos _____

  2 **A** preparing **B** walking **C** skiping **D** running _____

  3 **A** ladies **B** geese **C** crises **D** teeth _____

4 **A** disappoint **B** imature **C** pianos **D** candies _____

5 **A** trucksful **B** illiterate **C** regularly **D** overrate _____

6 **A** content **B** definitly **C** unaccustomed **D** truly _____

Part II Find the incorrectly spelled word in each paragraph. Write the word correctly on the line provided.

1 In the absense of any bargains, we left the store. A friend had referred us to it. Now we know that we have to do our own research. When we find a real bargain, we'll buy the item. _____

2 Without hesitancy, we said to the salesperson, "That delivery time is not feasable. We don't even leave work until an hour later." She said, "We'll try our best." _____

3 Our changeing schedule is a problem. Many times, no matter how seemingly competent the salesperson, the item arrives before we get home. We've almost given up on completing the transaction.

_____

4 We were complaining to a friend about our problem. He said, "I always ask for a guarantee of delivery at the promised time. I tell them that if I don't recieve it, they lose my business. It has always worked."

_____

5 We've decided to start all over again. This time, we don't intend to loose the battle!

Part III Find one incorrectly spelled word in each column.

Column A	Column B	Column C	Column D
really	themselves	unfold	visible
magazine	omission	pronunciation	omit
vision	studying	particular	whether
precede	weird	chief	usually
planing	efficiency	coming	defend
Wednesday	familiar	stubborness	wherever
preference	ignore	beggar	accomodate
reference	knowledge	height	challenge
salary	discipline	either	calendar
sufficient	noticable	women	ninety

Answer Key: Section 5

Practice 1

1. Éng-lish

2. com-pút-er

3. áb-sent
   4. yés-ter-day
   5. síg-na-ture
   6. con-tá-gious

Practice 2
   1. impossible
   2. illegal
   3. irreverent
   4. uncomplicated
   5. unavailable

Practice 3
   1. famous
   2. happiness
   3. noticeably
   4. truly
   5. carelessness

Practice 4
   1. **D** sunning
   2. **C** carelessness
   3. **A** developed
   4. **A** preference
   5. **C** badly

Practice 5
   1. occurred
   2. referred
   3. blank
   4. runner
   5. sunning

Practice 6
   1. relief
   2. niece
   3. seize
   4. deceived
   5. leisure

Practice 7
   1. **C** knives
   2. **A** fathers-in-law
   3. **C** children
   4. **D** radios
   5. **B** handfuls

Practice 8

1. supercedes
2. proceed
3. preceded
4. secede
5. exceeds

Spelling Review

PART I

1. **D** tomatoes
2. **C** skipping
3. No error
4. **B** immature
5. **A** truckfuls
6. **B** definitely

PART II

1. absence
2. feasible
3. changing
4. receive
5. lose

PART III

Column A	Column B	Column C	Column D
planning	noticeable	stubbornness	accommodate

Commonly Misspelled Words

Review the words that you have misspelled in the past. Try to learn ten words at a time. Use the techniques outlined in the beginning of this section.

STUDY TIP

Many Web sites offer lists of frequently misspelled words. In addition, you can find spelling lists in a large number of books on the English language. See Appendix B.

A

abnormal	acquaintance	ageless
abolition	acquiesce	aggravate
abscess	acquire	aggressive
absence	actually	aging
accede	adaptation	agitation
accommodation	adequate	agreeable
accumulate	adjacent	all right
acknowledgment	affix	already

A

amateur	apparently	attendants
amplification	appraisal	attorneys
analogous	appreciation	attribute
analysis	argument	auditor
analyze	assent	authentic
answer	assessment	autumn
anticipate	assistance	auxiliary
anxious	athletic	
apparatus	attendance	

B

bachelor	biased	boycott
bacteria	bimonthly	brief
bankruptcy	biographer	bulletin
barely	bisect	bureau
basically	bombard	burglaries
believe	bondage	business
belligerent	bookkeeper	
benefited	boundary	

C

cafeteria	collateral	conscious
calendar	colonization	consensus
campaign	colossal	consistent
canceled	column	consultant
cancellation	commentator	continually
candor	communal	controller
census	computerized	corporal
certainty	concede	correspondence
challenger	conceive	courtesies
chameleon	concession	courtesy
changeable	conflagration	credentials
chief	congenial	criticism
chronological	congruent	cross-reference
classification	connoisseur	crucial
classified	connotation	currency
coincidence	conscience	custody
collaborate	conscientious	

D

debtor	defendant	dependent
deceive	deferred	derogatory
decision	deficit	descendant
deductible	definite	desert
de-emphasize	deliberate	desperately
defective	delicious	dessert (food)

D

develop	disinterest	documentary
development	dispensable	dossier
dilemma	dissatisfied	drastically
disappear	dissimilar	durable
discipline	distasteful	dyeing

E

economical	enormous	excitable
economy	enthusiastic	exhaustible
effects	entrepreneur	exhibition
efficient	enumerate	exhibitor
elaborate	envious	exhilarate
embarrass	enzyme	existence
emergency	equipped	exonerate
emigrant	erroneous	exorbitant
eminent	error	external
emphasis	evasive	extraordinary
emphasize	exaggerate	extravagant
endorse	exceed	eyeing
endurance	excel	

F

facilitation	filament	fluorescent
facsimile	filmstrip	foliage
faculties	finalist	forcible
falsify	finally	foreign
familiarity	financial	foresee
fascinating	financier	forfeit
fastener	fissure	forty
fiendish	flecks	fourteen
fiery	flexible	function

G

gallery	glamour	grieve
galvanized	glucose	grievous
gauge	gnash	gruesome
generalization	government	guarantee
geographic	graft	guardian
geological	grammar	guidance
ghetto	grateful	guild
glamorous	gravitational	gymnast

H

handicapped	height	heterogeneous
handkerchief	helium	hindrance
harass	hemoglobin	homage
harassment	hemorrhage	hors d'oeuvre

H

hosiery	hygiene	hypocrisy
hostage	hygienic	

I

idiomatic	inference	intercede
ignorant	inflammatory	interim
illegitimate	influential	intermission
illustrator	infraction	interpretive
imminent	ingenuity	interruption
immovable	inhuman	intuition
impasse	innocuous	inverted
impenetrable	innuendo	involuntary
imprisonment	innumerable	irrelevant
inasmuch as	inoculate	irreparably
incidentally	input	irrigation
indict	insurance	irritable
indispensable	integrity	itemized
individual	intelligent	itinerary

J

jealous	jovial	jurisdiction
jeopardy	judgment	justice
journal	judiciary	

K

khaki	kindergarten	kinsman
kidney		

L

labeled	liable	linguist
laboratory	liaison	liquefy
ladies	libel	literally
latter	liberal	logical
league	liberate	loose
leased	license	lose
legion	lien	losing
legitimate	likeness	lovable
leisure	likewise	lucrative

M

maintain	medieval	millennium
maintenance	mediocre	miniature
maneuver	memento	minuscule
manual	merely	miscellaneous
marital	mileage	mischievous
mechanical	milieu	mislaid

M

misspell	mortgage	muscle
monkeys	movable	

O

oceanography	omitted	outdated
offense	optional	overview
omission	ordinary	overweight

P

pamphlet	picnicking	prerogative
panicky	pitiful	presume
paradigm	plagiarism	presumptuous
parallel	planned	pretense
parasite	playwright	previous
pastime	pneumonia	principal
patience	politician	privilege
patient	portable	probably
peculiar	possession	procedure
people's	possibilities	proceed
permissible	potato	profit
perseverance	potatoes	programmed
persistent	practically	promissory
persuade	preceding	pronunciation
phenomenal	preferable	pseudonym
phony	preferably	psychiatric
physical	preference	publicly
physician	preparation	pursue

Q

quantities	questionnaire	queue
quartet		

R

raisin	regrettable	resources
rarefy	reinforce	responsibility
realize	relevant	restaurant
reasonable	rendezvous	rhapsody
receipt	repetitious	rhetorical
receive	rescind	rhyme
recognizable	resemblance	rhythm
recommend	resilience	rhythmic
reconcile	resistance	

S

sacrilegious	similar	subtlety
salable	sincerely	subtly
salaries	skeptic	succeed
salient	skillful	successor
satellite	souvenir	summarize
scenes	specialized	supersede
schedule	specifically	surprise
scissors	sponsor	surreptitious
seize	stationary (fixed)	surveillance
separate	stationery (paper)	symmetrical
siege	statistics	
sieve	strength	

T

tariff	tempt	threshold
taunt	theater	totaled
taxiing	theory	tragedy
technical	thesis	traveler
technique	thoroughly	
temperament	thought	

U

unanimous	unfortunately	unnecessary
unauthorized	uniform	unwieldy
unbearable	unify	usage
unconscious	unique	
undoubtedly	unmanageable	

V

vacancy	valuing	vinyl
vaccinate	vegetable	visible
vacillate	vengeance	volume
vacuum	verbal	voluntary
vague	villain	voucher

W

warrant	wholly	woeful
weather	width	woman's
Wednesday	wield	women's
weird	wiring	woolly
welfare	withhold	wrapped
whether	witnesses	wretched

Y

yacht	yield	yoke

Posttests

Reading

You may have heard about this famous story or even read it. The story is called "The Gift of the Magi"; its author is O. Henry. O. Henry, an American, wrote in the late 1800s and early 1900s. Read a portion of the story and answer the questions.

One dollar and eighty-seven cents. That was all. And sixty cents of it was in pennies. Pennies saved one and two at a time by bulldozing the grocer and the vegetable man. One's cheeks burned with the silent charge of cost cutting that such close dealing implied. Three times Della counted it. One dollar and eighty-seven cents and the next day was Christmas.

There was clearly nothing to do but flop down on the shabby little couch and howl. So Della did it. Which sets off the idea that life is made up of sobs, sniffles, and smiles with sniffles in the majority.

While the mistress' tears gradually decrease, take a look at the home. A furnished flat, at $8 per week. It did not make description impossible, but it certainly had a beggary look.

In the hall below was a letter box with the name *Mr. James Dillingham Young.* But whenever Mr. Young came home and reached his flat, he was called Jim and greatly hugged by Mrs. Dillingham, or Della. Which is all very good.

Della finished her cry and tended to her cheeks with the powder rag. She stood by the window. She looked out dully at a gray cat walking a gray fence in a gray backyard. Tomorrow would be Christmas Day, and she had only $1.87 with which to buy Jim a present. She had been saving every penny she could for months, and with this result.

Twenty dollars a week doesn't go far. Expenses had been greater than she had calculated.

Now there were two possessions of the Youngs in which they took great pride. One was Jim's gold watch that had been his father's and his grandfather's. The other was Della's beautiful hair.

Suddenly she whirled from the window to see herself in the mirror. Rapidly she pulled down her long hair. It fell to its full length. Della went pale, and did it up again. A tear or two splashed on the new carpet.

On went her old brown jacket. On went her old brown hat. With a whirl of skirts, she went down the stairs to the street.

Where she stopped the sign read: Mme. Sofronie. Hair Goods of All Kinds. One flight up Della ran. She saw Mme. Sofronie and said, "Will you buy my hair?"

Adapted from *The Gift of the Magi,* by O. Henry.

1 O. Henry creates a dark atmosphere by

A Having Della whirl toward the mirror

B Making the rent $18 a week

C Using the colors brown and gray over and over again

D Talking about Christmas presents over and over again

2 You can conclude that Della and Jim live

A Well above their means

B On a very tight budget

C In one of the very best apartments in town

D Apart for most of the time

3 What do the words "such close dealing" mean in this context?

A Living close together

B Overspending regularly

C Playing cards

D Bargaining

4 How much rent did the couple pay?

A $8 a month

B $80 per week

C $8 per week

D $2800 per year

5 The author describes Jim's and Della's loving relationship. She sobs over her lack of money for a gift. The author's description

A Leads to her leaving Jim for another man

B Builds to Della's need to take extreme action

C Leaves Della unable to move

D Forces Della to buy herself a new dress

6 From reading Paragraphs 1 and 3, you can describe Della as

A Embarrassed about bargaining, but very caring about her husband

B Very sorry about marrying Jim

C Ready to look for a new apartment the next day

D Someone who can't get her work done

7 After reading this part of the story, what do you think Della will do next?

A She will sit and sob until Christmas.

B She will hurry home to clean the apartment.

C She will decide that buying a gift is unnecessary.

D She will sell her hair and buy a gift for Jim.

Read the application below and answer Questions 8 through 12.

Adapted for use in this exercise from OMB document # 18451.

FAFSA: Free Application for Federal Student Aid

FAFSA Page 2

Notes for questions 13–14 (page 3)

If you are an eligible noncitizen, write in your eight- or nine-digit Alien Registration Number. Generally, you are an eligible noncitizen if you are: (1) a U.S. permanent resident and you have an Alien Registration Receipt Card (I-551); (2) a conditional permanent resident (I-551C); or (3) an other eligible noncitizen with an Arrival-Departure Record (I-94) from the U.S. Immigration and Naturalization Service showing any one of the following designations: "Refugee," "Asylum Granted," "Indefinite Parole," "Humanitarian Parole," or "Cuban-Haitian Entrant." If you are in the U.S. on only an F1 or F2 student visa, or only a J1 or J2 exchange visitor visa, or a G series visa (pertaining to international organizations), you must fill in oval **c**. If you are neither a citizen nor eligible noncitizen, you are not eligible for federal student aid. However, you may be eligible for state or college aid.

Notes for questions 17–21 (page 3)

For undergraduates, full time generally means taking at least 12 credit hours in a term or 24 clock hours per week. 3/4 time generally means taking at least 9 credit hours in a term or 18 clock hours per week. Half time generally means taking at least 6 credit hours in a term or 12 clock hours per week. Provide this information about the college you plan to attend.

Notes for question 29 (page 3) — Enter the correct number in the box in question 29.

Enter **1** for 1ˢᵗ bachelor's degree

Enter **2** for 2ⁿᵈ bachelor's degree

Enter **3** for associate degree (occupational or technical program)

Enter **4** for associate degree (general education or transfer program)

Enter **5** for certificate or diploma for completing an occupational, technical, or educational program of less than two years

Enter **6** for certificate or diploma for completing an occupational, technical, or educational program of at least two years

Enter **7** for teaching credential program (nondegree program)

Enter **8** for graduate or professional degree

Enter **9** for other/undecided

Notes for question 30 (page 3) — Enter the correct number in the box in question 30.

Enter **0** for never attended college & 1st year undergraduate

Enter **1** for attended college before & 1st year undergraduate

Enter **2** for 2nd year undergraduate/sophomore

Enter **3** for 3rd year undergraduate/junior

Enter **4** for 4th year undergraduate/senior

Enter **5** for 5th year/other undergraduate

Enter **6** for 1st year graduate/professional

Enter **7** for continuing graduate/professional or beyond

2002-2003

FAFSA^{SM}

Free Application for Federal Student Aid
For July 1, 2002 — June 30, 2003

OMB # 1845-0001

Step One: For questions 1–34, leave blank any questions that do not apply to you (the student).

1–3. Your full name (as it appears on your Social Security card)

| 1. LAST NAME | 2. FIRST NAME | 3. MIDDLE INITIAL |

4–7. Your permanent mailing address

4. NUMBER AND STREET (INCLUDE APT. NUMBER)

5. CITY (AND COUNTRY IF NOT U.S.)   6. STATE   7. ZIP CODE

8. Your Social Security Number

9. Your date of birth

/ / 1 9

10. Your permanent telephone number

( ) –

11–12. Your driver's license number and state (if any)

11. LICENSE NUMBER   12. STATE

13. Are you a U.S. citizen? Pick one. **See page 2.**

a. Yes, I am a U.S. citizen. **Skip to question 15** .... ◯ 1

b. No, but I am an eligible noncitizen. **Fill in question 14.** ...... ◯ 2

c. No, I am not a citizen or eligible noncitizen. .... ◯ 3

14. ALIEN REGISTRATION NUMBER

A

15. What is your marital status as of today?

I am single, divorced, or widowed ..... ◯ 1

I am married/remarried .... ◯ 2

I am separated .... ◯ 3

16. Month and year you were married, separated, divorced, or widowed

MONTH   YEAR

/

For each question (17 – 21), please mark whether you will be full time, 3/4 time, half time, less than half time, or not attending. **See page 2.**

17. Summer 2002	Full time/Not sure ◯ 1	3/4 time ◯ 2	Half time ◯ 3	Less than half time ◯ 4	Not attending ◯ 5
18. Fall 2002	Full time/Not sure ◯ 1	3/4 time ◯ 2	Half time ◯ 3	Less than half time ◯ 4	Not attending ◯ 5
19. Winter 2002–2003	Full time/Not sure ◯ 1	3/4 time ◯ 2	Half time ◯ 3	Less than half time ◯ 4	Not attending ◯ 5
20. Spring 2003	Full time/Not sure ◯ 1	3/4 time ◯ 2	Half time ◯ 3	Less than half time ◯ 4	Not attending ◯ 5
21. Summer 2003	Full time/Not sure ◯ 1	3/4 time ◯ 2	Half time ◯ 3	Less than half time ◯ 4	Not attending ◯ 5

22. Highest school your father completed	Middle school/Jr. High ◯ 1	High school ◯ 2	College or beyond ◯ 3	Other/unknown ◯ 4
23. Highest school your mother completed	Middle school/Jr. High ◯ 1	High school ◯ 2	College or beyond ◯ 3	Other/unknown ◯ 4

24. What is your state of legal residence?

STATE

25. Did you become a legal resident of this state before January 1, 1997?

Yes ◯ 1   No ◯ 2

MONTH   YEAR

/

26. If the answer to question 25 is **"No,"** give month and year you became a legal resident.

27. Are you male? (Most male students must register with Selective Service to get federal aid.)

Yes ◯ 1   No ◯ 2

28. If you are male (age 18–25) and not registered, answer "Yes" and Selective Service will register you.

Yes ◯ 1   No ◯ 2

29. What degree or certificate will you be working on during 2002–2003? **See page 2** and enter the correct number in the box.

30. What will be your grade level when you begin the 2002–2003 school year? **See page 2** and enter the correct number in the box.

8 From what you have read in this application form, you can tell that an applicant

    A Must know his or her Social Security Number

    B Can get as much funding as he or she needs

    C Must be at least 29 years old to qualify

    D Must be married

9 Your permanent mailing address is

    A Where your mother lives

    B Where you used to live

    C Where you live

    D Where you are planning to move

10 If you are a citizen, you can

    A Answer Question 14

    B Skip Question 13

    C Skip to Question 15

    D Answer only questions about citizenship

11 According to the information on page 2, one of the conditions for being an eligible non-citizen is

    A That you are a U.S. permanent resident and have an Alien Registration Receipt Card (I-551)

    B That you must be a U.S. permanent resident and have an Alien Registration Receipt

    C That you must have an F1 or F2 student visa only.

    D That you must have lived in the United States for 12 years.

12 You know that Mike Rinaldi graduated from high school three months ago, and that he has expressed a strong interest in working with computers. You can conclude that he may choose one of the following answers to Question 29:

    A 1, 2, or 7

    B 2, 4, or 7

    C 1, 2, or 4

    D 3, 5, or 6

Michelle decided to learn how to use her hometown library as well as the one on campus. She was very excited to learn that she could also research from home. Now all she had to do was learn how to do it! Her local library offered these instructions regarding online research from home. First, scan the instructions, and then answer Questions 13 through 17.

Online Research from Home

1) *Go to our home page at*

2) *http://www.clan.lib.ri.us/nki/index.htm*

3) *Click on "Online Research."*

4) *Click on the link for the subject you would like to research (e.g., click on "health" to look for health information. You may also choose "magazine and newspaper articles," "encyclopedia articles," "maps," or "photographs and images.")*

5) *Click on the link for the online resource that you would like to use.*

6) *Type in your 14-digit North Kingstown Free Library Card number with no spaces between the numbers. (The card needs to be a North Kingstown card. If you have moved to North Kingstown and you have been using a CLAN card that you received from another library, you will need to get a new card by registering at the circulation desk.)*

7) *Start your research!*

8) *If you have any questions, call the Reference Desk at 294-3306.*

Be sure to check out our selected Web sites page at http://www.clan.lib.ri.us/nki/websites.htm
Courtesy of North Kingstown Free Library, North Kingstown, RI 02852

13 The main idea of this instruction sheet is to

- **A** Do all your shopping online
- **B** Learn how to get your diploma
- **C** Learn how to copy answers from books
- **D** Learn how to do online research from home

14 To start looking for information, do this first:

- **A** Call the library immediately.
- **B** Click on "maps."
- **C** Go to the library's home page.
- **D** Click on "Online Research."

15 If you plan to use the library or its online services, you can conclude that you will need to have

- **A** A CLAN card that was issued at this library
- **B** A new home address
- **C** A brand-new computer
- **D** An appointment with a librarian

16 If you were looking for a recent article in the *Boston Globe,*

- **A** You would click on the link called "magazine and newspaper articles."
- **B** You would first call the *Boston Globe.*
- **C** You would get a CLAN card from the *Boston Globe.*
- **D** You would click on "health information."

17 Scan the instructions for the special selected Web sites page. What is its Web address?

- **A** http://www.clan.lib.ri.us/nmi/index.htm
- **B** http://www.clan.lib.ri.us/nki/websites.htm
- **C** http://www.clan.lib.ny.us/ny/websites.htm
- **D** http://www.clan.lib.ma.us/bos/wesites.htm

Michelle clicked on Online Research and went immediately to the page below. Read the information and answer the questions that follow.

North Kingstown Free Library
Online Research

HELP! I don't know where to go.
Search for information in the following subjects & categories:

CLAN Catalog (Cooperating Libraries   Magazine & Newspaper Articles
   Automated Network)

Encyclopedia Articles   Literature & Authors

Biography (Past & Present)   Geography (Countries & States)

Health   History

Science & Math   Social Issues & Current Events

Maps (world & state)**   Photographs & Images

**For street maps & driving directions, sign up at the reference desk to use the Internet.

NKFL Home Page   Online Resources (in alphabetical order)   Reference Desk
Fiction Page   Young Readers' Page   Teen Page

   For help with online research, please ask at the reference or young reader's desks.

   This computer does not allow access to the Internet. To use a computer with Internet access, please sign in at the reference desk.

---

18 If Michelle does not know what step to take next, she should

   A Leave immediately

   B Click on every underlined word on the screen

   C Call Mike

   D Click on HELP

19 One of the first things Michelle noticed is that even her young children could find books by clicking on

   A Maps

   B Science & Math

   C Young Reader's Page

   D Social Issues & Current Events

20 Before Michelle and Mike can access occupational information online at this library they need to

   A Sign up at the reference desk

   B Click on Encyclopedia Articles

   C Click on Maps

   D Click on CLAN Catalog

21 What does Michelle have to do to get back to this library's home page?

   A Click on any subject matter

   B Get help from the reference desk

   C Click on NKFL Home Page

   D Get help from her professor

Read the following information on learning. Then answer Questions 22 through 25.

Learning experts agree that some habits help you learn while others hinder your progress. For example, studies done with high school students revealed some interesting data. The studies showed that students did best in their most difficult classes at 11 A.M. Yet math homework was best done at 6:30 P.M. At that hour, students dealt best with calculations. When are you at your peak for math?

Experts also suggested that breaks in the study routine were important. A 5-minute break in every 30 minutes worked well. That means, for example, getting up to stretch, walking around, or taking a drink of water. A different kind of break is important too. That is a break to review what you have studied. If you review what you have learned every 10 minutes, you will greatly increase future recall. Of course, reviewing at the end of a week also helps.

More good advice from the learning experts: Take care of your body and your mind. Exercising boosts the growth of new cells in the part of the brain called the hippocampus. That part of the brain is responsible for memory and learning. Two activities, however, work against the brain. Social drinking three or more times a week decreases cognitive, or knowledge gaining, skills. Smoking pot daily destroys your ability to attend to a task.

Variety is the spice of life—and great for your brain function. Doing puzzles, for example, sharpens analytical skills. They also improve memory and learning. In addition, occasionally you should try looking at everyday things differently. Take a different route to work or school. You'll force your brain to use its mapping ability. To stimulate your brain, wear your watch upside down. You'll force yourself to see things differently.

22 In the first paragraph, *calculations* means

    A Taking advantage of someone

    B Answers that are obviously wrong

    C Getting enough exercise while you're studying

    D Steps in working out the answer to a math problem

23 The opposite of the word *variety* (used in the last paragraph) is

    A Mixture

    B Assortment

    C Diversity

    D Sameness

24 Including exercise in your schedule and variety in the way you do things

    A Effect your brain positively

    B Result in being too tired to study

    C Are not effective tools for students

    D Guarantee success in your studies

25 A major point made by some learning experts is that

    A All habits hinder your learning

    B Some habits help you learn while others hinder it

    C Everyone has the same habits

    D The only good habit is to review often

To the Student: As you check your answers, record the results in this chart. Use the three columns next to the Answer Key to mark your answers as *Correct, Error,* or *Skipped.* Use the other columns to record additional information you want to remember about the individual questions. Total the number of your responses in each column at the bottom of the chart. Then read the recommendations that follow.

Reading Skills Assessment: Answers and Skills Analysis

Item Answers	Correct T	Error X	Skipped O	I have this question.	I need instruction.	Refer to these lessons	Reading Skill Categories*
1 C						6	5
2 B						5	4
3 D						5	5
4 C						6	4
5 B						6	5
6 A						6	4
7 D						6	5
8 A						2	3
9 C						4	1
10 C						2	3
11 A						2	3
12 D						5	4
13 D						2	3
14 C						2	3
15 A						5	4
16 A						3	5
17 B						2	3
18 D						3	5
19 C						2	3
20 A						2	3
21 C						3	5
22 D						4	2
23 D						4	2
24 A						6	3
25 B						2	3
TOTALS	correct	errors	skipped	Questions	Instruction	Lessons	Skills

* Key to Reading Skill Categories

1 Interpret Graphic Information   2 Words in Context   3 Recall Information

4 Construct Meaning   5 Evaluate/Extend Meaning

Note: These broad categories of reading skills are broken down into subskill categories. Question numbers are aligned with the subskill titles as well as the lesson to which you can return for a review.

READING SKILLS ANALYSIS

Interpret Graphic Information
REFERENCE SOURCES

LIBRARY CATALOG CARD DISPLAY

Maps

| Forms | 9 | (See Lesson 4) |

WORDS IN CONTEXT

| Same Meaning | 22 | (See Lesson 4) |
| Opposite Meaning | 23 | (See Lesson 4) |

RECALL INFORMATION

Details	8, 11, 17, 19	(See Lesson 2)
Sequence	14, 10, 20	(See Lesson 2)
Stated Concepts	25	(See Lesson 2)

CONSTRUCT MEANING

| Character Aspects | 6 | (See Lesson 6) |
| Main Ideas | 13 | (See Lesson 2) |

Summary/Paraphrase

| Cause/Effect | 24 | (See Lesson 2) |

Compare/Contrast

| Conclusion | 2, 3, 12, 15 | (See Lesson 5) |
| Supporting Evidence | 4 | (See Lesson 6) |

EVALUATE/EXTEND MEANING

Fact/Opinion

| Predict Outcomes | 7, 24 | (See Lesson 6) |
| Apply Passage Element | 16, 18, 21 | (See Lesson 3) |

Generalizations

Effect/Intentions

| Author Purpose | 5 | (See Lesson 6) |

Point of View

| Style Techniques | 1 | (See Lesson 6) |

Genre

To discover your areas for skills improvement in the Reading Section, do three things:

1. Total your number of correct answers out of the 25 possible answers. You should have 90 to 95 percent correct (or 23 to 24 correct answers).
2. Total the correct answers in each subset of skills. For example, in the subset *Recall Information*, there are eight correct answers. Again, you should have 7 correct answers.
3. Wherever your score is below 95 percent, go back to that lesson (indicated in parentheses) and review the skill.

Language

For Questions 1 to 3, decide which punctuation mark, if any, is needed in the sentence.

1 She said, "I'll pay the bridge toll"; I was shocked!

   A   ,

   B   ?

   C   "

   D   None

2 Before I start working at my desk, I turn on the computer turn on the printer, and turn off the phone.

   A   ,

   B   .

   C   ;

   D   None

3 "Which of these projects," Luis asked, should we consider our number one priority?"

   A   !

   B   .

   C   "

   D   None

For Questions 4 to 5, choose the phrase that best completes the sentence.

4 Yesterday, my children and I _____ too early to see the main show.

   A   was arriving

   B   am arriving

   C   will be arriving

   D   had arrived

5 Some of the machines in the garage _____, but others were overlooked.

   A   were fixed

   B   was fixed

   C   has been fixed

   D   is fixed

For Questions 6 through 11, choose the sentence that is written correctly and shows the correct capitalization and punctuation. Be sure the sentence you choose is complete.

6

   A   I can't be anymore clearer than that.

   B   I ain't got anything else to say.

   C   What haven't you told me about yourself?

   D   I haven't got nothing to say.

7

   A   I rung the bell and left.

   B   He had not swore to tell the truth.

   C   Do you always throw your clothes around like that?

   D   Barney gone East on route 195.

8

    A   The children have sitted in their chairs too long.

    B   Iowa City has always been my hometown.

    C   Walking through the building mumbling.

    D   Michael breaked his promise.

9

    A   Did he ask, "What do you got for your schedule this week?"

    B   I called the doctor and she ain't returned my call by noon.

    C   I seen his book called, *30 Days to a better vocabulary?*

    D   I saw a new set of knives in the drawer.

10

    A   Trimming the hedges, mowing the grass, and then I remove the weeds which is not my favorite things to do.

    B   Trimming the hedges, mowing the grass, removing the weeds.

    C   Removing the weeds, mowing the grass, trimming the hedges.

    D   Trimming the hedges, mowing the grass, and removing the weeds are not my favorite things to do.

11

    A   Nervous test-takers seen no chance for a good result.

    B   I done a great deal to do, nevertheless I will make time for our meeting.

    C   Bring these with you: your introduction, your statement of need, and your proposal for change.

    D   I done it right the first time.

Read each paragraph and answer Questions 12 through 21. In Paragraph III, you will also need to fill in a blank.

I. A cover letter always effects your résumé. Why? While your résumé states facts, the cover letter speaks direct to the person doing the hiring. Obviously, you want to grab that person's attention; otherwise, they may go right on to the next résumé.

12 Which word in the first sentence is an incorrect choice as a verb?

   A résumé

   B cover

   C effects

   D your

   E No error

13 Which descriptive word is in the wrong form?

   A grab

   B next

   C obviously

   D direct

   E No error

14 Which pronoun in the paragraph does not agree in number with a noun that comes before it?

   A they

   B you

   C us

   D your

   E no error

15 Which mark of punctuation is incorrect?

   A Obviously,

   B Why?

   C attention;

   D résumé.

   E No error

II. **While writing your cover letter, and including your personal strengths. The strengths need to relate directly to the job for which you are applying. Then of course your qualifications is backed up by the facts in your résumé. Each one, the cover letter and the résumé, need to be strong.**

16 Which one of the sentences in the paragraph is incomplete?

   A 1

   B 2

   C 3

   D 4

   E No error

17 In the third sentence, where should commas be placed?

   A Then,

   B backed up, by

   C facts,

   D Then, of course,

   E No error

18 In the third sentence, there is a subject-verb agreement error. How would you correct it?

   A   change *facts* to *fact*

   B   change *résumé* to *résumés*

   C   delete *up*

   D   change *is* to *are*

   E   No error

19 Look at the fourth sentence. Choose the answer that shows the correct subject and the verb.

   A   cover letter need

   B   résumé needs

   C   Each needs

   D   No error

III. Some people who are searching for jobs has come up with a very clever way to reach more people. They create and distributes 3 × 5 cards that hold a lot of important information. The card include name, phone number, job related skills, job objective, training/education/or certification, special skills. _____

It goes out attached to every résumé or application.

It is used as a business card.

It is given to people to whom the job-seeker is referred.

It is given to relatives and friends as well as the person's entire network.

It is left at the interview and attached to the thank you note that follows the interview.

20 In the first three sentences of this paragraph, there are three verb agreement errors (in number). Choose the answer that includes the three.

   A   has, distributes, include

   B   searching, has, hold

   C   come up, include, training

   D   reach, important, include

   E   No error

21 Which of the following sentences should fill the blank in the paragraph?

   A   Always wear a suit to the interview.

   B   Write a thank you note after each interview.

   C   In addition, the card is used in a number of ways:

   D   You will need a portfolio.

   E   No error

For Questions 22 and 23, choose the answer that best develops the topic sentence.

22 Our grandfathers worked for companies that tended to stay the same for many years, but in our own work experience, that's not often the case.

   A Companies today strive for stability. They can afford to remain unchanged for the foreseeable future.

   B When change comes to your workplace, resist it with all your might. If you are strong enough, you'll win the battle.

   C When things change at work, tell someone that you know better. Suggest a way to keep all the old ways in tact.

   D Today, companies look for people who are comfortable with change. Employees who are cooperative and productive in the midst of change are highly valued.

23 To commemorate Black History Month, the class developed themes on the subject of historic contributions made by African American women in science.

   A Professor Dale Emeagwali (a-MAG-wali) contributed to the fields of microbiology, molecular biology, and biochemistry. Her greatest achievement, however, was the discovery of an enzyme found in the blood of cancer patients.

   B Professor Dale Emeagwali (a-MAG-wali) contributed to the fields of microbiology, molecular biology, and biochemistry. Her husband, Dr. Phillip Emeagwali is often referred to as the father of the internet.

   C Professor Dale Emeagwali (a-MAG-wali) is working to dispute the statement that science can be understood by only a few of our school children.

   D Professor Dale Emeagwali (a-MAG-wali) is working hard with her husband to make some small contribution to science. She expects a breakthrough shortly.

For Answers 24 and 25, read the underlined sentences. Then choose the answer that best combines those sentences into one.

24 The board members considered safety the most important issue. They thoroughly discussed fire evacuation routes.

  A The board members considered safety the most important issue and then they thoroughly discussed fire evacuation routes.

  B They thoroughly discussed fire evacuation routes while the board members considered safety the most important issue.

  C The board members considered safety the most important issue; therefore, they thoroughly discussed fire evacuation routes.

  D The board members chose fire evacuation routes. They discussed them.

25 I will get up earlier to open the office. You could open it since you live so much closer to town.

  A I will get up earlier to open the office and you could do it too since you live so much closer to town.

  B Either I will get up earlier to open the office or you could since you live so much closer to town.

  C Either I will get up earlier to open the office. Or you could.

  D I could get up earlier to open the office, you could open the office, you live closer to town.

For Questions 26 through 28, read the paragraph. Then choose the sentence that best fills the blank in the paragraph.

26 _____. We suggest that you check our online manual of training courses. You will find many courses that will help you update your skills. If you have any questions about the course work, please ask the Human Resources Manager for more information.

A Training is always much more fun in a classroom.

B Our company offers many opportunities for gaining the skills you need.

C There are very few courses to choose from.

D Every employee we hire is fully prepared for all departments the day he or she starts the job.

27 On the other hand, you may have a specific training need. _____ In our manual, there are online courses of all lengths. Your need may be very specific and require only a few hours from start to finish. However, no matter what the length of the course, you will receive credit for it.

A Sometimes, that need can be filled by a short term, online tutorial, or teaching session.

B You must always go to another teaching location for the training course.

C Our company does not believe in computer based training.

D Every course we offer is four to six weeks long.

28 Our online courses have a number of characteristics that make your training easier. First, courses are very easy to sign up for. After you are assigned a password, you can go online and start your training portfolio. Once you have found the training you want, you will be given very clear procedures to follow. _____

A Immediately start the training.

B The first item on the procedures list is to record in your portfolio the name of the training course you have chosen.

C Always take a break at this point.

D Don't do a thing until you call a friend.

To the Student: As you check your answers, record the results in this chart. Use the three columns next to the Answer Key to mark your answers as *Correct, Error,* or *Skipped.* Use the other columns to record additional information you want to remember about the individual questions. Total the number of your responses in each column at the bottom of the chart. Then read the recommendations that follow.

Language Skills Assessment: Answers and Skills Analysis

Item Answers	Correct T	Error X	Skipped O	I have this question.	I need instruction.	Refer to these lessons	Reading Skill Categories*
1 D						5	32
2 A						5	5
3 C						5	28
4 D						2	3
5 A						2	4
6 C						5	9
7 C						2	5
8 B						2	3
9 D						2	5
10 D						6	13
11 C						2	3
12 C						2	5
13 D						4	8
14 A						3	2
15 E						5	24
16 E						2	11
17 D						5	25
18 D						2	4
19 C						2	4
20 A						2	4
21 C						6	15
22 D						6	15
23 A						6	15
24 C						6	12
25 B						6	2
26 B						6	14
27 A						6	15
28 B						6	18
TOTALS	Correct	Errors	Skipped	Questions	Instruction	Lessons	Skills

* Key to Language Skill Categories
1 Usage
2 Antecedent Agreement
3 Tense
4 Subject/Verb Agreement
5 Easily Confused Verbs
6 Adjective
7 Adverb
8 Choose Between Adjective/Adverb
9 Use Negatives
10 Sentence Formation
11 Sentence Recognition
12 Sentence Combining
13 Sentence Clarity
14 Paragraph Development, Topic Sentence
15 Supporting Sentences
16 Sequence
17 Unrelated Sentence
18 Connective/Transition
19 Capitalization
20 Proper Noun
21 Name
22 Title of Work
23 Punctuation
24 End Mark
25 Comma
26 Semicolon
27 Writing Conventions
28 Quotation Marks
29 Apostrophe
30 City/State
31 Letter Part

Note: These broad categories of language skills are broken down into subskill categories. Question numbers are aligned with the subskill titles as well as the lesson to which you can return for a review.

Language Skills Analysis

Usage

Pronoun

Objective

Possessive

Antecedent Agreement	14	(See Lesson 2)
Tense		
Past	8	(See Lesson 2)
Future		
Perfect	4, 11	(See Lesson 2)
Progressive		
Subject/Verb Agreement	5, 18, 19, 20	(See Lesson 2)
Easily Confused Verbs	7, 9, 12	(See Lesson 2)
Adjective		
Comparative		
Superlative		
Adverb		
Superlative		
Choose Between Adjective/Adverb	13	(See Lesson 4)
Use Negatives	6	(See Lesson 3)
Sentence Formation		
Sentence Recognition		
Complete/Fragment/Run-on	16	(See Lesson 2)
Sentence Combining		
Adding Modifier		
Coordinating	24, 25	(See Lesson 6)
Subordinating		
Sentence Clarity		
Misplaced Modifier		
Nonparallel Structure	10	(See Lesson 6)
Verbosity/Repetition		
Paragraph Development	26 (Topic)	(See Lesson 6)
Supporting Sentences	21, 22, 23, 27	(See Lesson 6)

Sequence		
Unrelated Sentence		
Connective/Transition	28	(See Lesson 6)
Capitalization		
Proper Noun		
Name		
Geographic Name		
Title Of Work		
Punctuation		
End Mark	15	(See Lesson 5)
Question Mark		
Comma		
Series	2	(See Lesson 5)
Appositive		
Introductory Element		
Parenthetical Expression	17	(See Lesson 5)
Semicolon		
Writing Conventions		
Quotation Marks	1, 3	(See Lesson 5)
Comma with Quotation		
End Marks with Quotation		
Apostrophe		
Possessive		
City/State		
Letter Part		
Date		
Address		

```
Salutation
Closing _____
```

To discover your areas of skills improvement in language, do three things:

1. Total your number of correct answers out of the 28 possible answers. You should have 90 to 95 percent correct (or 25 to 27 correct answers).

2. Total the number of correct answers in each subset of skills. For example, in the subset *Supporting Sentences,* there are four correct answers. You should have 4 correct answers.

3. Wherever your score is below 95 percent, go back to that lesson (indicated in parentheses) and review the skill.

Spelling

For Numbers 1 through 20, choose the word that is spelled correctly and best completes the sentence.

1 We thought it was _____ to choose vacation weeks so early in the year.

   A unnecessary

   B unecessary

   C unnecesary

   D unecesary

2 The moviegoers stood in one _____ line.

   A continous

   B contenuos

   C continuous

   D continuius

3 Your work has made a _____ difference in the success of this department.

   A noticeible

   B noticeable

   C notiseable

   D notisable

4 The Human Resources Manager _____ me to the company's learning center for help in writing business letters.

   A refered

   B reffered

   C referes

   D referred

5 The directive said, "Handle the changes _____."

   A expediently

   B expediuntly

   C expediantly

   D expedintly

6 Your _____ are not a problem; they have all been for serious illness.

   A abbsences

   B abcenses

   C absences

   D absunces

7 "_____ the day!" has become a popular slogan.

   A sieze

   B siece

   C seize

   D seise

8 You need to have a _____ driver's license for this job.

   A valid

   B vallid

   C valud

   D vallud

9 Our country has faced many _____ in the past few years.

   A crices

   B crises

   C crisses

   D cryses

10 We expect _____ of materials to arrive at the receiving dock.

   A truckfuls

   B truckfulls

   C trucksful

   D trucksfulls

11 She is a _____ to our team's relation-ships.

   A detriment

   B detrament

   C detrement

   D detrament

12 A _____ under the picture in the newspaper gave everyone's names.

   A capshon

   B capsion

   C capcion

   D caption

13 A room for 100 people will _____ all of us at the meeting.

   A acommadate

   B accommodate

   C accomadate

   D acommadate

14 Every time we hire a new employee, we make a _____ decision.

   A crucial

   B crusial

   C crutial

   D crusiel

15 Be careful; that ink is _____.

   A indelable

   B indellible

   C indellable

   D indelible

16 Your new plan has been an _____ for all of us.

   A insperation

   B innspuration

   C inspiration

   D inspuration

17 Those two computer programs are _____.

   A interchangable

   B intrachangeable

   C interchangeible

   D interchangeable

18 At Mike's company, 12 hours of entry level training are _____.

   A compulsery

   B compulsory

   C compulsry

   D compulsury

19 He is well prepared for a job that requires _____ thinking.

   A analytical

   B anilitical

   C anilical

   D analytucle

20 With your help, I have been able to face many _____.

   A emergencys

   B amergencies

   C emergencies

   D emurgencies

Spelling Posttest Answer Key

1. A; unnecessary
2. C; continuous
3. B; noticeable
4. D; referred
5. A; expediently
6. C; absences
7. C; seize
8. A; valid
9. B; crises
10. A; truckfuls
11. A; detriment
12. D; caption
13. B; accommodate
14. A; crucial
15. D; indelible
16. C; inspiration
17. D; interchangeable
18. B; compulsory
19. A; analytical
20. C; emergencies

To the Student: As you check your answers, record the results in this chart. Use the three columns next to the Answer Key to mark your answers as *Correct, Error,* or *Skipped.* Use the other columns to record additional information you want to remember about the individual questions. Total the number of your responses in each column at the bottom of the chart. Then read the recommendations that follow.

Spelling Skills Assessment: Answers and Skills Analysis

Item Answers	Correct T	Error X	Skipped O	I have this question.	I need instruction.	Spelling Skill Categories*
1 A						2
2 C						2
3 B						3
4 D						2
5 A						3
6 C						2
7 C						1
8 A						1
9 B						2
10 A						3

TOTALS	Correct	Errors	Skipped	Questions	Instruction	Skills
11 A						3
12 D						2
13 B						2
14 A						2
15 D						1
16 C						1
17 D						3
18 B						1
19 A						1
20 C						3

* Key to Spelling Skill Categories

1 Vowels   2 Consonants   3 Structural Units

Note: These categories of spelling skills are broken down into subskill categories as well. On the next page, question numbers are aligned with the subskill titles as well. Return to Section 5 to review the rules.

Spelling Skills Analysis

Vowel

Short	8
Long	7
Schwa	15, 16, 18, 19

Consonant

Variant Spelling	2, 6, 9, 12, 14
Silent Letter	
Double Letter	1, 4, 13

Structural Unit

Homonym	
Similar Word Part	5, 11
Root	10
Suffix	3, 17, 20

To discover your areas of skills improvement in the Spelling Section, do three things:

1. Total your number of correct answers out of the possible 20 answers. You should have 95 percent correct (or 19 correct answers).

2. Total the number of correct answers in each subset of skills. For example, in the subset *Schwa,* there are four correct answers. To score a passing grade, you should have 95 percent correct (or 3 correct answers).

3. Keep a list of your spelling errors and follow the directions for improvement in the Study Tip on page 296.

Math

Part I: Computation

No Calculators Permitted. Suggested Time Limit: 10 minutes. Start Time _____

1 $60 - 24.8 =$
- **A** 352.0
- **B** 35.2
- **C** 84.8
- **D** 45.2
- **E** None of these

2 $(5 + 3)(8 - 3) =$
- **A** 40
- **B** 13
- **C** 31
- **D** 61
- **E** None of these

3 $0.75 \times 7.5 =$
- **A** 5.125
- **B** 5.625
- **C** 56.25
- **D** 5,125
- **E** None of these

4 $\dfrac{7}{8} \div \dfrac{1}{2} =$
- **A** $\dfrac{7}{16}$
- **B** $1\dfrac{3}{4}$
- **C** $1\dfrac{3}{8}$
- **D** $3\dfrac{3}{4}$
- **E** None of these

5 $6(7 - 5) + {-4} =$
- **A** 12
- **B** 16
- **C** 8
- **D** 33
- **E** None of these

6 $5\dfrac{3}{4} + 12\dfrac{3}{8} =$
- **A** $17\dfrac{1}{8}$
- **B** $18\dfrac{1}{8}$
- **C** $16\dfrac{3}{8}$
- **D** $18\dfrac{3}{4}$
- **E** None of these

7 $-12 \times -3 =$
- **A** 36
- **B** −36
- **C** −15
- **D** 15
- **E** None of these

8 $5x(x + y) =$
- **A** $6x + 5xy$
- **B** $5x^2 + 5xy$
- **C** $5x^2y$
- **D** $5x^2 + y$
- **E** None of these

9 $20 - (-10) =$

   A   10

   B   −10

   C   30

   D   −30

   E   None of these

10 10 percent of _____ = $90

   A $9.00

   B $9,000

   C $80.00

   D $100.00

   E   None of these

11 What percent of $30.00 is $6.00?

   A   60 percent

   B   150 percent

   C   5 percent

   D   20 percent

   E   None of these

12 $24 \div -3 =$

   A   −8

   B   −6

   C   8

   D   21

   E   None of these

13 $6^2 + 9 \div 3 - 5 =$

   A   36

   B   2

   C   34

   D   10

   E   None of these

14 $|-5 \times 6| - |-25| =$

   A   −5

   B   55

   C   −55

   D   5

   E   None of these

15 $6\frac{1}{2}$ percent of $500.00 =

   A $35.20

   B $325.00

   C $32.50

   D $77.00

   E   None of these

16 $19c + c = 154 - 2c$

   A   c = 132

   B   c = 7

   C   c = 8

   D   154 − 22c

   E   None of these

Stop Time: _____

Math

Calculator Use Permitted. Suggested Time Limit: 30 to 35 minutes
Start Time: _____

1 It takes approximately 1,480 watts of electrical energy to operate a desktop computer and its monitor for 4 hours. How many kilowatts is that?

   A   Less than 1 kilowatt

   B   Between 1 and 2 kilowatts

   C   Between 10 and 20 kilowatts

   D   More than 14 kilowatts

2 Find the width of a field that has an area of 4,800 square meters and a length of 120 meters.

   A   30 meters

   B   40 meters

   C   45 meters

   D   None of the above

3 In 2002, the estimated population of the United States was 287,367,280. Round this population statistic to the ten thousands place.

   A   287,368,000

   B   290,000,000

   C   287,000,000

   D   287,370,000

4 A machine shaft revolves at 245 rpm (revolutions per minute). It is necessary to slow it down by 20 percent. What will the rpm of the shaft be after the reduction? Choose the expression that is set up to find the answer to this question.

   A $245 - (0.20 \times 245)$

   B $245 - (20 \times 245)$

   C $245 + (0.20 \times 245)$

   D $245 + (20 \times 245)$

5 What is the circumference of a swimming pool that has a radius of 6 feet? ($C = \pi d$. Use $\frac{22}{7}$ for π.)

   A $37\frac{5}{7}$ ft.

   B   38 ft.

   C   56 ft.

   D   None of the above

Refer to this advertisement to answer Question 6.

> **Dinette Set: Take it Home Today for Only $15.90!***
>
> Table and 4 Chairs Sale Price: $159.00 + 8% tax
>
> * Installment Plan 10% down $15 per week for 12 weeks
>
> * Plan includes tax.

6 How much more will it cost to buy the dining set on the installment plan than it will to buy it on a cash basis?

A $195.90

B $171.72

C $24.18

D $36.90

7 Shawn wants to buy a CD player that costs $48.00. If he has already saved $30.00, what percent of the price of the CD player has he saved?

A $62\frac{1}{2}$ percent

B 50 percent

C 75 percent

D 57 percent

8 Driving on the North West Expressway, Debbie averaged 62 miles per hour for $3\frac{1}{4}$ hours. How far did she drive?

A 195.2 miles

B 201.5 miles

C 120.25 miles

D 200.25 miles

Questions 9 and 10 are based on the passage and diagram that follow.

LOOKING FOR A SHORTCUT

> A group of hikers stopped along the trail to make a decision. They studied their map to figure out the shortest route from where they stood to Base Camp. They noticed that the two established trails leading to Camp intersected in a perpendicular manner. Further map reading, and use of a protractor and a compass, convinced the hikers they could take an off-trail shortcut through the woods, directly to Base Camp.

$\overline{DA} \approx 15$ miles

$\overline{AB} \approx 8$ miles

$\overline{DB}$ = the shortcut

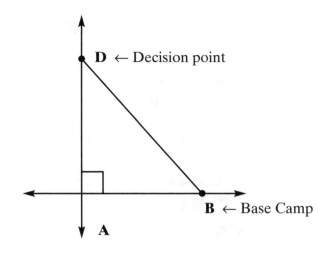

D ← Decision point

B ← Base Camp

A

9 About how many miles do the hikers hope to *eliminate* from their trek by taking the off-trail shortcut?

   A   17 miles

   B   12 miles

   C   8 miles

   D   6 miles

10 In order to start heading southeast at the correct angle, the hikers needed to find the approximate value of $\angle$BDA. They placed a protractor on the map to measure the number of degrees in that angle. Which statement about the measurement of $\angle$BDA makes the most sense?

   A $\angle$BDA = 45° or less

   B $\angle$BDA = 46° or more

   C $\angle$BDA $\approx$ 180°

   D $\angle$BDA = Between 75° and 89°

11 Ed bought his dog a 10-pound bag of food. The first time she was fed, the dog ate $1\frac{3}{8}$ pounds of food. How much dog food was left?

   A   8 lbs

   B $7\frac{5}{8}$ lbs

   C $8\frac{5}{8}$ lbs

   D   None of the above

12 In an election, the winning candidate had 1,200 more votes than the loser. The total number of votes cast was 36,568. Select the pair of equations below that can be used to answer this question: How many votes did the winner receive?

   A   W = 2L + 1,200
        L = 36,568 − 12,000

   B   W = L + 1,200
        W + L = 36,568

   C   W = L − 1,200
        36,568 = L + 1,200

   D   W = L + 12,000
        L + W + 1,200 = 36,568

Refer to this bar graph as you respond to Questions 13 and 14.

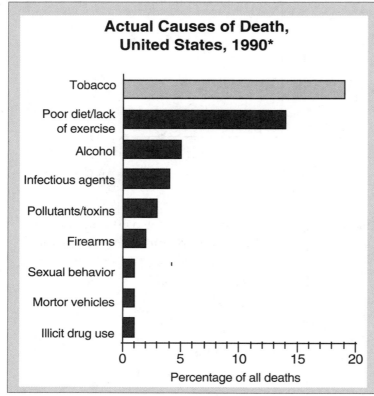

Actual Causes of Death, United States, 1990*

Percentage of all deaths

*The percentages used in this figure are composite approximations derived from published scientific studies that attributed deaths to these causes. Source: McGinnis JM, Foege WH. Actual causes of death in the United States. *JAMA* 1993;270:2207–12.

Source: Centers for Disease Control and Prevention. http://www.cdc.gov/tobacco/overview/oshsummary02.htm

---

13 Approximately what percent of deaths in the United States in 1990 were caused by tobacco and alcohol combined?

A   45 percent

B   40 percent

C   25 percent

D   20 percent

14 Select the number that will complete this sentence: Poor diet and lack of exercise caused about _____ times as many deaths as firearms.

A   5

B   7

C   12

D   16

15 John gets paid on an hourly basis for his work. If he works 52 hours one week and makes *d* dollars an hour, which expression represents his gross income for that week?

A   35/*d*

B   g + 52*d*

C   *d* + 52

D   52*d*

16 What number could *y* represent to make this inequality true? $y - 5 < 18$

A   The number 22 only

B   The number 24 only

C   Any number less than 23

D   Any number greater than 24

Refer to this circle graph to respond to Questions 17 and 18.

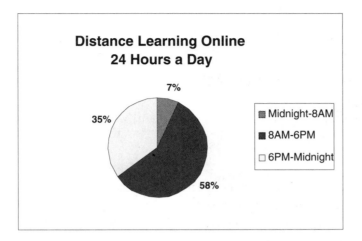

17 A popular distance learning program delivered lessons to over 370,000 Internet users during a two-year period. What fraction of those learners chose to work online between the hours of 6 PM and midnight?

   A $\frac{5}{7}$

   B $\frac{7}{13}$

   C $\frac{7}{20}$

   D $\frac{1}{3}$

18 Approximately how many learners were online between midnight and 8 AM?

   A   259,000

   B   214,600

   C   58,000

   D   25,900

19 Dominique says that when the outside temperature reaches 25°C, it's picnic time. Use the following formula to convert that temperature reading from °Celsius to °Fahrenheit: $F = 1.8C + 32$. In °F, that outside temperature would be

   A   65°

   B   67°

   C   77°

   D   None of the above

Use the data in this table and the information below to answer Questions 20 to 22:

Water Pump Rental Rates
Hoses and Connections Included

Pumps # Item	Flow Rate	Rate per Day	Pumps # Item	Flow Rate	Rate per Day
# 1	1.5 Gal/Min	$45	# 3	500 Gal/Min	$150
# 2	2.0 Gal/Min	$95	# 4	800 Gal/Min	$200

Torrential rains swept up the coast, leaving several low-lying properties under water. Terry and Rob woke to the sound of water gushing into their basement. Part of their house's foundation had caved in. When the water stopped rising, it covered the basement to a depth of 4 feet. They acted quickly to locate a place that rented water pumps.

"How much water are we talking about?" asked the man at Liberty Rental. "Figure that out, and I can advise you which of these four pumps will do the job." He handed them a conversion table with this information circled: 1 cubic foot = 7.4805 gallons.

"Our basement measures 24 feet by 28 feet," said Rob as he took out a notepad, a pen, and a calculator. Using the formula for the volume of a rectangular solid, V = *lwh*, Rob and Terry began to calculate. They hoped to rent a water pump with a flow rate that would remove the standing water as soon as possible—without emptying their wallet.

The manager offered them a deal: "If you can return the pump before noontime, I'll only charge you for half a day, no matter which pump you choose. I'm sure I'll be able to rent it out again this afternoon."

20 Terry and Rob used the conversion chart and rounded the numbers to figure the approximate number of gallons of water in their basement. Which of the following expressions did they key into their calculator?

 A 7.49×2800

 B 7.48×27000

 C 7.5×2700

 D 7.4805×2670

21 They figured they had about 20,000 gallons of water to remove. Next, they looked at the flow rates of the four water pumps. How many gallons of water per hour can pump #3 remove?

 A   30,000 gallons per hour

 B   500 gallons per hour

 C   5,000 gallons per hour

 D   800 gallons per hour

22 Rob and Terry hurried home with pump #3. The pump did the job in

A About $3\frac{1}{2}$ hours

B Less than 1 hour

C Less than $\frac{1}{2}$ an hour

D About 2 hours

23 Which three numbers will complete the spaces in the following number pattern? 100, 98, 94, _____, _____, 70, _____, 44

A 90, 86, 66

B 88, 82, 56

C 88, 80, 58

D 92, 88, 68

Questions 24 and 25 refer to the following passage and line graph.

CARS, SPEED, AND STOPPING DISTANCE

"It takes the average driver about 0.75 second to react before actually stepping on the brakes. Once the brake pedal is depressed, it takes additional time for the car to come to a complete stop."*

Here is the formula for finding the total stopping distance of a car traveling on dry, level concrete when an alert driver is behind the wheel: Total Stopping Distance $= (1.1 \times s) + (0.06 \times s^2)$. s represents **_speed_** in miles per hour. $(1.1 \times s)$ represents the *reaction time distance*, in feet. $(0.06 \times s^2)$ represents the **_braking time distance_**, in feet.

*Source: National Science Teachers Association.
http://www.nsta.org/Energy/fn_braking.html.

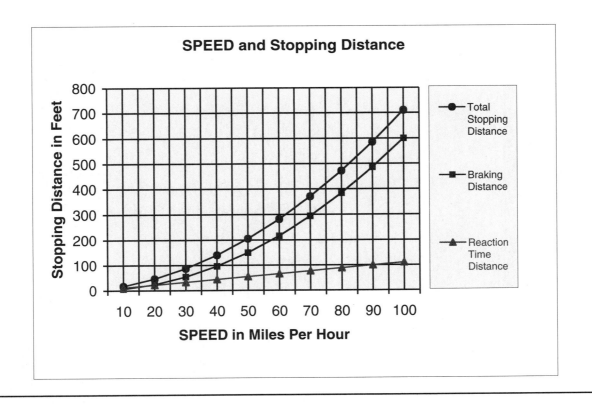

SPEED and Stopping Distance

24 Use the Total Stopping Distance formula to calculate how many feet it takes a car to come to a complete stop when that car is being driven at 65 miles per hour under the controlled conditions described above.

   A   310.5 feet

   B   318.5 feet

   C   321 feet

   D   325 feet

25 Examine the relationship between the Stopping Distance and Speed as pictured in the graph. Look at the trend lines to help you complete this statement: As *speed* in miles per hour *doubles*, the *braking distance* _____

   A   increases by 29 feet

   B   doubles

   C   triples

   D   quadruples

Math Skills Posttest Answer Key

To the Student: Check your answers and record your results in this chart. Use the three columns next to the Item Answers to mark your responses as *Correct, Error,* or *Skipped.* Use the other columns to record information you want to remember about the individual math problems. Total the number of your responses in each column at the bottom.

Answer Key and Skills Analysis: Part I, Computation

Item Answers	Correct T	Error X	Skipped O	I have this question.	I need instruction.	Refer to these lessons	Math Skill Objectives*
1 B						5	1
2 A						3	5
3 B						5	1
4 B						5	2
5 C						7	3
6 B						5	2
7 A						7	3
8 B						8	5
9 C						7	3
10 E						5	4
11 D						5	4
12 A						7	3
13 C						3	5
14 D						8	5
15 C						5	4
16 B						8	5
Totals	Correct	Errors	Skipped	Questions	Lessons to Review		

*Key to Math Skill Objectives:
1 Decimals 2 Fractions 3 Integers 4 Percents 5 Algebraic Operations

Answer Key and Skills Analysis: Part II, Application

Item Answers	Correct T	Error X	Skipped O	Questions	Need instruction	Refer to these lessons	Math Skill Objectives*
1 B						6	6, 8
2 B						4, 8	5
3 D						3	1, 8
4 A						3, 5	4

Item Answers	Correct T	Error X	Skipped O	Questions	Need instruction	Refer to these lessons	Math Skill Objectives*
5 A						4, 5	5
6 C						8, 5, 2	3
7 A						5, 6	7, 1
8 B						5, 6	7
9 D						4, 3	3, 6
10 A						4, 2	3, 6
11 C						4	7, 1
12 B						8	4
13 C						2, 5	3
14 A						2, 5	3, 2
15 D						8	4
16 C						3	4
17 C						5	3, 7
18 D						5	3, 8
19 C						6, 8	5, 4
20 C						6, 4	5, 4
21 A						6	3, 5
22 B						2, 6	5
23 C						7	4
24 D						8	4
25 D						7	3
Totals	Correct	Errors	Skipped	Questions	Lessons to Review		

*Key to Math Skill Objectives

1 Numeration	2 Number Theory	3 Data Interpretation
4 Pre-Algebra/Algebra	5 Measurement	6 Geometry
7 Computation in Context	8 Estimation	

Analyze Your Results

1 Write the number of your *correct* answers for Parts I and II in the spaces below.

2 Divide the number of correct answers by the total number of answers to figure your percentage of success.

Part I _____ Correct answers ÷ 16 Total answers = _____ = _____ %

Part II _____ Correct answers ÷ 25 Total answers = _____ = _____ %

Plan Your Review

This Posttest gives you a good idea of the types of items you will find on the TABE, Level A Forms 7 and 8. To be confident of doing well on this section of the TABE. Your goal is to answer between 88 and 100 percent of the items correctly.

Recommendation

For each item you answered incorrectly, skipped, or did correctly but still have questions about, review the pages of the lessons indicated. Then return to this Posttest and reread the test item you missed. Do you understand it now?

If your answer is *Yes*, practice your new understanding:

- Check out math books at your public library or learning center
- Browse math web sites
- Ask fellow students or a teacher about practice possibilities

If your answer is *No*,

- Help yourself. Review the learning/study strategy tips in this book.
- Ask for help. A fellow student or your teacher will be pleased to be asked.

 FYI

The TABE math test will have items you have not directly prepared for. This will be true as well for other tests that cover content similar to the TABE. Take a deep breath if you see a problem that looks unfamiliar. Relax. Look at it again. Approach it with logic and common sense.

Testing Strategies and Tips

If you read and responded to questions regarding your test taking "know-how" in Section 1, you have seen these test-taking strategies and tips. Each strategy/tip is followed by a brief explanation and/or an example of how to use it. If you did not respond to the questions in Section 1, you may want to go there after you familiarize yourself with these strategies/tips and see how you feel about your abilities. Using these strategies and tips will help make your test-taking experience a better one.

1. *Visualize success for self-confidence and best results.*
   Have you ever heard of the term "self-fulfilling prophecy"? In essence, it means that if you think you *can* do something, you have a better chance of being able to, and if you think you can't do something, you have less of a chance of being able to. So, using the principle of self-fulfilling prophecy, tell yourself that you *can* do well. Talk to yourself in positive terms, not negative ones.

2. *Prepare physically for the test day.*
   Even if you are prepared for the content of the test, you may not do well if you are not well rested. So, get to bed early the night before, or spend a quiet evening at home (it's probably not a good idea to go out to a party!).

3. *Identify key words in questions & directions.*
   During the test, look out for important words that will help you understand directions and the questions being asked. Don't rush through either the directions or each test question, because you risk reading them incorrectly and your responses may be wrong.

4. *Recognize pitfalls of multiple-choice tests.*
   Often the answers that you have to choose from in a multiple-choice test are similar. You must read each one carefully when selecting to make sure you choose the one you intended to.

5. *Use a process of elimination to check multiple-choice questions.*
   If you are having trouble deciding on an answer to a multiple choice question, first look at all the possible answers and see if any can be eliminated. Sometimes an answer just doesn't fit and you can eliminate it from consideration. This will narrow the items you have to choose from.

6. *Relax by using breathing techniques.*

   When you are sitting down to take a test and feel tense or nervous, take a moment to take a few deep breaths in through your nose and slowly exhale out through your mouth. This will help calm your nerves.

7. *Take one-minute vacations to relieve stress during the test.*

   Another way to reduce stress or nervousness during a test is to stop for a minute, close your eyes, and visualize a place that brings you peace or happiness. Try to envision being there or think about the sensation you feel when you are there. For example, if you love to be at the beach, try to see yourself sitting on the warm sand with the sun beating down on your face. Think of the sound of the gentle waves lapping at the shore. Feel better already, don't you?

8. *Pace yourself during the test to finish within the time limit.*

   As much as you might love to spend more than a minute on your mini-vacation, you do need to be mindful of the time limits of a test. Make sure you know how much time you can spend on each section, and stick to it. Don't linger too long on any item; you can always go back to it if you have time.

9. *Know when to leave a question that is giving you trouble.*

   As mentioned above, you can't linger too long on any item or you may end up having to rush through other questions. If you just can't seem to answer the question, move on and come back to it if you have the time at the end.

10. *Use any time that is left at the end to check your work.*

    If you should finish a test before the time allotted, go back to items you might have left blank first. Then proceed to check your work if you still have time left.

General TABE Information

The TABE is a multiple-choice test. The test is offered in either a Complete Battery or Survey version in two available forms (7 and 8) for Level A. The Survey version consists of one-half the number of questions that the Complete Battery version consists of. The Complete Battery version consists of the following sections and number of questions:

- Reading—50 questions
- Mathematics Computation—25 questions
- Applied Mathematics—50 questions
- Language—55 questions
- Spelling—20 questions

TABE is one of several approved "Ability-to-Benefit" Tests that is used to determine if an adult qualifies academically for Federal Financial Aid. Here are the current passing scores required for eligibility:

Test of Adult Basic Education (TABE):

Forms 5 and 6, Level A, Survey Version, and Complete Battery Version.

Passing Scores:

Reading Total (768), Total Mathematics (783), Total Language (714).

Test of Adult Basic Education (TABE):

Forms 7 and 8, Level A, Survey Version, and Complete Battery Version.

Passing Scores:

Reading (559), Total Mathematics (562), Language (545)

[FR Doc. 97-5686 Filed 3-6-97; 8:45 A.M.] Dated: February 28, 1997.

Web site:
http://www.ed.gov/legislation/FedRegister/announcements/
1997-1/030797a.html

APPENDIX B

Resources

English Language Reference Books

Bernstein, T. M. *The Careful Writer: A Modern Guide to English Usage.* New York: Atheneum, 1965.

Booher, D. D. *Communicate with Confidence: How to Say it Right the First Time Every Time.* New York: McGraw-Hill, 1994.

Brusaw, C. T., G. J. Alred, and W. E. Oliu. *The Business Writer's Handbook.* 5th ed. New York: St. Martin's Press, 1997.

Cazort, D. *Under the Grammar Hammer: The 25 Most Important Mistakes and How to Avoid Them.* Los Angeles: Lowell House, 1997.

Dutwin, P., and H. Diamond. *English the Easy Way.* 4th ed. Hauppauge, N.Y.: Barron's Educational Series, Inc., 2003.

Dutwin, P., and H. Diamond. *Grammar in Plain English.* 3d ed. Hauppauge, N.Y.: Barron's, 1997.

Dutwin, P., and H. Diamond. *Writing the Easy Way.* 3d ed. Hauppauge, N.Y.: Barron's, 2000.

Follett, W. *Modern American Usage: A Guide.* Edited and completed by Jacques Barzun and others. New York: Hill & Wang, 1998.

Kipfer, B. A. (editor). *Roget's International Thesaurus.* 6th ed. New York: Harper Collins, 2001.

Merriam-Webster Collegiate Dictionary. 10th ed. New York: Merriam-Webster, 1998.

Mersand, J., and F. Griffith. *Spelling the Easy Way.* 2d ed. Hauppauge, N.Y.: Barron's Educational Series, Inc., 1996.

Oliu, W. E., C. T. Brusaw, and G. J. Alred. *Writing that Works.* New York: St. Martin's Press, 1980.

Sabin, W. A. *Gregg Reference Manual.* 9th ed. New York: Glencoe McGraw-Hill, 2001. Godden, Nell and Erik Palma. Eds. (*Princeton Review*). *Grammar Smart: A Guide to Perfect Usage.* New York: Villard Books, 1993.

Strunk W. Jr, and E. B. White. The Elements of Style. 3d ed. Boston: Allyn and Bacon, 1975.

Turabian, K. L. *A Manual for Writers of Term Papers, Theses, and Dissertations.* 6th ed Chicago: University of Chicago Press, 1996.

Weiss, E. H. *The Writing System for Engineers and Scientists.* Englewood Cliffs, N.J.: Prentice Hall, 1982.

Information Technology

Note: Refer to Section 2, Lesson 4 for information on accessing the Internet. Refer to Section 2, Lesson 4 for information on using your library for researching on the Internet.

Look into Distance Education/Learning

Distance education is the process of providing instruction when students and teachers are separated by physical distance but united by computers. Distance education is often offered together with occasional face-to-face communication. Learning has traditionally taken place in the classroom (face to face) or as home schooling. Now distance education has created virtual classrooms, and it has a place in learning.

In a traditional classroom setting, instruction is accomplished through lecturing and interaction of students-to-students and students-to-teacher. However, recently, computers have become the medium through which instruction is given. Instructors can make and receive assignments by e-mail, which sends messages from one computer user to another. In addition, two special terms apply: Communication is said to be *asynchronous* when people do not interact simultaneously. Communication is *synchronous* when interaction between participants (such as a class "discussion") is simultaneous.

Many community colleges and universities, as well as some states, offer distance education as a way for adults to further their education more conveniently.

Inquire at Your Workplace about E-Learning as a Training Solution

Many companies offer training as needed through the use of computer courses. Computer assisted instruction (CAI) is used to enhance the learning experience by helping learners to gain mastery over a specific skill.

Community Services

Use your telephone book to find the following:

- Your local library.
- Your community center (for education and recreation)
- Your family services organization
- Your congressional representatives
- Your local school department
- Your local recreation department

Educational Opportunities

You will find educational opportunities and solutions by calling the appropriate department of your local and state school system. Also, access your state's Web site for information. You may find any or all of the following:

- State Adult Education Department (may sponsor distance education)
- Adult high school
- ABE/GED programs
- Career and technical high school
- Special education
- State Educational Opportunity Center

In addition, local libraries frequently offer literacy and ABE/GED classes, as well as many other courses and programs.

INDEX

Study tips (*Cont.*):
  graphs, 97
  greater than/less than, 168
  integers, 172
  last words in sentences, 283
  main idea, 29, 35
  motto for working smarter, 120
  multiplying/dividing signed numbers, 177
  multi-sensory experiences, 197
  patterns, 113
  pronouns, 260
  punctuation, 267, 273, 276
  reading/reflecting, 163
  root values, 131
  root words, 127, 131, 132
  sentence fragments, 267
  singular vs. plural, 260
  skimming and scanning, 31
  solving equations, 192
  spelling, 298, 307
  structure and neatness, 163
  templates for calculations, 100
  transition words, 288
  words in context, 47–49
Subjects, 226
  agreement of verb and, 227–230
  pronouns as, 238–239
Subordinating words, 283
Subordination, 280
Subtraction:
  of decimals, 146
  of fractions, 141–142
  of integers, 175–176
  of powers of the same base, 115
Succeed at learning, x–xiii
Suffixes, 300–301
Supplementary angles, 127–128
Support, sources of, 9–11
Supporting details, 30–37
  on graphs, 36
  skimming/scanning for, 31
Syllables, 299, 301
Symbols (as literary technique), 65
Synonyms, 47

TABE:
  general information on, 356–357
  score requirements for, 2, 357

Tables, 95
  details from, 96–97
  finding main ideas from, 36–37
Temperature, 155–156, 164
Tense, 231–234, 247–249
Test taking, 3–4, 17, 355–356
  self-assessment, 3–4
  for skills assessments, x
  strategies and tips, 355–356
3–times rule, xi
Topic sentences, 285–287
Transition words, 288–289
Transitional sentences, 29
Transversal line, 127
Triangles, 129, 134

Unknown, solving for, 189–194, 196
Using skills, xi

Vacations, one-minute, 356
Value(s):
  absolute, 167–168
  balancing, in equations, 190–192
  mathematical expression of,
    103–110
  and metric prefixes, 156–157
  place, 104–110
Variables, 160, 161, 190, 195
Verbs, 226
  action, 227–235
  agreement of subject with,
    227–230
  in contractions, 245–246
  irregular, 233
  linking (being/non-action), 238–246
  and pronouns, 241–246
  tense agreement with, 247–249
  tense of, 231–234
Visualization, 188–189, 355
Volume, 133–136
Vowels, 298, 299

Word problems, 97–98
Words in context, 46–50
Work habits (*see* Learning)
Writing (*see* Language)

Zero, 167, 168